Blue Laws

The History, Economics, and Politics of Sunday-Closing Laws

David N. Laband
Clemson University

Deborah Hendry Heinbuch

Lexington Books
D.C. Heath and Company/Lexington, Massachusetts/Toronto

For Anne, Kimberley and Shelley.
— *D.N.L.*

For Echele and Jeffrey.
— *D.H.H.*

Library of Congress Cataloging-in-Publication Data

Laband, David N.
  Blue laws.

  Bibliography: p.
  Includes index.
  1. Sunday legislation — United States — States.
  2. Sunday legislation — United States.   3.   Sunday
legislation.   I. Heinbuch, Deborah Hendry.   II.   Title.
KF2009.Z95L33   1987   344.73'012574   85–45930
                                      347.30412574
  ISBN 0–669–12416–8 (alk. paper)

Published simultaneously in Canada
Printed in the United States of America
Casebound International Standard Book Number: 0–669–12416–8
Library of Congress Catalog Card Number 85–45930

The paper used in this publication meets the minimum requirements of
American National Standard for Information Sciences — Permanence of
Paper for Printed Library Materials, ANSI Z39.48 1984. ∞™

87 88 89 90 91 8 7 6 5 4 3 2 1

Contents

Figures and Tables

Figures

Tables

1
Blue Laws:
An Introduction

On a Sunday some months ago, I broke my watchband. I was on my way to give a speech and without a watch to glance at, my speeches tend to go a little long.

Like until Tuesday.

So I quickly drove to the nearest department store, strode briskly to the doors and nearly wrenched my arm off. The store was closed.

A guard outside the building watched my antics. "Sunday," he said.

"So?" I said.

"Sunday," he said more emphatically. "Everything's closed on Sundays."

Immediately, the Good Roger within me formulated a reply.

"Why, yes, of course, how logical and proper," Good Roger wanted to say. "Things should close on Sunday. It is the work of the devil to engage in commerce on the Sabbath."

Instead, Bad Roger answered the guard.

"That's the dumbest thing I ever heard of," Bad Roger said. "I can go down the street and get a drink in a saloon on a Sunday, but I can't get a watchband? Besides, *you're* working, aren't you?"

The guard shrugged. "Somebody's got to tell people it's Sunday," he said.

Bad Roger is not pleased with the antiquated, bush-league, narrow-minded Sunday blue laws that affect certain stores in certain parts of this state.

Good Roger tried to explain it to him. "Sunday blue laws are designed to encourage a day of quiet contemplation and religious observance," he said.

"Oh, yeah?" Bad Roger said. "So how come every Sunday everybody's watching football on TV? What are they contemplating? Refrigerator Perry?"

"That's not the point," Good Roger said. "Sunday is a special day, a holy day."

"Only if you're a Christian," Bad Roger said. "Moslems say Friday is a holy day. Jews say Saturday is a holy day. Besides, how come blue laws are suspended just before one of the holiest days on the Christian calendar, Christmas?"

But Good Roger had done his research. That is one of the things that makes Good Roger good. Bad Roger just screams and shouts and writes about whatever he pleases.

How that guy got a column is beyond me.

"Observe these letters from decent, Godfearing citizens printed in *The Sun* on Feb. 25 of last year," Good Roger said. "For instance: 'Sunday remains the Sabbath day for Protestant and Catholic Christians, who make up the vast religious majority in this state. God granted the Sabbath to be a day set apart (holy) for rest, reflection and recreation, not because He needs it, but because we need it.'"

"Or this one: 'Our country is blessed. Should we not set aside one day to give thanks? What happened to "keep holy the Sabbath"?'"

Bad Roger was not impressed. "What happened to the separation of church and state?" he asked. "How come the state of Maryland is in the religion business?"

Good Roger stamped his foot. "But pity the poor workers," he said. "Many fear they will be forced to work on Sundays without blue laws."

"Let's pity the poor unemployed," Bad Roger said. "Those people would kill for part-time employment on Sundays. Besides, I worked on Sundays for years."

"And that is why you turned out so bad," Good Roger said. "In most homes on Sundays, the family returns from church and gathers together in the rumpus room. Father leads a discussion on the meaning of life. Sally and Billy review what they have learned in school that week. Mom makes fudge and Spot sits in front of the fire, wagging his tail."

"Have you been sniffing the oven cleaner again?" Bad Roger said. "This is America. Dad is out bowling, Mom is at the aerobics class, Sally is on her way to a Madonna concert, Billy is doing 20 months for drug possession and Spot was eaten by a hungry family down the street."

Good Roger burst into tears of rage. "You make me so mad I could spit," he sobbed. "Not only religious people and workers, but small businessmen are also in favor of the blue laws!"

"Of course they are, dumbo," Bad Roger said. "The small businessmen are in favor of blue laws because they don't want shoppers going out to the big malls on Sunday. And they know how to influence the state legislators."

Good Roger was stunned. "A Maryland legislator could not be influenced by special interests," he said.

"A Maryland legislator could be influenced by a Big Mac and a large fries," Bad Roger said. "You know why small businessmen have the clout to defeat a repeal of the blue laws? Because they are the ones who buy tickets to the political fund raisers. Government is cash-and-carry these days."

Good Roger dried his eyes. "I suppose you have a better idea?" he said.

"Yeah," Bad Roger said. "Throw out the blue laws. Those who want to go to church, go to church. Those who want to shop, shop. Those who want to play Parcheesi, play Parcheesi. It's called choice. It's what America is all about."

Good Roger was very nearly speechless. "You keep up this kind of talk," he whispered, and you are going straight to hell."

"Well, if I am going on a Sunday, the law will let me buy a *Hustler* magazine and a bottle of whiskey on the way," Bad Roger said. "But if I need a watchband, I'm out of luck."

—Roger Simon,
The Baltimore Sun, 12-9-85

There are many local and state laws that prohibit or restrict individuals from engaging in certain acts on Sunday and impose legal sanctions on violators. These regulations are commonly referred to by many names: "blue laws," "Sunday legislation," Sunday-closing laws," or "Sunday statutes." The range of behavior that is restricted covers a broad spectrum. Boxing and wrestling are prohibited on Sunday in a number of states, as are sales of alcohol, barbering, horse racing, hunting, motor vehicle sales, labor, and retail sales. Bingo, billiards, bowling, butcher shops, card playing, cock fighting, dancing, digging clams or oysters, fresh meat sales, gaming, pawnbrokers, polo, raffles, serving civil process, and tobacco warehouse sales are all prohibited activities in at least one state on Sundays.

Sunday-closing laws in America date back to the colonial period; the laws of that time were derived from similar laws that existed in England. More generally, laws restricting behavior of individuals date back more than two thousand years. A number of states have repealed their Sunday-closing laws since the turn of the twentieth century. Such repeal and attempted repeal has not been taken lightly by especially interested individuals and groups on both sides of the issue. Attempts to change the law in one respect or the other are invariably accompanied by acrimonious debate and extensive coverage in local media. The media attention is understandable—large numbers of individuals are affected by certain types of restrictions. In Maryland, for example, several counties prohibit Sunday sales of most items by retail sellers who employ more than six employees. Major department stores are forced to close, which puts a crimp in the shopping plans of thousands, perhaps tens of thousands, of Marylanders each weekend.

Despite the widespread incidence of Sunday-closing laws among the states and localities, and the obvious impact that such laws have on the lives of individuals living within the political jurisdictions affected, formal analysis of blue laws is virtually nonexistent. The effects of blue laws on the well-being of families, workers, and businessmen have never been formally investigated, as far as we have been able to determine. For that matter, there is not even a readily accessible compilation of laws governing Sunday-trading behavior.

The public policy issue continues to occupy the time and attention of public officials from law enforcement personnel to state legislators. A book that explores the issues, the arguments, and the interest groups in favor of, and opposed to, blue laws is not only needed, but timely.

In the pages that follow, we present a comprehensive examination of Sunday-closing laws. Chapter 2 leads off the discussion with a legislative/judicial history of blue laws, with particular attention paid to important developments in English and colonial American law. In chapter 3 we present a detailed summary of current state laws that regulate individuals' selling behavior on Sundays. We focus specifically on legislation that restricts commercial activity as one category, and legislation that regulates liquor sales and sales of automobiles as a separate category. General types of regulation are recognized, and we examine the nature and extent of enforcement of the law across affected political boundaries. The arguments voiced by special-interest groups in favor of, and opposed to, blue laws are introduced and discussed in chapter 4. A positive analysis of the validity of these various arguments is presented in chapter 5, via comparison between a sample of ten blue law states and ten non–blue law states across a wide spectrum of variables measuring social and economic well-being.

In brief, we find little evidence to support the claim that individuals are better off when they are required to take a day of rest, and we find mixed evidence with respect to the impact of blue laws on churches. The data on business activity and effects on the labor force are much clearer: production by small, relatively inefficient businesses is subsidized by Sunday-closing legislation and in terms of earnings and employment, people are better off when the state provides an unrestricted commercial environment on Sundays.

Chapter 6 reviews the history of blue laws in three other major English-speaking countries: England, Australia, and Canada. Concluding thoughts are offered in chapter 7.

We wish to emphasize that neither author has a vested interest in one side or the other. It is true that a free-market economist (which Laband is) is trained from Adam Smith onwards to abhor the type of interference in the operation of a free economy represented by Sunday-closing laws, or any type of government-imposed closing laws. Recognition of this potential source of biased judgment provided a constant incentive to take scrupulous care that the investigation proceeded in the true spirit of academic inquiry. The presentation is positive, that is, factual, as opposed to normative. Decisions with respect to what public policy ought to be are better left to those with greater interest in such matters than we have. Our work proceeded without the financial or moral encouragement of, or, indeed, the knowledge of, Marylanders for Blue Law Repeal, Maryland Citizens for Sunday Shopping, the Downtown [Baltimore] Merchants Association, the Voters Interest League, the Highlandtown Merchants Association, the Mayor's Advisory Committee on Small Business, or any other group in favor of, or opposed to, repeal of blue laws in Maryland or any other state. We hope that the information contained in this volume will provide valued assistance to policy makers who confront the issue of instituting or repealing Sunday closing legislation. If government regulation of an otherwise free market is abhorent to a free-market economist, even more abhorent is government regulation by politicians making decisions based on ignorance.

2
A History of Blue Laws

Remember the Sabbath day, to keep it holy.

Six days shalt thou labor, and do all thy work.

But the seventh day is the Sabbath of the Lord thy God: thou shalt not do any work, thou, nor thy son, nor thy daughter, thy manservant, nor thy maid servant, nor thy cattle, nor thy stranger that is within thy gates.

For in six days the Lord made heaven and earth, the sea, and all that in them is, and rested the seventh day: wherefore, the Lord blessed the Sabbath day, and hallowed it.

—Exodus 20:8–11

S abbath laws have an extensive history among inhabitants of the Western world. Prohibitions against a wide array of practices can be found in both books of the Bible, Codex Justinian, Codex Theodosian, the medieval councils (e.g., Tarragon, Orleans, Auxerre, Macon II, Mayence, and Rheims), laws and canons set down by the church, the statutes of English monarchs, American colonial law, statutes of the fifty states of America, and statutes of the other English-speaking countries of the Western world. In modern times, that is, the post-Constitution period in America, the legality of blue laws has been challenged repeatedly in the courts. In virtually all cases, the legality of the principle that a state may itself regulate individual citizens' behavior on Sunday for "the common good" or may delegate that authority to local political jurisdictions has been recognized by the courts. Specific wording of certain statutes has, however, resulted in the courts invalidating that legislation. Convicted Sabbath-breakers, those individuals who profaned the Sabbath, could receive punishments as severe as death, and history has recorded a number of actual cases where this was so. Despite the occasional severity of meted punishment, there is ample evidence from all periods of time that civil disobedience to this regulation of individual activity on Sunday has been the rule rather than the exception.

The purpose of this chapter is to survey, in chronological fashion, the development of Sabbath laws from their inception to the middle of the twentieth century among the English-speaking peoples. We examine not only the law itself, but also the stated penalties and, insofar as evidence is available, the actual punishments exacted.

Where Does the "Blue" in Blue Laws Come From?

It was during the colonial period that the term "blue law" was coined, although there is some historical disagreement with respect to its origin. According to Henman [1838] "blue law" refers to the color of the paper upon which was printed the code of laws of the New Haven colony in 1665. No printing establishment had, by that time, been established in the colonies, and the various laws were announced to the assembled citizenry on specified lecture days by local constables, who received the only written copies of the laws. This mode of enacting and declaring the laws continued until the colony's laws became so numerous as to render their recollection by both the people and the courts inconvenient and difficult. Accordingly, in 1665 the General Court of the Colony ordered that an "able, judicious, and godly man" should be appointed to codify the laws of the New Haven colony. Then-Governor Eaton was appointed to this task, and the Court ordered five hundred copies to be printed (in England) for use by the New Haven colonists. The first printed laws in the New Haven colony were returned on blue-colored paper.

The dissenting voice of Trumbull [1876] argues that the blue referred to by the term "blue law" bears testimonial to the strictness with which the laws were observed by the Puritans and other schismatic groups. "True Blue will never stain" runs an old proverb that refers to a person of rigid devotion to his or her principles. Just as a "true blue" color or dye never fades or changes its color, so a person of fixed principles, firmly grounded upon the reasonableness and justice of the same, will not be easily swayed to depart from them. Blue, then, is the color of constancy and fidelity. According to Trumbull (p. 9), nothing was more unpopular at the court of Charles the Second than constancy in virtue and adherence to convictions of duty. "True blue" became a term of reproach, reserved for, among others, the puritans.

The Origins of Sunday Laws

Although there is a long and strong tradition of association between the Christian church and observation of a day of rest on the Sabbath, Sunday was recognized as a day of rest long before any mention was made of it as the

"Lord's Day." The Sunday holiday was as much a part of pagan life as other holidays sprinkled at odd times throughout the year; the difference lay in the weekly regularity of the event. The earliest edict regarding behavior on Sunday was laid down by Constantine in the year 321:

> Let all judges and all city people and all tradesmen rest upon the *venerable day of the sun*. But let those dwelling in the country freely and with full liberty attend to the culture of their fields; since it frequently happens that no other day is so fit for the sowing of grain, or the planting of vines; hence the favorable time should not be allowed to pass, lest the provisions of heaven be lost.
>
> Given the seventh of March, Crispus and Constantine being consuls, each for the second time.
>
> "Codex Justin," lib. iii, tit. xii, 1.3.[1]

Sunday is mentioned only by its pagan name, "venerable day of the sun." Nothing is said of any relation to Christianity; no reference is made to the Sabbath or the Fourth Commandment. The law, which applied to every subject throughout the Roman Empire, was apparently found to be too strict and was almost immediately relaxed by Constantine:

> As it seemed unworthy of the day of the sun, honored for its own sacredness, to be used in litigations and baneful disputes of parties, so it is grateful and pleasant on that day for sacred vows to be fulfilled. And, therefore, let all have the liberty on the festive day of emancipating and manumitting slaves, and besides these things let not public acts be forbidden.
>
> Published the 5th, before the nones of July, at Caralis, in the consulship of Crispus II and Constantine II (321).
>
> "Codex Theo.," lib.ii, tit. v111, lex 1.[2]

Lewis [1888] provides detailed and compelling evidence that this first Sunday legislation was purely pagan in origin and that the influence of Christianity in the Roman Empire at that date was not sufficient to produce such a proclamation. Indeed, the term "Lord's Day" does not appear in any civil legislation concerning Sunday for more than sixty years after Constantine's proclamation. In the year 386 a law was passed respecting Sunday behavior that makes passing reference to divine worship as well as the day of the sun. Later that same year the joint emperors Gratianus, Valentinianus, and Theodosius issued the first civil proclamation acknowledging both the Christian and pagan influence on behavior:

> On the day of the sun, properly called the Lord's day by our ancestors, let there be a cessation of lawsuits, business, and indictments; let no one exact a debt due either the state or an individual; let there be no cognizance of

disputes, not even by arbitrators, whether appointed by the courts or voluntarily chosen. And let him not only be adjudged notorious, but also impious who shall turn aside from an institute and rite of holy religion.

Published the third before the nones of November, at Aquilia; approved at Rome the eighth before the calends of December, in the consulship of most noble, most pious Honorius, and most illustrious Euodius.

"Codex Theo.," lib. viii, tit. viii, lex 3.[3]

The Early History of Sabbath Laws in England

Samples of many, not all, Sabbath laws enacted during the fourth through the eighteenth centuries are presented now in chronological order. They are meant to stand on their own merit, as they present a strong flavor for the prevailing conditions and sentiments of their respective periods. The year of issue is reported, followed by the text of the proclamation and the issuer.

399   The two august emperors Arcadius and Honorius, to Aurelianus, pretorian prefect:

On the Lord's day, which derives its name from the respect due it, let there be no celebration of theatrical sports, nor races of horses, nor any shows in any city, which are found to enervate the mind. But the natal days of the emperors, even if they fall on the Lord's day, may be celebrated.

Dated the first of September, at Constantinople, in the consulship of most illustrious Theodosius.

"Codex Theo.," lib. ii, tit. viii, lex 23.[4]

409   The two august emperors, Honorius and Theodosius, to John, pretorian prefect:

On the Sabbath and other days, during which the Jews pay respect to their own mode of worship, we enjoin that no one shall do anything or ought to be sued in any way; with regard to public taxes and private litigations, it is plain that the rest of the days can suffice.

Dated the seventh before the calends of August, at Ravenna, our lords Honorius VIII and Theodosius III, both august, being consuls.[5]

409   Let the judges take care and ascertain by inquiry that the debtors are brought out of prison on all of the Lord's days, lest humane treatment be denied these through the bribery of the guards of the prison. Let them cause food to

be supplied to those not having it, two or three pence daily, or as many as they may deem sufficient, having been assigned to the keeper of the prison, since the provisions of the poor are enough for their support. These ought to be conducted to the bath under faithful guards; a fine of twenty pounds of gold being imposed upon the judges, and the same amount upon their assistants, and also a fine of three pounds of gold being denounced against the commanders if they shall treat with contempt these most salutory enactments. A praiseworthy care shall not be wanting to the bishops of the Christian religion to impress this admonition for observing the ordinance upon the judges.

Dated the 12th day before the calends of February, at Ravenna, in the consulship of Honorius VIII and Theodosius III.[6]

"Codex Theo.," lib. vi, tit. iv, lex 29.

425   The august emperors Theodosius and Valentinianus, to Asclepiodotus, pretorian prefect:

On the Lord's day, which is the first day of the whole week, and on the days of the nativity and the Epiphany of Christ, and also on the days of Pentecost and of Easter, as long as the celestial light and the (white) garments testify of the new light of sacred babtism (in our souls); at which time also the memory of the passion of the apostles, the supreme teachers of Christianity, is rightly celebrated by all; all the pleasures of the theatres and of the circus throughout all cities, being denied to the people of the same, let the minds of all faithful Christians be employed in the worship of God. If any, even now, through the madness of Jewish impiety or the error and folly of dull paganism are kept away, let them learn that there is one time for prayer and another for pleasure. Let no one think himself compelled, as by a great necessity, in honor of our power or imperial office, lest he exalt the work of the shows to the contempt of divine religion; neither let him fear that he will come under the condemnation of our highness, if he shall show less of devotion to us than is customary; and let no one wonder because reverence is then turned away from our excellency, human born, to God the omnipotent and deserving, to whom the allegiance of the whole world ought to be paid.

Given at Constantinople, February 1st.

"Codex Theo.," lib. xv, tit. v, lex 5.[7]

469   The august emperors, Leo and Anthemis, to Armasius, pretorian prefect:

We wish the festal days dedicated to the Majesty Most High, to be employed in no voluptuous pleasures, and profaned by no vexatious exactions.

I. Therefore, we decree that the Lord's Day shall always be so held in honor and veneration, that it shall be free from all prosecutions, that no chastisement shall be inflicted upon anyone, that no bail shall be exacted, that public service shall cease, that advocacy shall be laid aside, that this day shall be free from judicial investigations, that the shrill voice of the crier shall cease, that litigants shall have rest from their disputes, and have time for compromise, that antagonists shall come together without fear, that a vicarious repentance may pervade their minds, that they may confer concerning settlements and talk over terms of agreement. But, though giving ourselves up to rest on this religious day, we do not suffer any one to be impure pleasures. On this day the scenes of the theatre should make no claims for themselves, neither the games of the circus nor the tearful shows of the wild beasts; and if the celebration should happen to fall on our birthday it may be postponed.

He shall suffer the loss of his office and the confiscation of his estate, who shall attend the games on this festal day, or shall, as a public servant, under pretense of public or private business, cause these enactments to be treated with contempt.

Dated December 13, at Constantinople, Zeno and Matiuanus being consuls.[8]

"Codex Justin," lib. iii, tit. xii, lex. 11.

516   Let not any bishop or presbyter or any of the inferior clergy hear causes on the Lord's day . . . but let them be occupied in the performance of the solemnities ordained in the honor of God.

"Council of Tarragon," chap. iv, can. xv;
Binias tome x, p. 625.[9]

538   Whereas the people are persuaded that they ought not to travel on the Lord's day with the horses, or oxen and carriages, or to prepare anything for food, or to do anything conducive to the cleanliness of houses or men, things which belong to Jewish rather than Christian observances;

we have ordained that on the Lord's day what was before lawful to be done may still be done. But from rural work, i.e., plowing, cultivating vines, reaping, mowing, thrashing, clearing away thorns or hedging, we judge it better to abstain, that the people may the more readily come to the churches and have leisure for prayers. If anyone be found doing the works forbidden above, let him be punished, not as the civil authorities may direct, but as the ecclesiastical powers may determine.

> "Council of Orleans III," can. xxviii; Binius, tome xi, p. 496.[10]

578   On the Lord's day it is not permitted to yoke oxen or to perform any other work except for appointed reasons.

> "Council of Auxerre," can. xvi, Binius tome xiii, p. 44.[11]

585   . . . Keep the Lord's day whereon ye were born anew and freed from all sin. Let no one spend his leisure in litigation; let no one continue the pleading of any cause. Let no one under the plea of necessity allow himself to place a yoke on the neck of his cattle. Let all be occupied in mind and body in hymns, and in the praise of God. If anyone dwells near a church, let him go thereto, and upon the Lord's day engage with prayer and tears. Let your eyes and hands on that day be lifted up to God. For this is the day of perpetual rest. This is shadowed to us in the seventh day in the law and the prophets. It is right, therefore, that we should all celebrate this day, through which we are made to be what we were not; for we were in sin, but through this we were made righteous. Let us then yield a willing service to the Lord, through whom we know ourselves to have been freed from the bonds of error. Not because our Lord requires it of us that we should celebrate this day by constraint of the body, but seeks obedience, by which, trampling on earthly things, we may be lifted to heaven through his mercy. If anyone shall disregard this wholesome exhortation, or treat it contemptuously, he shall, in the first place, draw upon himself the wrath of God; and secondly, the unappeasable anger of the clergy. If he be an advocate, let him wholly lose the privilege of pleading the cause; if a countryman or a slave, let him be soundly beaten with whips; if a clerk or monk, let him be suspended from the society of his brethren for the space of six

months. For all these things may we be rendered pleasing unto God.

> "Council Macon II," can. ii, Binius, tome
> xiii, pp. 75–6.[12]

696   Law 9. If a slave (esne) do any servile labor, contrary to his lord's command, from sunset on Sunday eve till sunset on Monday eve, let him make a compensation (bot) of eighty shillings to his lord.

Law 10. If an esne so do of his own accord on that day, let him make a "bot" of six to his lord, or his hide.

Law 11. But if a freeman [so do] at the forbidden time, let him be liable to his heals-fang (a fine paid to save himself from the pillory), and the man who detects him, let him have half the fine (wite) and the work.

> Withread, King of Kentishmen.[13]

871–901   Law 7. If anyone engage in Sunday marketing, let him forfeit the chattel, and twelve ores (192 pence), among the Danes, and thirty shillings among the English. If a freeman work on a festival day, let him forfeit his freedom, or pay a fine (wite or lah-slit). Let a theow-man (slave) suffer in his hide, or hide-gild. If a lord oblige his theow to work on a festival day, let him pay lah-slit within the Danish law, and wite among the English.

> Alfred, King of Wessex.[14]

924   Law 24. And that no marketing be on Sundays; but if any one do so, let him forfeit the goods, and pay thirty shillings as wite.

> "Council of Greatanlea," under King
> Aethelstane.[15]

1017   Sunday traffic we forbid everywhere, and every folkmote (general assembly), and every work, and every journey, whether in a wain, or on a horse, or as a burthen.

> Canute, King of Denmark, King of all
> England.[16]

1354   It is accorded and established, that showing of wools shall be made at the staple every day of the week, except the Sunday and solemn feasts of the year.

> Edward III, statute 28.[17]

1409   He that playeth at unlawful games on Sundays and other festival days prohibited by the statute shall be six days imprisoned.

Henry IV, statute 11.[18]

1448   Considering the abominable iniquities and offenses done to Almighty God and to his saints, always aiders and singular assisters in our necessities, because of fairs and markets open their high and principal feasts, as in the feast of the Ascension of our Lord, in the day of Corpus Christi, in the day of Whitsunday, in Trinity Sunday, with other Sundays, and also in the high feast of the Assumption of our Blessed Lady, the day of All Saints, and on Good Friday, accustomably and miserably holden and used in the realm of England in which the principal and festival days for great earthly covetise, the people is more willingly vexed, and in bodily labor foiled, than in other ferial days, as in fastening and making their booths and stalls, bearing and carrying, lifting and placing their wares outward and homeward, as though they did nothing, remember the horrible defiling of their souls in buying and selling, with many deceitful lies and false perjury, with drunkenness and strifes, and so specially withdrawing themselves and their servants from divine service; the aforesaid lord the king, by advice and assent of the lords spiritual and temporal and the commons of this realm of England, being in the said Parliament, and by the authority of the same Parliament, hath ordained that all manner of fairs and markets in the said principal feasts and Sundays and Good Fridays, shall clearly cease from all showing of any goods and merchandises (necessary victual only excepted) upon pain of forfeiture of all the goods aforesaid so showed, to the lord of the franchise or liberty where such goods, contrary to this ordinance be or shall be showed (the four Sundays in harvest excepted). Nevertheless, of his special grace, by authority aforesaid, granteth them power which of old time had no day to hold their fair or market, but only upon the festival days aforesaid, to hold by the same authority and strength of his old grant, within three days next before the said feasts, or next after, proclamation first made to the simple common people, upon which day the aforesaid fair shall be holden, always to be certified, without any fine or fee to be taken to the king's use. And they which of old time have, by special grant, sufficient days before the feasts aforesaid or after, shall in like manner, as aforesaid, hold their fairs and markets the full number of their days, the said festival days and Sundays and Good Fridays excepted.

Henry VI, statute 27.[19]

1469   Because of keeping of holy days and divine service, which are greatly broken, and namely, in the collection of customs and annual rents, in-casting and out-casting of tenants, which cause great dissension, and causes ofttimes great gatherings and discord upon solemn days if Whit-Sunday and Martin-mas; for the eschewing of the which, it is thought expedient in this present Parliament, that the said collecting of customs and annual rents, in-casting and out-casting of tenants, be deferred to the third day after Whit-Sunday and Martin-mas, without prejudice of any persons, and in likewise there be no fairs holden on holy days, but on the morning after.

Fifth Parliament of King James III.[20]

1579   For inasmuch as it is enacted and ordained by a good and godly Act, made in the days of King James IV, our Sovereign Lord's grandfather, of worthy memory, that there be no markets nor fairs holden upon holy days, nor yet within churches or churchyards upon holy days or other days, under pain of forfeiting of the goods; which Act our Sovereign Lord and his three estates ratifies and approves and ordains the same to have effect and execution in time coming. And seeing that the Sabbath day is now commonly violated and broken, as well within burghs as in the country, to the great dishonor of God, by holding and keeping of the said markets and fairs on Sabbath days, using of hand-labor, and working thereon, as on the remaining days of the week, and by gaming and playing, passing to taverns and ale-houses, and the wilfull remaining from their parish church in time of sermon and prayers on the Sabbath; Therefore, his Majesty, and his three estates, in this present Parliament enact and ordain, that there be no markets nor fairs holden upon the Sabbath day, nor yet within churches or church-yards, that day or any other day, under the pain of forfeiture of the goods to the use of the poor within the parish. And likewise, that no hand-laboring, nor working be used on the Sabbath day, nor no gaming and playing, passing to taverns and ale-houses, or selling of meat or drink, or wilfull remaining from their parish church in the time of sermon or prayers on the Sabbath day be used, under the pains following: that is to say, of every person, for the hand-laboring and working, commonly used by the poorest sort, ten shillings, and for gaming, playing, passing to taverns and ale-houses, selling of meat and drink, and wilfull remaining from their parish church in time of sermon or prayers on the Sabbath day, of every person twenty shillings, to be applied to the help and relief of the poor of the parish. And in the case of the refusal, or inability of any person offending in the premises, to pay the said pains respectively, presently and promptly, upon their apprehension or conviction, after lawful trial, he or she shall be put and holden in the stocks, or such other engine devised for public punishment, for the space of twenty-four hours. And for execution hereof, the King's Majesty's commission of Justice shall be granted to some person in every parish, best fitted and able to perform the same, at the request of the minister.

Sixth Parliament of King James VI.[21]

1594 Our Sovereign Lord and estates of this present Parliament ratify and approve the Acts made by his Highness of before, concerning the discharging of holding of markets upon the Sabbath day, with this admonition: That whosoever profanes the Sabbath day by selling, or presenting, or offering to be sold upon the said day, any goods or gear, or whatsoever merchandise by themselves or any other in their name, and is three several times lawfully convicted thereof, either before the provost and bailies within the burgh, where the profanation shall happen to be committed, or before certain commissioners and justices in every Presbytery, to be appointed by the King's Majesty, with advice of his privy council, their whole goods and gear shall be forfeited to his Majesty's use, and their persons punished at the will of his Majesty, with advice of his secret council.

Fourteenth Parliament of King James VI.[22]

1656 Forasmuch as God hath appointed one day in seven to be kept holy unto himself, and that in order thereunto man should abstain from the works of his ordinary calling, and hath intrusted the Magistrate amongst others, to take care thereof within his gates; and whereas it is found by daily experience, that the first day of the week (being the Lord's-day, and since the resurrection of Christ to be acknowledged as the Christian Sabbath) is frequently neglected and prophaned to the dishonor of Christ, and Profession of the Gospel; therefore for the better observation of the said Day, and preventing in some measure such Prophanation thereof for the future, be it enacted by his Highness the Lord Protector, and the Parliament of the Commonwealth of England, Scotland, and Ireland, and the Dominions thereunto belonging, that whatsoever person or persons within this commonwealth shall be found guilty according to this act, of doing and committing the offenses hereafter mentioned upon the said Lord's-day, that is to say, betwixt twelve of the clock on Saturday night and twelve of the clock Lord's-day night, shall be adjudged, deemed, and taken to be guilty of prophaning the Lord's-day; that is to say every person being a waggoner, carrier, butcher, higler, drover, or any of their servants travelling or coming by land or water, into his or their inn, house, or lodging within the times aforesaid; and every innkeeper victualler, or ale-house keeper, who shall lodge and entertain any such waggoner, carrier, butcher, higler, drover or their servants, coming and travelling as aforesaid; Every person using or employing any Boat, Wherry, Lighter, Barge, Horse, Coach of Sedan or travelling or labouring with any of them upon the day aforesaid (except it be to and from some place for the service of God, or except in case of necessity, to be allowed by some Justice of the Peace); Every person being in any Tavern, Inn, Alehouse, Victualling house, Strongwater house, Tobacco house, Celler or Shop, (not lodging there, nor upon urgent necessity, to be allowed by a Justice of the Peace) or fetching or sending for any wine, ale or beer, tobacco, strongwater, or other strong liquor unnecessarily, and to tipple within any other house or shop; And the keepers or owners of every such houses, cellars or shops, keeping or causing to be kept their doors ordinarily and usually open upon the Day aforesaid; every person dancing or prophanely singing or playing upon musical instruments, or tippling in any such houses, cellars or shops or elsewhere upon the day aforesaid, or harbouring or entertaining the persons so offending; Every person grinding or causing to be ground any corn or grain in any mill, or causing any fulling or other mills to work upon the day aforesaid; And every person working in the washing, whiting, or drying of clothes thread or yarn, or causing such work to be done, upon the day aforesaid; Every person setting up, burning or branding beef, turf or earth, upon the day aforesaid; Every person gathering of rates, loans, taxations, or other payments upon the day aforesaid (except to the use of the poor in the public collections); Every chaundler melting, or causing to be melted, tallow or wax belonging to his calling; and every common brewer and baker, brewing and baking, or causing bread to be baked, or beer or ale to be brewed upon the day aforesaid; And every butcher killing any cattle, and every butcher, coffermonger, poulterer, herb seller, cord wayner, shoemaker or other persons selling, exposing or offering to sell any their wares or commodities, and the persons buying such wares or commodities, upon the day aforesaid; All tailors and other tradesmen, fitting or going to fit, or carry and wearing apparel or other things; and barbers trimming upon the day aforesaid; All persons keeping, using or being present upon the day aforesaid at any Fairs, Markets, Wakes, Revels, Wrestlings, Shootings, Leaping, Bowling, Ringing of Bells for pleasure, or upon any other occasion (save for calling people together for the public Worship) Feasts, Church Ale, May-Poles, Gaming, Bear-Baiting, Bull-Baiting, or any other Sports and Pastimes; All persons unnecessarily walking in the Church or Church-Yards, or elsewhere in the time of Public Worship; And all persons vainly and profanely walking, on the day aforesaid; And all persons travelling, carrying Burthens, or doing any worldly labour or work of their ordinary Calling on the day aforesaid, shall be deemed guilty of prophaning the Lord's-day.

And it is enacted by the Authority aforesaid, that every person being of the age of fourteen years or upwards, offending in any of the premises, and being convicted thereof by confession, or the view of any Mayor, Head-Officer or Justice of the Peace, or upon the testimony of one or more witnesses upon oath, before any such Mayor, Head-Officer or Justice of the Peace in the County, City, Division or place where the offense shall be committed (which oath the said Mayor, Justice of Peace or Head Officer, shall and may administer) shall for every such offense whereof he shall be so convicted, forfeit the sum of ten shillings; Besides which forfeitures, all and every person and persons selling, exposing, or offering to sell any wares or commodities upon the day aforesaid, and in like manner duly convicted, shall have their wares and commodities so sold, exposed or offered to be sold, seized and disposed of as is by this act appointed.

Provided, and is hereby enacted and declared, that nothing in this act contained, shall extend to the prohibiting the dressing of meat in private families, or the dressing or sale of victuals in a moderate way in Inns, Victualling-houses, or Cooks' Shops, for the use of such as cannot otherwise be provided for, or to the crying or selling of milk before nine of the clock in the morning or after four of the clock in the afternoon, from the tenth of September, till the tenth of March; or before eight of the clock in the morning, or after five of the clock in the afternoon, from the tenth of March till the tenth of September, yearly, nor to hinder any other works of piety, necessity or mercy, to be allowed by a Justice of the Peace.

And whereas many navigable rivers or waters extend themselves into, or are the bounds of more counties than one, by reason whereof some doubts have been raised, whether the Justices of the Peace of any County lying on the one side of such river have any, or how far they may have, jurisdiction or power upon or over the same; be it therefore enacted by the Authority aforesaid, that the Justices of the Peace of any such county, or the Constable or other officers of any Parish lying on either side of such river, shall have power, and are hereby authorized and required to put this Act into execution, for the apprehension and punishing of all Water-Men, Barge-Men or other persons whatsoever, who shall on the said day be found contrary to this Act, travelling, rowing or working in or with any boat, lighter, barge, or other smaller vessel on any part of such river, and the said boats, lighters, barges and other vessels, shall seize and stay, or cause to be seized and stayed, until twelve of the clock of the said night, and until the penalties hereby inflicted on such person or persons as shall be discovered to have offended therein, be duly paid and satisfied to the officer or officers of that town or parish (on either side of such river) as shall first discover and attempt the pursuing, seizing and staying thereof.

And it is enacted by the Authority aforesaid, that all elections, swearing and taking of place of Mayors, Sheriffs, Bayliffs, Aldermen, or other officer whatsoever, in any city, borough, town corporate, or any other place within this Commonwealth, that after the first day of August next ensuing, by virtue or color of any Act of Parliament, charter, custom, prescription, or otherwise, should or might fall out to be upon a Lord's-day; and all commissions and courts, which by means of any adjournment or other cause; and all returns of writs which shall fall out to be upon any Lord's-day as aforesaid, shall be, and are hereby authorized and required to be kept, had and done, sat upon, and executed upon the next day which shall ensue such Lord's day; and all Mayors, Recorders, Stewards, Town Clerk, or other officers or persons whatsoever, that have, or after the said first day of August next, shall have power and authority to elect, swear, or give any charge or oath for taking any such place, oath or office, or to keep any courts, shall and may, and are hereby authorized and required to make such elections, give such oath and charge, and take such oaths, places or offices, or keep such courts as above said, upon the day next ensuing such Lord's-day; and that all customs, rents, and services due to lords of mannors, which by virtue of any custom, prescription or otherwise, are, or ought to be done, performed, and paid upon any Lord's-day, shall, after the said first day of August next, be done, performed and paid upon the day next following such Lord's-day, and shall be as valid and effectual to all intents and purposes whatsoever, as if the same had been done upon the said Lord's-day; and that all rents, sums of money, covenants and conditions, payable or performable upon any Lord's-day, shall and may be paid and performed upon the day next ensuing such Lord's-day, and that such payment and performance thereof, shall be as good and effectual in the Law, to all intents and purposes, to save all penalties, re-entries or forfeitures whatsoever, as if the same had been made and performed at or upon the day limited or appointed in or by any bond, lease, covenant, indenture, or other deed or agreement whatsoever, any law, usage or custom to the contrary hereof notwithstanding.

And that no Fair, Market, or Proclamation of any Fair or Market shall be had, made or used upon any Lord's-day, but upon the day next ensuing, nor shall any person or persons serve, or cause to be served, any writ, process, warrant, order, judgement or decree (except in cases of treason, felony, breach of the peace, and prophanation of the Lord's-day) upon pain that every person and persons bodies politic and corporate, offending in any of the particulars last mentioned, shall forfeit the sum of five pounds to be recovered in name of the Lord Protector, by bill, plaint, writ or action of debt in any Court of Record, or upon information or indictment before the Justices of the Peace in the open Sessions, who have thereby power to hear and determine the same, and to be disposed; viz. One moyety to the use of His Highness, the Lord Protector, and the other moyety to the use of him or them that will sue or prosecute for the same; and that the service of every such writ, action, process, warrant order, judgment or decree shall be void to all intents and purposes whatsoever.

And whereas many Fairs and Markets are kept upon Saturdays and Mondays, whereby is often occasioned the prophanation of the Lord's-day, it is hereby enacted by the Authority aforesaid, that all and every person and persons resorting to sell or buy commodities in any such Fairs and Markets, shall in due time come to and depart from the same, and strictly observe the laws and rules of the Markets, that the observation of the Lord's day may not thereby be violated, upon pain that every person travelling to or from such Fairs or Markets upon the Lord's-day, and duly convicted as aforesaid, before one or more Justices of the Peace, who have hereby power by their own view, confession of the parties, or the oath of one or more witnesses (which oath they may administer) to hear and determine the same, shall forfeit for every offense the sum of ten shillings.

And to the end this Act may be duly observed and henceforth put into execution, be it enacted by the Authority aforesaid, that all and every Mayor, Head Officers and Justices of the Peace within their respective Counties, limits and jurisdictions, are hereby enjoyned and authorized from time to time under their hands and seals, to appoint and require such Churchwardens, Overseers of the Poor, Constables, and other persons within their several jurisdictions, as they shall think fit, to seize and secure such wares and commodities as shall be sold, exposed, cryed or offered to sale contrary to this Act, upon the day aforesaid, and to search for, discover, secure, apprehend and bring before them or any other Justice of the Peace of the County or place where they shall be apprehended, all and every person and persons whom they shall find prophaning and violating, or shall know or be informed to have prophaned and violated the Lord's-day in any of the particulars herein mentioned, or shall just cause to suspect for the same; which said warrant so received, the said Constables, Tythingmen, Churchwardens, Overseers of the Poor, or either of them to whom the said warrant is or shall be directed, shall make publication of in said Parish-Church or Chapel fourteen days before execution of the same, and after such publication and end of the said fourteen days, the said Constables, Tythingmen or Overseers of the Poor so authorized, and every of them, are hereby required and authorized to do and perform their duties accordingly, without expecting any particular warrant for the same, upon such pains and penalties as are hereafter in this Act inflicted upon willful neghlecters of their duty.

And for the better execution of the powers aforesaid, the Constables, Churchwardens or Overseers of the Poor so authorized, are hereby required and authorized to demand entrance into any dwelling-house or other place whatsoever suspected by them to harbor, entertain or suffer to be any person or persons prophaning the Lord's-day; and if such entrance be either willfully delay or refused, all and every person or persons so delaying or refusing, being convicted thereof (as by this Act is appointed) shall forfeit the sum of twenty shillings.

And all Churchwardens and Overseers of the Poor, and Constables within their several limits, are hereby enjoyned and authorized upon their own view and knowledge, as well with warrant as without, to seize, and secure all such wares and commodities, sold, exposed or offered to be sold, and to apprehend, secure and stop all offenders against this law, with their horses and carriages (if any such shall be) and after apprehension, to bring such offenders before any Justice of the Peace, to be dealt with according to the directions of this Act unless the offender shall forthwith pay the penalty forfeited by this Act to such officer.

And it is enacted by the Authority aforesaid, that if any

children or servants under the age of fourteen years, offending in any of the offenses within this Act mentioned, and thereof convicted before any Mayor, Head-officer, or any one or more Justices of the Peace as aforesaid, the parents, guardians, masters, mistresses or tutors of all such children and servants shall forfeit the sum of one shilling for every such servant or child so offending and thereof convicted as aforesaid, unless such parent, guardian, master, mistress or tutor, shall in the presence of the Church-wardens, Overseers of the Poor, or other officer, or one of them, give or cause to be given unto such child or servant so offending, due correction.

And to the end that no prophane licentious person or persons whatsoever may in the least measure receive encouragement to neglect the performance of Religious and Holy duties on the said day, by colour of any law or laws giving liberty to truly tender consciences; be it enacted by the Authority aforesaid, that all and every person and persons shall (having no reasonable excuse for their absence, to be allowed by a Justice of the Peace of the County where the offense shall be committed) upon every Lord's-day diligently report to some Church of Chappel where the true worship and service of God is exercised, or shall be present at some other convenient Meeting place of Christians, not differing in matters of faith from the publique profession of the nation, as it is expressed in the humble petition and advice of the Parliament to His Highness, the Lord Protector, where the Lord's-day shall be duly sanctified, according to the true intent and meaning of this act, upon pain that all and every such person or persons so offending, shall for every such offense, being thereof convicted forfeit the sum of two shillings and six-pence.

And it is enacted by the Authority aforesaid, that no person being the minister or publique preacher of or in any Church, Chappel or publique congregation within this Commonwealth, and officiating and doing his duty therein upon any Lord's-day, or at any other times, shall be molested, hindered or disturbed therein by any person whatsoever; and if any person or persons shall after the first day of August next ensuing, maliciously, wilfully, or of purpose molest, let, disturb, disquiet or otherwise trouble any such minister or publique preacher in the doing and performing the duty of their respective places, or in his going to or returning from such place, or make or cause to be made any publique disturbance in any part of the Lord's-day in any of the places aforesaid, it shall, and may be lawful to and for any Churchwarden, Overseer of the Poor, or Constable of the Parish and place where such molestation, disturbance and disquieting shall be, and they are hereby enjoyned to apprehend all and every person and persons offending therein; or in the case of escape before such apprehension, for the Churchwardens, Overseers of the Poor, or Constables of any Parish or place where such offender shall be found, to apprehend them and every of them, as well without warrant as with warrant, and bring them before the Mayor, or any Justice of the Peace or Head-Officer where any such person or persons shall be apprehended, and if such Mayor, Justice or Head officer shall find cause upon his own view, confession of the party, or the oath of one or more sufficient witnesses (which oath he shall have hereby power to administer) then he shall commit such person to prison, there to remain without bail or mainprize until the next general Sessions of the Peace to be holden for the County, City or place where the offense shall be committed; and if upon information, presentment or indictment, such person or persons shall at the General Sessions of the Peace (who have hereby power to hear and determine the same by confession or oath of two or more sufficient witnesses) be found guilty for maliciously, willfully or of purpose molesting, letting, disturbing or otherwise troubling such minister or public preacher, or making any disturbance as aforesaid, every person so convicted, shall forfeit the sum of five pounds, one moyety to the use of High Highness, the Lord Protector, and the other moyety to him or them that will sue or prosecute for the same; or at the discretion of the said Justices, shall be sent to the House of Correction or Work-house, to be set at hard labour; with such moderate correction, as in the discretion of the said Justices shall be thought fit, for some time, not exceeding six months.

And it is enacted by the Authority aforesaid, that all persons contriving, printing or publishing any papers, books or pamphlets for allowance of sports and pastimes upon the Lord's-day, or against the morality thereof, shall forfeit the sum of five pounds, or be committed to the House of Correction as aforesaid.

And it is enacted by the Authority aforesaid, that in

case any wares, or commodities shall be seized and secured for being sold, exposed, or offered to be sold, contrary to this Act and the offenders therein convicted as aforesaid, all such wares and commodities, or the value thereof, at the discretion of the Mayor, Head Officer of Justice, shall be disposed of to the use of the poor of the parish where such wares shall be first seized, saving that it shall be in the power of such Mayor, Justice of Peace or Head-Officer, out of the same to reward any person that shall inform, or otherwise prosecute any person for the said offense, according to their discretion, so as such reward exceed not the third part of the wares and commodities so seized, and so as no reward be given to any person upon whose oath only the offender shall be convicted; and all sums of money and forfeitures not otherwise disposed of by this Act, shall be employed for the use of the poor of the Parish where the several offenses shall be committed, saving only that it shall be lawfull to and for any Mayor, Justice of Peace or Head Officer, out of the said forfeitures to reward any such persons that shall inform, or otherwise prosecute any persons for the same, according to their discretion, so as such reward exceed not the third part of the forfeiture, and so as no reward be given to any person upon whose oath only the offender shall be convicted.

Provided always, that no person or persons shall be impeached or molested for any offense within this Act, unless he or they be thereof convicted within one month after the offense committed.

And it is enacted by the Authority aforesaid, that all Mayors, Justices of the Peace, Head Officers, the Governors of Inns of Court and Chancery, all masters and Governors of schools, and families and the governors of the Company of Water-men for the river of Thames (who for the purposes in the Act mentioned shall have the power of Constables upon the said river, and upon any keys, wharfs or banks thereof) and all other officers and persons herein concerned, are hereby enjoined and authorized within their several limits and jurisdictions, to see this Act put in due and speedy execution, upon pain that all and every person and persons neglecting to do his and their respective duties, in putting this Act in due and speedy execution, being thereof duly convicted by bill, plaint, writ or action of debt, in any Court of Record, or upon presentment, information or indictment before any Justices of the Peace in their open sessions (who have hereby power to hear and determine the same) shall forfeit the sum of five pounds; one moyety whereof shall be to the use of His Highness, the Lord Protector, and the other moyety to him or them that will prosecute for the same.

And it is hereby enacted by the Authority aforesaid, that no writ of Certiorari shall be granted or allowed for the removing any action, suit presentment, information, indictment, or any other proceedings against any person for offending against this law; and that in any action brought against any Justice of Peace, Churchwardens, Overseers of the Poor, Constables, or any other officers or persons whatsoever, for acting or doing, or commanding to be acted or done, any matter or thing in pursuance to this Act, or for being aiding or assisting thereunto, the defendant in every such action shall and may plead the general issue, and give the special matter in evidence, and upon Non suit of the Plaintiff, or verdict passing for the Defendant, the Defendant shall have and recover his and their treble costs.

And it is lastly enacted, that the Churchwardens or other officers of every parish within this Commonwealth, do at the charge of the Parish procure one or more of these acts to be safely kept in their respective parishes; and the ministers of each Parish are hereby enjoyned in every year, that is to say, upon the first Lord's-day in March yearly, immediately before the morning sermon to read, or cause to be read, this present Act.

Provided, that this act shall not extend to authorize or impower any constables or officer, without the special warrant of one or more Justice or Justices of the Peace, to enter, or demand entrance into any house upon pretence of execution of his or their office by virtue of this act, other than into taverns, inns, ale-houses, tobacco shops, victualling-houses, or tippling-houses, anything in this Act to the contrary notwithstanding.

Enacted by the Parliament Commencing
17 Sept. 1656.

1661   The King's Majesty, considering how much it concerns the honor of God that the Sabbath day be duly observed, and all abuses thereof restrained, and that notwithstanding of several Acts of Parliament, made in that behalf, particularly the third Act of the Sixth Parliament of King James VI, of blessed memory, the said day has been much profaned by salmon-fishing, running of salt-pans, mills and kilns, hiring of shearers, and using of merchandise on that day, and other ways. Therefore, our Sovereign Lord, with advice and consent of his estates of Parliament, made for observation of the Sabbath day, and against the breakers thereof: and by these presents inhibits and discharges all salmon-fishing, running of salt-pans, mills and kilns, all hiring of shearers, carrying of loads, keeping of markets, or using any sorts of merchandise on the said day, and all other profanation thereof whatsoever, under the pains and penalties following, viz.: The sum of twenty pounds Scots for the running of each salt-pan, mill or kiln on the said day, to be paid by the heritors and possessors thereof, and the sum of ten pounds for each shearer and fisher of salmon, on the said day, the one-half thereof to be paid by the hirers and conductors, and the other half to be paid by the persons hired; and the said sum of ten pounds for every other profanation of the said day; and which fines and penalties are to be uplifted and disposed of, in manner contained in the Act and instructions concerning the justices of peace; and if the party offending be not able to pay the penalties aforesaid, then to be exemplarily punished in his body, according to the merit of his fault.

The First Parliament of Charles II.[23]

1676   For the better observation and keeping holy the Lord's day, commonly called Sunday, be it enacted by the King's most excellent majesty, and by and with the advice and consent of the lords, spiritual and temporal, and of the commons in this present Parliament assembled, and by the authority of the same, that all the laws enacted and in force concerning the observation of the day, and repairing to the church thereon, be carefully put in execution; and that all and every person and persons whatsoever shall upon every Lord's day apply themselves to the observation of the same, by exercising themselves thereon in the duties of piety and true religion, publicly and privately; and that no tradesman, artificer, workman, laborer, or other person whatsoever, shall do or exercise any worldly labor or business or work of their ordinary callings upon the Lord's day, or any part thereof (works of necessity and charity only

excepted), and that every person being of the age of fourteen years or upwards offending in the premises shall, for
every such offense, forfeit the sum of five shillings; and
that no person or persons whatsoever shall publicly cry,
show forth, or expose for sale any wares, merchandise,
fruit, herbs, goods, or chattels whatsoever, upon the Lord's
day, or any part thereof, upon pain that every person so
offending shall forfeit the same goods so cried or showed
forth or exposed for sale.

2. And it is further enacted that no driver, horse-
courser, wagoner, butcher, higgler—they or any of their
servants—shall travel or come into his or their inn or lodging upon the Lord's day, or any part thereof, upon pain
that each and every such offender shall forfeit twenty shillings for every such offense; and that no person or persons
shall use, imploy, or travel upon the Lord's day with any
boat, wherry, lighter, or barge, except it be upon extraordinary occasion to be allowed by some justice of the
peace of the county, or some head officer, or some justice
of the peace of the city, borough, or town corporate, where
the fact shall be committed, upon pain that every person so
offending shall forfeit and lose the sum of five shillings for
every such offense.

6. Provided, also, that no person or persons upon the
Lord's day shall serve or execute, or cause to be served or
executed, any writ, process, warrant, order, judgment, or
decree (except in case of treason, felony, or breach of the
peace), but that the service of every such writ, process,
warrant, order, judgment, or decree, shall be void to all
intents and purposes whatever; and the person or persons
so serving or executing the same shall be as liable to the
suit of the party grieved, and to answer damages done to
him for the doing thereof, as if he or they had done the
same without any writ, process, warrant, order, judgment,
or decree at all.

Twenty-Ninth Parliament of King
Charles II.[24]

Early Sunday Laws in America

The Act enacted by the twenty-ninth Parliament of Charles II was the prevailing law of the British colonies in America up to the time of the American
Revolution. It provided the basis for most of the early American Sunday

laws. The first Sunday law passed by British subjects on American soil was enacted by the Colony of Virginia in 1610. Colonial laws are presented, by colony, in chronological order.

VIRGINIA

1610   Every man and woman shall repair in the morning to the divine service and sermons preached upon the Sabbath day, and in the afternoon to divine service, and catechising, upon pain for the first fault to lose their provision and the allowance for the whole week following; for the second, to lose the said allowance and also be whipt; and for the third to suffer death.[25]

1623   Whosoever shall absent himself from divine service any Sunday, without an allowable excuse, shall forfeit a pound of tobacco, and he that absenteth himself a month shall forfeit 50 lbs of tobacco.[26]

1705   If any person of full age shall absent from divine service at his or her parish church or chapel, the space of one month (except such Protestant dissenters as are exempted by the act of Parliament made in the first year of King William and Queen Mary) and shall not, when there, in a decent and orderly manner continue till the service be ended: and if any person shall on the Lord's day, be present at any disorderly meeting, gaming, or tippling, or travel upon the road, except to and from church (cases of necessity and charity excepted) or be found working in their corn, tobacco, or other labor of their ordinary calling, other than is necessary for the sustenance of man or beast; every such person being lawfully convicted of any such default or offence, by confession or otherwise, before one or more justice or justices of the county, within two months after such default or offense made or committed, shall forfeit and pay five shillings, or fifty pounds of tobacco for every such default or offence; and on refusal to make present payment, or give sufficient caution for payment thereof at the laying of the next parish levy, shall, by order of such justice or justices, receive, on the bare back, ten lashes, well laid on.[27]

1786   If any person on Sunday shall himself be found labouring at his own or any other trade or calling, or shall employ his apprentices, servants or slaves in labour, or other business, except it be in the ordinary household offices of daily necessity, or other work of necessity or charity, he shall forfeit the sum of ten shillings for every such offence, deeming every apprentice, servant or slave so employed, and every day he shall be so employed as constituting a distinct offence.[28]

MASSACHUSETTS

1650   Further be it enacted that whosoever shall prophane the Lords day be doeing any servill worke or any such like abusses, shall forfeite for every such default tenn shillings or be whipte.[29]

1671   9. This court taking notice of great abuse, and many misdemeanours, committed by divers persons in these many wayes, Profaning the Sabbath or Lords day, to the great dishonour of God, Reproach of Religion, and Grief of the Spirits of God's People.

Do therefore Order, That whosoever shall profane the Lord's-day, by doing unnecessary servile Work, by unnecessary travailing, or by sports and recreations, he or they that so transgress, shall forfeit for every such default forty shillings, or be publickly whipt: But if it clearly appear that the sin was proudly, Presumptuously and with a high hand committed, against the known Command and Authority of the blessed God, such a person therein despising and reproaching the Lord, shall be put to death or grievously punished at the Judgement of the court.

10. And whosoever shall frequently neglect the public Worship of God on the Lord's-day, that is approved by this Government, shall forfeit for every such default convicted of, ten shillings, especially where it appears to arise from negligence, Idleness, or Prophaneness of Spirit.[30]

1797   Whereas the observance of the Lord's day is highly promotive of the welfare of a community, by affording necessary seasons for relaxation from labour and the cares of business; for moral reflections and conversations on the duties of life, and the frequent errors of human conduct; for public and private worship of the Maker, Governor and Judge of the world; and for those acts of charity which support and adorn a Christian society: And whereas some thoughtless and irreligious persons, inattentive to the duties and benefits of the Lord's day, profane the same, by unnecessarily pursuing their worldly business and recreations on that day, to their own great damage of the community, by producing dissipation of manners and immoralities of life:

1. Be it enacted by the Senate and House of Representatives, in General Court Assembled, and by the authority of the same, That no person or persons whatsoever shall keep open his, her or their shop, warehouse, or workhouse, nor shall, upon land or water, do any manner of labor, business or work (works of necessity and charity only excepted) nor be present at any concert of music, dancing, or public diversion, show or entertainment, nor use any sport, game, play, or recreation, on the Lord's day, or any part thereof, upon penalty of a sum not exceeding twenty shillings, nor less than ten shillings, for every offense.[31]

CONNECTICUT

1656

Whosoever shall profane the Lord's day, or any part of it, either by sinful servile work, or by unlawful sport, recreation, or otherwise, whether wilfully or in a careless neglect, shall be duly punished by fine, imprisonment, or corporally, according to the nature, and measure of the sin, and offence. But if the court upon examination, by clear and satisfying evidence find that the sin was proudly, presumptuously, and with a high hand committed against the known command and authority of the blessed God, such a person therein despising and reproaching the Lord, shall be put to death, that all others may feare and shun such provoking rebellious couises.[32]

1721

Whatsoever person shall be guilty of any rude and unlawful behavior on the Lord's Day, either in word or action, by clamorous discourse, or by shouting, hollowing, screaming, running, riding, dancing, jumping, winding horns or the like, in any house or place so near to any publick meeting house for divine worship that those meet there may be disturbed, shall be fined forty shillings.[33]

MARYLAND

1692–
1715

Be it enacted . . . that from and after the publishing of this law, no person or persons whatsoever within this

Province, shall work or do any bodily labor or occupation upon the Lord's Day, commonly called Sunday . . . (the works of absolute necessity and mercy always excepted) . . . nor shall abuse or profane the Lord's Day by drunkenness, swearing . . . And if any person or persons . . . shall offend in any or all of these premises, he . . . shall forfeit and pay for every such offense the sum of one hundred pounds of tobacco.[34]

1723   Be it enacted, That no person whatsoever shall work or do any bodily labor on the Lord's day, commonly called Sunday, and that no person having children, servants, or slaves, shall command, or wittingly or willingly suffer any of them to do any manner of work or labor on the Lord's day, (works of necessity and charity always excepted) nor shall suffer or permit any children, servants, or slaves, to profane the Lord's day by gaming, fishing, fowling, hunting, or unlawful pastimes or recreations; and that every person transgressing this act, and being thereof convict by the oath of one sufficient witness, or confession of the party before a single magistrate, shall forfeit two hundred pounds of tobacco, to be levied and applied as aforesaid.[35]

PENNSYLVANIA

1682   But to the end That Looseness, irreligion, and Atheism may not Creep in under the pretense of Conscience in this Province, Be It further Enacted by the Authority aforesaid, That, according to the example of the primitive Christians, and for the ease of the Creation, Every first day of the week, called the Lord's day, People shall abstain from their usual and common toil and labour, That whether Masters, Parents, Children, or Servants, they may the better dispose themselves to read the Scriptures of truth at home, or frequent such meetings of religious worship abroad, as may best sute their respective persuasions.[36]

NEW YORK

1695   Whereas the true and sincere service and worship of God, according to his holy will and commandments, is often profaned and neglected by many of the inhabitants and sojourners within this Province, who do not keep holy the Lord's day, but in a disorderly manner, accustom themselves to travel, laboring, working, shooting, fishing, sporting, playing, horseracing, frequenting of tippling-houses, and the using of many other unlawful exercises and pastimes upon the Lord's day, to the great scandal of the holy Christian faith:

Be it therefore enacted . . . that there shall be no travelling, servile laboring and working, shooting, fishing, sporting, playing, horse racing, hunting, or frequenting of tippling-houses, or the use of any other unlawful exercises or pastimes, by any of the inhabitants or sojourners within this Province, or by any of their slaves or servants, on the Lord's day; and that every person or persons offending in the premises shall forfeit for every offense the sum of six shillings . . . and in default of such distress, that the party offending, to be set publicly in the stocks by the space of three hours.[37]

NEW HAMPSHIRE

1700   That all and every person and persons whatsoever, shall on that day carefully apply themselves to duties of religion and piety, publicly and privately: and that no tradesman, artificer, or other person whatsoever, shall upon land or water, do or exercise, any labor, business, or work of their ordinary calling; nor use any game, sport, play, or recreation on the Lord's day, or any part thereof (works of necessity and mercy only excepted) upon pain that every person so offending shall forfeit five shillings . . .

And in case any such offender be unable or refuse to satisfy such fine, to cause him to be put in the cage, or set in the stocks, not exceeding three hours.[38]

GEORGIA

1762   Whereas there is nothing more acceptable to God than the true and sincere worship and service, according to his holy will, and that the keeping holy of the Lord's day is a principal part of the true service of God, which in this province is too much neglected by many . . . be it enacted . . . that all and every person and persons whatsoever, shall on every Lord's day, apply themselves to the observation of the same, by exercising themselves thereon in the duties of piety and true religion, publicly or privately, or having no reasonable or lawful excuse, on every Lord's day shall resort to their parish church, or some meeting or assembly of religious worship, tolerated and allowed by the laws of England, and there shall abide, orderly and soberly, during the time of prayer and preaching, on pain of forfeiture for every neglect of the sum of two shillings and sixpence Sterling.

II. That no tradesman, artificer, workman, laborer, or other person whatsoever, shall do or exercise any worldly labor, business or work of their ordinary callings upon the Lord's day, or any part thereof (works of necessity or charity only excepted) and that every person, being of the age of fifteen years or upwards, offending in the premises, shall, for every such offense, forfeit the sum of ten shillings. . . .

III. No drover waggoner, butcher, higler, they or any of their servants, or any other traveller, or person whatsoever, shall travel on the Lord's day . . . except it be to the place of religious worship, and to return again, or to visit or relieve any sick person, or unless the person or persons were belated the night before, and then to travel no farther than to some convenient inn or place of shelter for that day, or upon some extraordinary occasion for which he, she, or they shall be allowed to travel under the hand of some justice of the peace of this province.

VI. That the church-wardens and constables of each parish respectively, or any one or more of them, shall, once in the forenoon, and once in the afternoon, in the time of divine service, walk through the town of Savannah and the respective towns of this province, to observe, suppress and apprehend all offenders whatsoever contrary to the true intent and meaning of this act; . . . and all persons whatsoever are strictly commanded and required to aiding and assisting any constables, or other officers, in their execution of this act, on the penalty of ten shillings Sterling for every refusal.

VII. . . . In case of default of such distress, or in case of insufficiency or inability of the said offender to pay the said forfeiture or penalties, that then the party offending be set publicly in the stocks for the space of two hours.[39]

NORTH CAROLINA

1741   Whereas in well-regulated governments effectual care is always taken that the day set aside for public worship

be observed and kept holy; and, to suppress vice and immorality, Wherefore . . . be it enacted . . . that all and
every person and persons whatsoever shall, on the Lord's
Day, commonly called Sunday, carefully apply themselves
to the duties of religion and piety; and that no tradesman,
artisan, planter, laborer, or other person whatsoever, shall
upon the land or water do or exercise any labor, business,
or work of their ordinary callings, (works of charity and
necessity only excepted) nor employ themselves either in
hunting, fishing, or fowling, nor use any game, sport, or
play, on the Lord's Day aforesaid, or any part thereof,
upon pain that every person so offending, being of the age
of fourteen years and upwards, shall forfeit and pay the
sum of ten shilling.[40]

NEW JERSEY

1693

Whereas, it hath been the practice of all societies of
Christian professors to set aside one day in the week for the
worship and service of God, and that it hath been and is
the ancient law of England, (according to the practice of
the primitive Christians) to set apart the first day of the
week to that end, and finding by experience that the same
good practice and law hath been greatly neglected in this
province, to the grief of such as profess the Christian
religion, and to the scandal thereof. Be it therefore enacted
. . . that if any person or persons shall within this province
be found doing any unnecessary servile labor, or shall
travel upon the Lord's day, or first day (except to some
religious service or worship, or otherwise in case of necessity) or shall be found tippling, sporting, or gaming,
thereby profaning the Lord's day, or first day, shall, upon
conviction thereof before one justice of the peace, forfeit
and pay for every such offense six shillings.[41]

DELAWARE

1795

Whereas the penalties which have hitherto been
inflicted upon those who profane the Lord's Day, commonly called Sunday, have been found insufficient to deter
many persons from such immorality; therefore, Be it
enacted . . . that if any person or persons, after the passing
of this act, shall do or perform any wordly employment,
labor or business whatsoever, upon the Lord's Day, commonly called Sunday, (works of necessity and charity only

excepted) . . . such person or persons so offending, for every such offense, shall forfeit the sum of four dollars; and upon the refusal or inability to pay the said fine and the legal costs, he or she shall be imprisoned in the public goal of the county, for any space of time not exceeding twenty-four hours.[42]

RHODE ISLAND

1679   Be it enacted by the General Assembly, and by the authority of the same, That no person or persons within this Colony shall do or exercise any labor or business or work of their ordinary calling, nor use any game, sport, play or recreation on the first day of the week, nor suffer the same to be done by their children, servants or apprentices (works of necessity and charity only excepted), on the penalty of five shillings for every such offense . . . together with the reasonable charges accruing thereon; and in the case such offender shall not have sufficient to satisfy the same, then to be set in the stocks by the space of three hours.[43]

TENNESSEE

1803   If any person shall be guilty of exercising any of the common vocations of life, or of causing or permitting the same to be done by his children of his servants, acts of real necessity or charity excepted, on Sunday, he shall, on due conviction thereof before any justice of the peace of the county, forfeit and pay ten dollars ($10.00), one half to the person who will sue for the same, the other half for the use of the county.[44]

Enforcement

Captain Kemble of Boston, Massachusetts, in 1656 was locked in the public stocks for two hours for kissing his wife on the Sabbath after spending three years at sea. The charge was "unseemly behavior."[45]

In the 1800s, the following citizens of Arkansas were convicted of violating Sunday laws:[46]

James A. Armstrong : for "digging potatoes in his field" . . . was fined $26.50.

James A. Armstrong : for "working in his garden" . . . was fined
(a second time) $4.65.

F.N. Elmore : for "digging potatoes" . . . was fined $28.95.

William L. Gentry : for "plowing on his farm" . . . was fined
    $28.80.

John A. Meeks : for "shooting squirrels on Sunday" was fined
    $22.00.

J.L. Munson : for "cutting briars out of the fence corners at
    the back of his field" . . . was fined $14.20.

J.L. Shockey : for "hauling rails and clearing land" . . . was
(a second time)   fined $10.00.

James M. Pool : for "hoeing in his garden" . . . was fined
    $30.90.

John Neusch : for "gathering early peaches which were over-
    ripe and were in danger of spoiling" . . . was
    fined $25.00.

Alexander Holt : for "having worked on a farm in the northern
    part of Hot Spring County" . . . was fined
    $16.00.

I.L. Benson : for "painting the railroad bridge" . . . was
    fined $4.75.

Even George Washington, the then newly elected President of the United States was not immune from prosecution under Sabbath laws in 1789. While traveling from Connecticut to a town in New York to attend worship service one Sunday, Washington was challenged by a tithingman for violating Connecticut's law forbidding travel on Sunday.[47] That law prohibited anyone from walking or riding unnecessarily on the first day of the week. Washington was permitted to continue on his journey only after he promised to go no further than the town intended.

Although the fines mentioned do not seem high by standards in 1987, they represented substantial penalties in previous periods. Moreover, one could, for willful profanation of the Lord's Day, be put to death. If the punishments seem harsh by the standards of the twentieth century, perhaps they were not so severe as judged by the prevailing times. As reported by Trumbull [1876], 223 offenses were punishable by death in England in the year 1819. Only twelve offenses were declared to be capital by the earliest penal codes of Massachusetts (1641) and Connecticut (1642).

Despite the severity of the law, the specificity of their application, and the not-so-occasional meting out of punishment, there exists ample evidence of widespread civil disobedience to the early English and colonial American Sabbath laws. The titles of, and preambles to, a great many of these early statutes state the unambiguous intention of curbing the rampant profanation of the Lord's Day.

The disobedience in colonial America is a consequence ironic, albeit unsurprising, of the lack of freedom of religion in America. What those early Puritans demanded of English authority was freedom to exercise their religion, not freedom for others to practice as they would. Once they reached the shores of America, there was no toleration of competition from Baptists, other religious denominations, or atheism. Church attendance was mandatory, under penalty of severe fines. The preambles of many of the early Sabbath laws also address the religious character of those laws, especially the intent to enforce the church's monopoly vis-à-vis saving men's souls and collecting alms, from rich and poor alike. The central position of the church with respect to Sunday-closing laws has diminished considerably since the late 1700s, however, the restriction of competition theme has not. This issue will be taken up again in chapters 4 and 5.

Famous Court Decisions

There have been three principal challenges to the legality of blue laws over the decades: substantive, procedural, and preemptive. Substantive challenges center on claims that blue laws violate freedom of religion and unlawfully restrain trade. The preponderance of litigation has involved procedural issues, in which plaintiffs have argued violations of federal and state equal protection and due process provisions, discriminatory enforcement, and impermissable delegation of legal rule-making authority to local jurisdictions. The line of attack via the preemptive argument is that state-enacted blue laws are preemptive by conflicting federal legislation, especially the Sherman Act [1890], which forbids monopolization in restraint of trade and conspiracies to restrain trade.

The U.S. Supreme Court has consistently upheld the constitutionality of Sunday-closing laws, despite the barrage of litigation and the mixed record of blue laws decisions at the state level. The high court first considered the legality of blue laws in the case of *Soong v. Crowley* (1884), but it was not until 1961 that the Court ruled decisively on the issue, across the spectrum of appeals. In that year, four cases were argued before the Supreme Court; in all of them the constitutionality of blue laws was upheld, by wide majorities.

The first, and perhaps most significant, case to be decided was *McGowan v. Maryland* (1961). Challenges to the legality of Maryland's blue laws were raised on both substantive and procedural grounds, by a discount chain store. The store operators contended that the prohibition against Sunday-selling violated their rights under the First and Fourteenth Amendments. The store argued that Sunday was the Sabbath of predominantly Christian sects and that the purpose of the enforced stoppage of labor on that day was to facilitate or encourage, or both, church attendance. The First Amendment to the U.S. Constitution prohibits laws respecting an establishment of religion, or prohibiting the free exercise thereof. Writing for an eight-to-one majority, Chief Justice Earl Warren conceded that Sunday blue laws were originally motivated by religious forces, but held that, previous history notwithstanding, the state had a secular interest in setting one day apart as a day of rest, repose, recreation, and tranquility. That is, the State was recognized as maintaining a legitimate public interest in promoting the well-being of its citizenry; discretion in such promotion was left, of course, to the states. Moreover, the Court found, that Sunday laws involved no direct cooperation between the state and religious groups and did not entail the use of public money to aid a particular religion. Therefore, it concluded that Sunday-closing laws do not violate the establishment clause of the First Amendment.

The second case, *Two Guys from Harrison–Allentown v. McGinley* (1961) was also decided on First Amendment grounds. The plaintiffs challenged the Sunday closing law in Pennsylvania on the grounds that legislatively imposed sanctions inhibiting business on Sunday constituted a forbidden establishment of religion. The Court rejected their appeal because the appellants did not demonstrate injury to their own religious practices.

Both *Braunfeld v. Brown* and *Gallagher v. Crown Kosher Super Market* involved Orthodox Jewish Sabbatarian merchants who voluntarily closed their shops on Saturday, which is the Jewish Sabbath, but attempted to remain open on Sunday in violation of closing laws in Massachusetts and Pennsylvania, respectively. They argued that denial of Sunday as a day of business to a person who observes Saturday as his bona fide Sabbath inhibits the free exercise of religion. Both appeals were turned down by the Supreme Court, which found that Sunday-closing laws do not exert economic pressure which, by itself, is sufficient to amount to a constitutionally prohibited restraint on their free exercise of religion. Moreover, the Court determined that the secular purpose and interest in Sunday-closing laws outweighed, and therefore justified, any religious injury inflicted.

In response to the procedural challenge raised by *McGowan,* that implementation of the law arbitrarily affected certain individuals but not others, the Court responded:

> The Fourteenth Amendment permits the States a wide scope of discretion in enacting laws which affect some groups of citizens differently than others. The constitutional safeguard is offended only if the classification rests on

grounds wholly irrelevant to the achievement of the State's objective. State legislatures are presumed to have acted within their constitutional power despite the fact that, in practice, their laws result in some inequality. A statutory discrimination will not be set aside if any state of facts reasonably may be conceived to justify it.[48]

The "rational basis test" set forth in *McGowan* legitimizes blue laws if any state of fact can be conceived to justify them. It is precisely this issue that Roger Simon addresses in the quote that opens this book—can one conceivably argue that sales of an item are acceptable in one store but not in a different store, or that sales of certain items are permissible but not sales of similar items? Can one justify the fact that camera film can be sold but not cameras? Nails but not hammers? With this guideline, a number of state courts have invalidated Sunday-closing laws by determining that classifications in their state's respective schemes in fact rest on grounds wholly irrelevant to the achievement of the state's objective. In 1976, the New York Court of Appeals struck down New York's blue law for exactly this reason. Although the court recognized as valid in principle the state's secular interest in promoting Sunday as a day of rest, it found that the "gallimaufry of exceptions [to the law had] obliterated any natural nexus" between the law and its purpose.[49]

Unlike the courts in a number of other states, the Maryland high court declined to even acknowledge the possibility that numerous changes or exceptions to the state's blue laws could, at some point, destroy the law's rationality (in providing equal protection). Instead, the court absolved itself from responsibility by declaring that the enacting body, the legislature, maintained exclusive authority to remedy possible defects in the law:

> The Maryland Sunday Blue Laws have been soundly denounced by some persons. They have been characterized as unwise, complex, a patchwork, a crazy quilt, a labyrinth, a legal maze, unnecessarily befuddling statutory crabgrass, an inconvenience, a hypocrisy. But even if they were, they could not for those reasons be voided by the judiciary. As we have indicated, absent some constitutional infirmity the judiciary simply has no power to interfere. We have determined that sec. 534L and 534N, contrary to appellants' contentions, are constitutionally valid. The statutes must stand firm until the General Assembly of Maryland changes them. If it concludes that the public welfare requires that Sunday business activities can no longer be proscribed in Baltimore County and Anne Arundel County, or in fact in any other county, or city or town, *it has the power and the means to effectuate its conclusion.*[50] [Emphasis added]

Additional challenges to the legality of blue laws have been based on violation of due process charges, which are similar to, yet distinct from, the equal protection guarantees. For example, several states have struck down blue law provisions because the statutory language was unconstitutionally vague.[51] The violation of Fourteenth Amendment due process provisions results from the failure of the law to give merchants proper notice of prohibited behavior. On the other hand, arguably vague designations such as "emergency" repairs and "garden and lawn supplies" have been upheld by courts in other states.[52] Again, the unmistakeable grant of judicial approval for legislative vagueness was provided by the high court of Maryland in the *McGowan* case, in which the Court found that "business people of ordinary intelligence would be able to know what exceptions are encompassed by the statute . . . as a matter of ordinary commercial knowledge."[53]

The equal protection challenge to blue laws also arises in connection with the enforcement of the laws. When the plaintiff demonstrated that the law was enforced in an arbitrary or discriminatory manner, convictions under validly enacted blue laws have been overturned. In *New York v. Acme Markets, Inc.* (1975) the New York Court of Appeals found that the blue law in question violated the equal protection clauses of the federal and state constitutions because there was no general policy of enforcement and a history of prosecution only when private citizens complained to the enforcement authorities. In a similar vein, the Kentucky Court of Appeals found discriminatory enforcement of that state's blue laws in *City of Ashland v. Heck's, Inc.* (1966), since the department store in question was the only entity in the city found guilty of violating the law in twenty-five years. However, discriminatory purpose is not presumed by the courts, and according to Dilloff [1980, p. 711] such a defense is most successful when law enforcement officials only enforce the law when asked to do so by merchant-competitors or other special-interest groups.

In the late 1970s, Texas's blue law was challenged on the grounds that it was preempted by the Sherman Antitrust Act, a federal law that prohibits restraint of trade. The supremacy clause of the Federal Constitution (art. iv, sec. 2) provides that the Constitution of the United States shall be the supreme law of the land, not to be preempted by any other law, including, obviously, state law. The Texas Supreme Court rejected this argument in *Gibson Distributing Co. v. Downtown Development Association* (1978), on the grounds that state action affecting commerce is generally exempted from the Sherman Act, although the door was not slammed completely shut on this line of attack.

Concluding Thoughts

Almost from their earliest inception and for most of their history, blue laws have been closely and explicitly tied to the church. The separation of church and state mandated by the U.S. Constitution has, over the past two centuries, eliminated much of the overt religious support for Sunday-closing laws. The decline of the prominent role played by the church in supporting the enact-ment and enforcement of blue laws did not, however, bring about a corre-sponding decline in the importance of those laws. Instead, the states, for a variety of reasons which will be further investigated in chapter 4, insisted upon their right to regulate Sunday trading for secular reasons.

It is abundantly clear from the judicial record that state legislatures are accorded full authority to regulate Sunday trading in order to promote the general public well-being. Only when the regulations themselves are violative of rights granted under the U.S. Constitution or enforcement of the statutes is discriminatory have the courts deigned to overrule state authority on the issue. By and large, then, the real public policy issues must be fought out in the state legislatures. The results of past lobbying and politicking are, of course, observable as today's state laws. These are presented in the next chapter. The issues at stake and the interested parties on both sides are identi-fied in chapter 4 and analyzed for empirical veracity in chapter 5.

Notes

1. A.H. Lewis [1888], p. 19.
2. Ibid., p. 34.
3. Ibid., pp. 36–7.
4. Ibid., pp. 39–40.
5. Ibid., pp. 41–2.
6. Ibid., p. 43.
7. Ibid., pp. 45–6.
8. Ibid., pp. 47–8.
9. Ibid., p. 64.
10. Id.
11. Id.
12. Ibid., pp. 65–6.
13. Ibid., p. 71.
14. Ibid., pp. 72–3.
15. Ibid., p. 73.
16. Ibid., p. 78.
17. Ibid., p. 82.
18. Ibid., p. 90.
19. Id.
20. Ibid., p. 144.
21. Ibid., pp. 145–6.
22. Ibid., p. 148.
23. Ibid., pp. 148–9.
24. Ibid., pp. 108–9; see also, *Maryland Law Review,* Vol. 39, No. 1, 1979, "Never on Sundays."

25. W.A. Blakely [1970], p. 33.

26. Ibid., p. 34.

27. Ibid., pp. 34–5.

28. 366 U.S. 420, McGowan et al. v. Maryland [1960]. Other statutes cited in 366 U.S. 420 include: 1629; 1642–1643 (traveling, shooting); 1657: The Sabboth to bee kept holy (traveling, shooting, lading); 1661–1662: Sundays not to bee profaned; 1691: An act for the more effectual suppressing the severall sins and offences of swaring, cursing, profaineing Gods holy name, Sabbath abuseing, drunkenness, ffornication, and adultery; 1786: An act for punishing disturbers of Religious Worship and Sabbath breakers.

29. Blakely, *supra* note 25, p. 36; Lewis, p. 161.

30. Ibid., pp. 36–7; see also 366 U.S. 617.

31. Ibid., pp. 40–1; 366 U.S. 420 provides the following additional references: 1650: Prophanacon the Lord's Day, Compact with the Charter and Laws of the Colony of New Plymouth; 1658: traveling; 1671: General Laws of New Plymouth; 1653: Sabbath, Colonial Laws of Massachusetts (traveling, sporting, drinking); 1668: For the better Prevention of the Breach of the Sabbath; 1692: An Act for the better Observation and Keeping the Lord's Day; 1761: An Act for Repealing the several Laws now in Force which relate to the Observation of the Lord's-Day, and for making more effectual Provision for the due Observation thereof; 1782: An Act for Making More Effectual Provision for the Due Observation of the Lord's Day; 1792: An Act providing for the due Observation of the Lord's Day.

32. Ibid., p. 42.; see also, Hinman [1838], p. 132.

33. Prince [1899], p. 124. Additional references from 366 U.S. 420 include: 1668: Public Records of the Colony of Connecticut, 1665–1678 (traveling, playing); 1672: Prophanation of the Sabbath, Laws of Connecticut, 1673; 1676: Public Records of the Colony of Connecticut, 1665–1678; 1750: An Act for the due Observation, and keeping the Sabbath, or Lord's Day; and for Preventing, and Punishing Disorders, and Prophaneness on the same, Acts and Laws of His Majesty's English Colony of Connecticut in New-England; 1784: An Act for the due Observation of the Sabbath or Lord's Day, Acts and Laws of the State of Connecticut; 1796: An Act for the due Observation of the Sabbath or Lord's-Day, Acts and Laws of the State of Connecticut.

34. Blakely, *supra* note 25, p. 45.

35. Ibid., p. 46. Additional references from 366 U.S. 420 include: 1649: An Act concerning Religion; 1654: Concerning the Sabboth Day; 1674: An Act against the Prophaning of the Sabbath day; 1692: An Act for the Service of Almighty God and the Establishment of the Protestant Religion within this Province; 1696: An Act for Santifying & keeping holy the Lord's Day Commonly called Sunday; 1723: An Act to punish Blasphemers, Swearers, Drunkards, and Sabbath-Breakers.

36. See 366 U.S. 582. Additional references from 366 U.S. 420 include: 1682: The Great Law or the Body of Laws; 1690: The Law Concerning Liberty of Conscience; 1700: The Law Concerning the Liberty of Conscience; 1705: An Act to Restrain People from Labor on the First Day of the Week; 1779: An Act for the Suppression of Vice and Immorality; 1786: An Act for the Prevention of Vice and Immorality; 1794: An Act for the Prevention of Vice and Immorality.

37. Blakely, *supra* note 25, p. 50. Additional references from 366 U.S. 420

include: 1685: A Bill against Sabbath breaking; 1695: An Act against profanation of the Lord's Day, called Sunday; 1788: An Act for Suppressing immorality.

38. Ibid., p. 51. Additional references from 366 U.S. 420 include: 1700: An Act for the better Observation and Keeping the Lords Day; 1715: An Act for the Inspecting and Suppressing of Disorders in Licensed Houses; 1785: An Act for the Better Observation and Keeping the Lords Day; 1789: An Act for the better Observation of the Lord's day; 1799: An Act for the better observation of the Lords day.

39. Ibid., pp. 51–3. Additional references from 366 U.S. 420 include: 1762: An Act For preventing and punishing Vice, Profaneness, and Immorality, and for keeping holy the Lord's Day, commonly called Sunday.

40. Ibid., pp. 53–4. Additional references from 366 U.S. 420 include: 1741: An Act for the better observation and keeping of the Lord's Day; commonly called Sunday; and for the more effectual suppression of vice and immorality.

41. Ibid., p. 54. Additional references from 366 U.S. 420 include: 1683: Against prophaning the Lord's Day; 1693: An Act for preventing Profanation of the Lords Day; 1704: An Act for Suppressing of Immorality; 1790: An Act to promote the Interest of Religion and Morality, and for suppressing of Vice; 1798: An Act for suppressing vice and immorality.

42. Ibid., p. 56. Additional references from 366 U.S. 420 include: 1740: An Act to prevent the Breach of the Lord's Day commonly called Sunday; 1795: An Act more effectually to prevent the profanation of the Lord's day, commonly called Sunday.

43. Ibid., p. 57. Additional references from 366 U.S. 420 include: 1679: An Act Prohibiting Sports and Labours on the First Day of the Week; 1798: An Act prohibiting Sports and Labour on the First Day of the Week.

44. Tennessee Code Annotated, sec. 39-4001 (1803).

45. Ripley's Believe It or Not, *Greenville News,* September 16, 1986, p. 3c.

46. Blakely, pp. 656–63.

47. For the original text of this incident, see "The President and the Tithing-man," *Columbian Centinel,* December 1789. In Earle [1891], pp. 74–75.

48. 366 U.S. at 425–26.

49. 366 N.Y.S. 2d at 662.

50. 286 Md. 611, 409 A.2d 250 (1979), *Supermarkets General Corp. v. Maryland.*

51. See, for example, *Minnesota v. Target Stores, Inc.,* 279 Minn. 447, 156 N.W. 2d. 908 (1968); *Henderson v. Antonacci,* 62 So. 2d. 5 (Florida 1952).

52. See, for example, *Malibu Auto Parts v. Virginia,* 218 Virginia 467 (1977) and *Genesco, inc. v. J.C. Penney Co.,* 313 So. 2d 20 (Mississippi 1975).

53. 366 U.S. at 428.

3
Sunday-Closing Laws:
State by State

The purpose of this chapter is to provide readers with a comprehensive review of state and local statutes, current to 1985, that restrict individual behavior on Sundays. The survey classifies Sunday-closing legislation into one of three categories: 1) restrictions on commercial activity, 2) restrictions on the sale of alcohol, and 3) restrictions on sales of automobiles. We preface the state-by-state survey with a brief discussion of the types of restrictions imposed by the various states, and close out the chapter with a discussion of the question of enforcement of the statutes.

Types of Sunday-Closing Legislation

In general, Sunday-closing laws have been enacted by the state legislatures, although a number of states permit municipalities or other units of local government to regulate Sunday activities.[1] Of course, such local restrictions cannot circumvent or otherwise interfere with state prohibitions.[2] Local regulations characteristically supplement the state statutes, but some states have delegated partial or complete responsibility for regulation of Sunday activities to local governments, including the ability to exempt themselves from state regulations provided they receive approval from the local electorate. Several counties in Maryland, for example, have voted to abolish their blue laws via referendum elections. The latest strategy in the battle to repeal blue laws, particularly in Louisiana, is to concentrate not on complete repeal of the laws, but rather, to solicit the political support needed to rewrite the state legislation to pass the mantle of responsibility for regulation from the state to the localities. The feeling of opponents of blue laws is that it is easier, politically, to beat many small localities individually on this issue than it is to change the law at the state level.

In practice, state regulation of Sunday activity has been accomplished by two general methods. A number of states and municipalities have enacted a general ban on all business and labor activity. In Kentucky, for example, "any person who works on Sundays at his own or at any other occupation or employs any other person, in labor or other business, whether for profit or amusement," is subject to a fine of between $2 and $50.[3] The state of Maryland prohibits retail activity by all outlets employing more than six employees and two guards. Virtually all states permit specific exemptions and exceptions to these general restrictions. These exceptions typically include works of "necessity" and "charity" in addition to individuals who worship on a day other than Sunday. Exemptions are made also for retail outlets that contribute to the ability of the public to take full advantage of Sunday as a day of relaxation, recreation, or religious observance.[4] Additional exceptions have been granted to special interest groups with strong enough lobbying influence in the corridors of the state capital, although the nominal reasons specified by the legislature for granting such exceptions typically refer back to public necessity or public convenience reasons, or both.

The second way in which politicians regulate Sunday activity is to impose specific prohibitions on identified activities. This requires the writing of a separate statute for each activity that is regulated, and the types of restrictions are (apparently) limited only by the imaginations of the legislators. Certain states restrict the hours during which alcoholic beverages may be sold on Sundays. Many others prohibit the sale of specific items or the engaging in specific activities such as boxing, wrestling, or hunting. Back when the city of Baltimore still had a National Football League team, the city used to regulate the starting times of the football games at Memorial Stadium. To be specific, games played there were not legally permitted to kick off before 1:00 p.m. on Sunday, so as to not compete with churches for the attendance (and money) of potential patrons. Table 3–1 identifies those states with general restrictions, and those states with specific restrictions, on Sunday activities.

Despite the general trend in recent years toward repeal of blue laws, most states still have some sort of statute that regulates Sunday activity. As of 1985, thirty-nine states restricted Sunday activities, in some fashion. It should be pointed out, however, that the number of states with general restrictions has undergone a steady decline since the early 1960s. In 1961, general Sunday regulations were in effect in thirty-four states, whereas in 1985 only twenty-two states still maintained general restrictions on Sunday behavior. Sunday-closing legislation is more prevalent in the East and South, while states with no restrictions or limited restrictions tend to be located in the Midwest and West. Aside from limited sales of alcohol, only ten states have no other regulations governing Sunday behavior. These states are Alaska, Arizona, California, Florida, Montana, Nebraska, New Mexico, Oregon, South Dakota, and Washington.

Many of the states that have passed general restrictions on Sunday activities also single out specific activities for prohibition under separate statutes. Boxing and wrestling, barbering, and hunting have draw particular attention

Table 3–1
States with General and Specific Blue Laws

General	Specific
Alabama	Colorado
Arkansas	Delaware
Connecticut	Hawaii
Georgia	Idaho
Kentucky	Illinois
Louisiana	Indiana
Maine	Iowa
Maryland	Kansas
Minnesota	Michigan
Mississippi	Missouri
New Hampshire	Nevada
New York	New Jersey
North Carolina	Ohio
North Dakota	Texas
Oklahoma	Utah
Pennsylvania	Wisconsin
Rhode Island	Wyoming
South Carolina	
Tennessee	
Vermont	
Virginia	
West Virginia	

in this regard across the fifty states, as have a number of sporting activities, even though one of the stated purposes of blue laws is to encourage recreational activity on Sunday. Similarly, states which have repealed their general blue laws very often continue to restrict specific activities. New Jersey, for example, which repealed its general Sunday-closing laws in 1978, continues to prohibit, on Sunday, bingo playing, raffles, pawnbrokers, barbers, beauty parlors, hunting, and the digging of oysters and other shellfish under separate statutes.

By far and away the most common type of restriction concerns the sale of alcoholic beverages on Sunday. In most states which dispense liquor through state-run outlets, legislation prevents these stores from opening on Sundays. Roughly one-third of all states prohibit any sale of alcoholic beverages. Other states prohibit the sale of hard liquor but permit the sale of beer and wine. Still others restrict the hours during which alcohol may be sold, where it may be sold, and how it may be sold. For example, liquor stores are closed on Sunday in Maryland by state law, but there are no restrictions on the types of alcoholic beverage one can order in a restaurant on Sunday.

As an overview of the specific laws detailed in the next section, table 3–2

Table 3–2
Types of Sunday-Closing Laws and Number of States

Restricted Activity	Number of States
Alcohol Sales (total ban)	15
Banking	4
Barbering	11
Beauty Shops	3
Billiard Rooms	2
Bingo	3
Bowling	3
Boxing and Wrestling	14
Card Playing	2
Cock Fighting	2
Dancing/Public Entertainment	5
Digging Oysters/Clams	2
Gaming	3
General Labor/Work	18
Horse Racing	9
Hunting	11
Motion Pictures	2
Motor Vehicle Sales	8
Moving Large Vehicles on Public Highways	2
Parades	1
Pawnbrokers	4
Polo	1
Raffles	1
Retail Sales	19
Sale of Fresh Meat	1
Serving Civil Process	3
Sports	4
Tobacco Warehouse Sales	1

Source: Statutes of the fifty states.

lists the various activities regulated by blue laws throughout the country and the number of states having a statute for each specific activity. Table 3–3 identifies the states that have restrictive statutes pertaining to each activity.

State-by State Survey of Laws

Alabama

Sunday laws that affect retail sales:

> Any person who compels his child, apprentice, or servant to perform any labor on Sunday, except the customary domestic duties of daily necessity or comfort, or works of charity or who engages in shooting, hunting, gaming, card playing or racing on that day, or

Table 3-3
State Restrictions by Activity—1985

Alcohol Sales	Bowling	Horse Racing
Arkansas	Maine	Alabama
Georgia	Maryland	Arkansas
Idaho	Rhode Island	Illinois
Illinois		Louisiana
Kansas		Maine
Kentucky	*Boxing and Wrestling*	Minnesota
Louisiana	Alabama	Mississippi
Maine	Arkansas	New Hampshire
Michigan	Delaware	New York
Mississippi	Idaho	
Missouri	Illinois	*Hunting*
North Dakota	Indiana	Alabama
Ohio	New Hampshire	Delaware
Rhode Island	North Dakota	Georgia
South Carolina	Oklahoma	Maryland
	Pennsylvania	Mississippi
	Rhode Island	New Jersey
Banks	Utah	North Carolina
Alabama	West Virginia	Ohio
Georgia	Wyoming	Pennsylvania
Nevada		Tennessee
Wisconsin		West Virginia
	Butcher Shops	
Barbering	Louisiana	*Labor*
Louisiana		Alabama
Maryland		Connecticut
Michigan	*Card Playing*	Louisiana
Minnesota	Alabama	Maine
New Jersey	Arkansas	Maryland
New York		Massachusetts
Ohio		Minnesota
Pennsylvania	*Cock Fighting*	Mississippi
Rhode Island	Arkansas	New Hampshire
Tennessee	Mississippi	Pennsylvania
		Rhode Island
		South Carolina
Beauty Shops	*Dancing*	Tennessee
Georgia	Georgia	Vermont
New Jersey	New Jersey	Virginia
Pennsylvania	New York	West Virginia
	South Carolina	
Billiard Rooms		*Motion Pictures*
Georgia	*Fresh Meat Sales*	Maine
Rhode Island	Pennsylvania	South Carolina
Bingo	*Gaming*	*Motor Vehicle Sales*
New Jersey	Alabama	Colorado
New York	Massachusetts	Connecticut
Oklahoma	South Carolina	

Table 3–3 (Continued)

Motor Vehicle Sales (Cont'd)	Polo	Retail Sales (Cont'd)
Iowa	Pennsylvania	Pennsylvania
Maine		Rhode Island
Michigan	*Raffles*	South Carolina
Oklahoma	New Jersey	Texas
Pennsylvania		
Rhode Island	*Retail Sales*	*Serving Civil Process*
	Alabama	Massachusetts
Moving Large Vehicles	Arkansas	New York
Kansas	Georgia	South Carolina
Wisconsin	Kentucky	
	Louisiana	*Sports (general)*
	Maine	Maine
Parades	Maryland	Massachusetts
New York	Massachusetts	New York
	Minnesota	South Carolina
Pawnbrokers	Mississippi	
Michigan	Missouri	*Tobacco Warehouse Sales*
New Jersey	New Hampshire	Georgia
Pennsylvania	New York	
Rhode Island	North Carolina	

who, being a merchant or shopkeeper, druggist excepted, keeps open store on Sunday, shall be fined not less than $10.00 nor more than $100.00, and may also be imprisoned in the county jail, or sentenced to hard labor for the county, for not more than three months. However, the provisions of this section shall not apply to the operation of railroads, airlines, buslines, communications, public utilities, or steamboats or other vessels navigating the waters of this state, or to any manufacturing establishment which is required to be kept in constant operation, or to the sale of gasoline or other motor fuels or motor oils. Nor shall this section prohibit the sale of newspapers, or the operation of newsstands, or automobile repair shops, florist shops, fruit stands, ice cream shops or parlors, lunch stands or restaurants, delicatessens or plants engaged in the manufacture or sale of ice; provided, that such business establishments are not operated in conjunction with some other kind or type of business which is prohibited by this section. It shall also be lawful to engage in motorcycle and automobile racing on Sunday, whether admission is charged or not; except, that this proviso shall not be construed to prevent any municipality from passing ordinances prohibiting such racing on Sunday. CODE OF ALABAMA (1852), sec. 73; CODE (1867), sec. 3614; CODE (1876), sec. 4443; CODE (1886), sec. 4045; CODE

(1907), sec. 7814; Acts (1923), No. 417, p. 559; CODE (1923), sec. 5539; CODE (1940), T. 14, sec. 420; Acts (1951), No. 433, 433m, p. 783, sec. 1; Acts (1953), No. 230, p. 297; CODE (1975), sec. 13-6-1; CODE (1975), sec. 13A-12-1 [1982 replacement Vol. 12].

Any person who opens, or causes to be opened, for the purpose of selling or trading, any public market or place on Sunday, or opens, or causes to be opened, any stall or shop therein, or connected therewith, or brings anything for sale or barter to such market or place, or offers the same for sale therein on that day, or buys or sells therein on that day, including livestock or cattle, shall, on conviction, be punished as prescribed in section 13A-12-1. Any place where people assemble for the purchase and sale of goods, wares and merchandise, provisions, cattle or other articles is a market house or place within the meaning of this section. CODE (1867), sec. 3615; CODE (1876), sec. 4444; CODE (1886), sec. 4046; CODE (1896), sec. 5543; CODE (1907), sec. 7819; CODE (1923), sec. 5541; CODE (1940), T.14, sec. 422; CODE (1975), sec. 13-6-2; CODE (1982), sec. 13A-12-2 [1982 replacement Vol. 12].

Alaska

Sunday laws that affect retail sales—none in general.

Exceptions:
(a) Liquor sales—none.
(b) Motor vehicle sales—none.

Arizona

Sunday laws that affect retail sales—none in general.

Exceptions:
(a) Liquor sales—It is unlawful for an on-sale or off-sale retail licensee or an employee of such licensee to sell, dispose of, deliver or give spirituous liquor to a person between the hours of one o'clock a.m. and twelve o'clock noon on Sundays. It is unlawful for an on-sale retail licensee or an employee of such licensee to allow a person to consume spirituous liquors on the premises between the hours of one fifteen a.m. and twelve o'clock noon on Sundays. ARIZ. REV. STAT. ANN. sec. 4-244, (Supp. 1985).
(b) Motor vehicle sales—none.

Arkansas

Sunday laws that affect retail sales—none in general. However, the city council or board of managers of any city or incorporated town in this State shall have the authority, by ordinance, to regulate that operation of businesses within such cities or towns on Sunday. Acts (1957), No. 367; ARK. STAT., sec. 19-2335 [1980 replacement, Vol. 2B].

Exceptions:

(a) Liquor sales: The sale of intoxicating liquor on Sunday is declared to be a misdemeanor, and any person who shall sell intoxicating liquor on Sunday shall be punished by a fine of not less than one hundred ($100.00) dollars nor more than two hundred and fifty ($250.00) dollars for the first offense; and for the second and subsequent offenses he shall be punished by a fine of not less than two hundred and fifty ($250.00) dollars nor more than five hundred ($500.00) dollars or by imprisonment in the county jail for not more than one year, or both such fine and imprisonment in the discretion of the jury or court. Acts (1943), No. 257, sec. 2; ARK. STAT., sec. 48-904 [1977 Replacement, Vol. 4A].

No agent or person engaged in the liquor business in the state of Arkansas shall solicit or take or accept any orders on the Sabbath for the purchase or delivery of any alcoholic beverages. Acts (1939), No. 352, sec. 5; ARK. STAT., sec. 48-905 [1977 Replacement, Vol. 4A].

It shall be unlawful for any person, persons, firm, or corporation to sell on Sunday any wine or beer. Acts (1943), No. 281, sec. 1; ARK. STAT., sec. 48-906 [1977 Replacement, Vol. 4A].

Any person, persons, firm or corporation violating Section 1 [48-906] shall be punished by a fine of not less than $50.00, nor more than $100.00, and for the second offense be punished by fine and shall have the license revoked and forfeit all money paid for by said license and the trial court shall make a finding in its orders as to whether it is the first or second offense. Acts (1943), No. 281, sec. 2; ARK. STAT., sec. 48-907 [1977 Replacement, Vol. 4A].

(b) Motor vehicle sales—none.

California

Sunday laws that affect retail sales—none in general.

Exceptions:

(a) Liquor sales—none.

(b) Motor vehicle sales—none.

Colorado

Sunday laws that affect retail sales—none in general.

Exceptions:
(a) Liquor sales—(2) It is unlawful for any person licensed as a manufacturer or as a limited winery licensee pursuant to this article: (a) To make any delivery of malt, vinous, or spiritous liquors on Sunday, on general election day, or on any of the following legal holidays: New Year's Day, Memorial Day, Independence Day, Labor Day, or Christmas day, but nothing in this paragraph (a) shall apply to sales, shipments or deliveries made in interstate commerce to a wholesaler by a manufacturer of malt, vinous, or spiritous liquors; (4) It is unlawful for any person licensed to sell at wholesale pursuant to this article: (a) To make any delivery of malt, vinous, or spiritous liquors on Sunday, on general election day, or on any of the following legal holidays: New Year's Day, Memorial Day, Independence Day, Labor Day, Thanksgiving day, or Christmas day; (5) It is unlawful for any person licensed to sell at retail pursuant to this article: (b) To sell, serve, or distribute any malt, vinous, or spiritous liquors on any primary or general election day, as defined by article 1 of title 1, C.R.S. during polling hours, or on Sunday and Christmas except as permitted by paragraph (c) of this subsection (5). The provisions of this paragraph (b) shall not apply to any other election held in this state, including, but not limited to, elections held pursuant to title 22, title 23, parts 2 and 3 of article 20 of title 30, article 10 and parts 5 and 6 of article 25 of title 31, and title 32 (except article 8) C.R.S., or to a public transportation system. (B) For consumption on the premises, on Sundays and Christmas, beginning at 12 midnight until 2 a.m. and from 8.00 a.m. until 8 p.m. (II) Notwithstanding the provisions of subsubparagraph (B) of subparagraph (1) of this paragraph (c), hotel and restaurant licensees, beer and wine licensees, tavern licensees, club licensees, and arts licensees, upon the payment of an additional annual fee of two hundred dollars to the local licensing authority, may obtain a special license to sell, serve, or distribute malt, vinous, and spiritous liquors by the drink after the hour of 8 p.m. and until 12 midnight on Sundays and Christmas. Co. Rev. Stat., Vol. 5, 1985 Replacement Vol., Commerce IV, sec. 12-47-128.
(b) Motor vehicle sales—No person, firm, or corporation, whether owner, proprietor, agent, or employee, shall keep open, operate, or assist in keeping open or operating any place or premises or residences whether open or closed, for the purpose of selling, bartering, or exchanging or offering for sale, barter, or exchange,

any motor vehicle, whether new, used, or secondhand, on the first day of the week commonly called Sunday. This part 3 shall not apply to the opening of an establishment or place of business on the said first day of the week for other purposes, such as the sale of petroleum products, tires, or automobile accessories, or for the purpose of operating and conducting a motor vehicle repair shop, or for the purpose of supplying such services as towing and wrecking.

Any person, firm, partnership, or corporation who violates any of the provisions of this part 3 is guilty of a misdemeanor and, upon conviction thereof, shall be punished by a fine of not less than seventy-five dollars nor more than one thousand dollars, or by imprisonment in the county jail for not more than six months, (or the court, in its discretion, may suspend or revoke the Colorado motor vehicle dealer's license issued under the provisions of part 1 of this article), or by such fine and imprisonment and suspension or revocation. Co. REV. STAT., Vol. 5, 1985 Replacement Vol., Commerce IV, secs. 12-6-302 and 12-6-303.

Connecticut

Sunday laws that affect retail sales — none in general.

Exceptions:
(a) Liquor sales — (a) The sale or the dispensing or consumption or the presence in glasses or other receptacles suitable to permit the consumption of liquor by an individual of alcoholic liquor in places operating under hotel permits, cafe permits, restaurant permits for catering establishments, bowling establishment permits, racquetball facility permits, club permits, coliseum permits, coliseum concession permits, special sporting facility guest permits, special sporting facility concession permits, special sporting facility bar permits, golf country club permits and charitable organization permits shall be unlawful on Saturday between two o'clock a.m. and nine o'clock a.m. and Sunday after two a.m., or on Christmas, except when any Sunday is December thirty-first or January first, except that alcoholic liquor may be sold on Christmas for consumption on premises when served with hot meals, and except that any town may, by a vote of a town meeting or by ordinance, (1) allow the sale of alcoholic liquor between the hours of twelve o'clock noon on Sunday and one o'clock a.m. on Monday in hotels, restaurants, cafes, catering establishments, bowling establishments, racquetball facilities, clubs, golf country clubs and places operating under charitable organization

permits, a university permit, a coliseum permit, coliseum concession permit, a special sporting facility restaurant permit, a special sporting facility employee recreational permit, a special sporting facility guest permit, a special sporting facility concession permit or a special sporting facility bar permit and (2) prohibit the sale of alcoholic liquor from twelve o'clock midnight on Saturday until two a.m. on Sunday; and such sale or dispensing or consumption or presence in glasses or other receptacles suitable to permit the consumption of alcoholic liquor by an individual shall be unlawful on any other day between the hours of one o'clock a.m. and nine o'clock a.m., except that such sale shall be lawful on January first until three o'clock in the morning. Notwithstanding any other provisions of this section to the contrary, such sale or dispensing or consumption or presence in glasses in places operating under a bowling establishment permit shall be unlawful before five p.m. on any day, except in that portion of the permit premises which is located in a separate room or rooms entry to which, from the bowling lane area of the establishment, is by means of a door or doors which shall remain closed at all times except to permit entrance and egress to and from the lane area. Any alcoholic liquor sold or dispensed in a place operating under a bowling establishment permit shall be served in transparent containers such as, but not limited to, clear plastic or glass. When any Sunday falls on December thirty-first or January first, sale of alcoholic liquor in any club, golf country club, restaurant, cafe, catering establishment, bowling establishment, racquetball facility, coliseum, hotel or place operating under charitable organization permit shall not begin before twelve o'clock noon. The sale or dispensing or consumption or the presence in glasses or other receptacles suitable to permit the consumption of liquor by an individual or alcoholic liquor in places operating under night club permits may not be allowed except during the hour immediately following the closing time established under this section for the other permits listed in section 30-21a and on the days allowed under other such permits. Any town may, by vote of a town meeting or by ordinance, reduce the number of hours during which sales under this subsection shall be permissable.

(b) The sale or dispensing of alcoholic liquor in places operating under package store permits, drug store permits or grocery store beer permits shall be unlawful on Decoration Day, Independence Day, Labor Day, Thanksgiving Day, New Year's Day, Sunday or Christmas or, if Independence Day, Christmas, or New Year's Day occurs on a Sunday, on the Monday next following such day except that such sale or dispensing shall be lawful on any Independence Day occurring on a Saturday; and such sale or dispensing of alcoholic liquor in places operating under package store permits, drug store permits, and grocery store beer permits shall be unlawful on any other day before eight o'clock a.m. and after eight o'clock p.m. Any town may, by a vote of town meeting or by ordinance, reduce the number of hours during which such sale shall be permissable.

(c) The sale or the dispensing or consumption or the presence in glasses or other receptacles suitable to permit the consumption of liquor by an individual of alcoholic liquor in places operating under a tavern permit shall be unlawful on Saturday between two o'clock a.m. and nine o'clock a.m. and Sunday after two a.m. or on Christmas; and such sale or dispensing or consumption or presence in glasses or other receptacles in such tavern shall be unlawful on any other day between the hours of one o'clock a.m. and nine o'clock a.m. Any town may, by a vote of a town meeting or by ordinance, reduce the number of hours during which such sale shall be permissable or prohibit the sale of alcoholic liquor from twelve o'clock midnight on Saturday until two a.m. on Sunday or allow the sale of alcoholic liquor between the hours of twelve o'clock noon on Sunday and one o'clock a.m. on Monday in places operating under a tavern permit. In the case of any tavern wherein, under the provisions of this section, the sale of alcoholic liquor is forbidden on certain days or hours of the day, or during the period when a tavern permit is suspended, it shall likewise be unlawful to keep such tavern open to, or permit it to be occupied by, the public on such days or hours.

(d) In all cases when a town, either by vote of a town meeting or by ordinance, has acted on the sale of alcoholic liquors or the reduction of the number of hours when such sale is permissable, such action shall become effective on the first day of the month succeeding such action and no further action shall be taken until at least one year has elapsed since the previous action was taken. Nothing in this section shall be construed to require any permittee to continue the sale or dispensing of alcoholic liquor until the closing hour established under this section.

(e) The retail sale of wine and the tasting of free samples of wine by visitors and prospective retail customers of a farm winery permittee on the premises of such permittee shall be unlawful on Sunday before eleven o'clock a.m. and after eight o'clock p.m. and on any other day before ten o'clock a.m. and after eight o'clock p.m. Any town may, by vote of a town meeting or by ordinance, reduce the number of hours during which sales and the tasting of free samples of wine under this subsection shall be permissable.

(f) The sale or the dispensing or consumption or the presence in glasses or other receptacles suitable to permit the consumption of liquor by an individual or alcoholic liquor in places operating under airport restaurant permits and airport bar permits shall be unlawful on Saturday between two o'clock a.m. and nine o'clock a.m., and Sunday between two o'clock a.m. and eleven o'clock a.m., and such sale or dispensing or consumption or presence in glasses or other receptacles suitable to permit the consumption of alcoholic liquor by an individual shall be unlawful on any other day between the hours of one o'clock a.m. and nine o'clock a.m., except that such sale shall be lawful on January first until three o'clock in the morning. The sale or dispensing or consumption or the presence in glasses or other receptacles suitable to permit the consumption of liquor by an individual of alcoholic liquor in places operating under night club permits in Bradley International Airport may not be allowed except during the hour immediately following the closing time established under this section for such permits.

In all cases where a town, either by vote of a town meeting or by ordinance, had, prior to April 30, 1971, authorized the sale of alcoholic liquor on Sunday between the hours of twelve o'clock noon and nine o'clock in the evening, such sale shall be authorized until the time specified in section 30-91 unless an earlier closing hour is established by town meeting or ordinance after April 30, 1971.

Nothing in section 30–91 shall be construed to supersede any action taken by a town prior to May 25, 1971, to prohibit the sale of alcoholic liquor in such town from midnight on Saturday until one a.m. on Sunday and such action shall be construed to prohibit such sale from midnight on Saturday until two a.m. on Sunday in such town.

In all towns in which the sale of alcoholic liquor on Sunday between the hours of twelve o'clock noon and the time specified in section 30-91 is permitted, prior to June 5, 1975, in a place operating under a hotel permit, a restaurant permit or a cafe permit, such sale shall be authorized on Sunday between such hours in a place operating under a tavern permit unless such sale is prohibited by town meeting or ordinance after June 5, 1975.

In all towns which have authorized the sale of alcoholic liquor on Sunday commencing at twelve o'clock noon, either by vote of a town meeting or by ordinance, such sale shall be permitted commencing at eleven o'clock a.m. in places operating under hotel, restaurant, cafe, club or country club permits unless a later opening hour is established by vote of a town meeting or by ordinance after July 1, 1981. General Statutes of Connecticut, revised to January 1, 1985, vol. 9, sections 30-91 and 30-91a.

(b) Motor vehicle sales—No person, firm or corporation

engaged in the business of buying, selling, exchanging, dealing or trading in new or used motor vehicles shall open any place of business or lot wherein he attempts to or does engage in the business of buying, selling, exchanging, dealing or trading in new or used motor vehicles, or buy, sell, exchange, deal, or trade in new or used motor vehicles as a business on Sunday. Any person who violates the provisions of this section shall be fined not more than fifty dollars for the first offense and not more than one hundred dollars for each subsequent offense. Any licensed motor vehicle dealer who violates the provisions of this section shall, in addition to the fine provided herein, be subject to suspension of license as provided in section 14-64. The general statutes of Connecticut, revised to January 1, 1985, Vol. 13, section 53-301.

District of Columbia

Sunday laws that affect retail sales—none in general.

Exceptions:
  (a) Liquor sales—none.
  (b) Motor vehicle sales—none.

Florida

Sunday laws that affect retail sales—none in general.

Exceptions:
  (a) Liquor sales—none.
  (b) Motor vehicle sales—none.

Georgia

Sunday laws that affect retail sales—none in general.

Exceptions:
  (a) Liquor Sales—In all consolidated governments of this state within the limits of which the sale of alcoholic beverages is lawfully authorized, such sales for consumption on the premises shall be authorized, at the discretion of the governing body of the consolidated government, at any time from 11:55 p.m. on Saturdays and the two hours immediately following such time.
    In each county having a population of 550,000 or more according to the United States decennial census of 1970 or any future such census in which the sale of alcoholic beverages is lawful:

(1) The county governing authority may authorize the sale of alcoholic beverages for consumption on the premises at any time from 11:55 p.m. on Saturdays and the three hours immediately following such time; and

(2) Alcoholic beverages may be sold on Sundays between the hours of 12:30 p.m. and 12:00 midnight in public stadiums, coliseums, and auditoriums with a seating capacity in excess of 3,500 persons and in eating establishments. As used in this paragraph, the term "eating establishment" means an establishment which is licensed to sell distilled spirits, malt beverages, or wines and which derives at least 50 percent of its total annual gross food and beverage sales from the sale of prepared meals or food.

In all municipalities having a population of 300,000 or more according to the United States decennial census of 1970 or any future such census in which the sale of alcoholic beverages is lawful:

(1) The municipal governing authority may authorize the sale of alcoholic beverages for consumption on the premises at any time from 11:55 p.m. on Saturdays and the three hours immediately following such time; and

(2) Alcoholic beverages may be sold on Sundays, as provided in paragraph (2) of the previous paragraph.

In all counties having a population of not less than 350,000 according to the United States decennial census of 1980 or any future such census in which the sale of alcoholic beverages is lawful:

(1) The county governing authority may authorize the sale of alcoholic beverages for consumption on the premises at any time from 11:55 p.m. on Saturdays and the three hours immediately following such time; and

(2) Alcoholic beverages may be sold and served by the drink on Sundays from 12:30 p.m. until 12:00 midnight in any licensed establishment which derives at least 50 percent of its total annual gross food and beverage sales from the sales of prepared meals or food in all of the combined retail outlets of the individual establishment where food is served and in any licensed establishment which derives at least 50 percent of its total annual gross income from the rental of rooms for overnight lodging.

In all counties having a population of not less than 170,000 nor more than 275,000 according to the United States decennial census of 1980 or any future such census in which the sale of alcoholic beverages is lawful and in all municipalities within such counties in which the sale of alcoholic beverages is lawful, the governing authority of the county or municipality, as appropriate, may authorize the sale of alcoholic beverages for consumption on the premises:

(1) At any time from 11:55 p.m. on Saturdays until 2.55 a.m. on Sundays; and

(1) In eating establishments which are located in the unincorporated area of the county, in the case of the county, or which are located in the corporate limits of the municipality, in the case of a municipality, on Sundays between the hours of 12:30 p.m. and 12:00 midnight. As used in this paragraph, the term "eating establishment" means an establishment which is licensed to sell distilled spirits, malt beverages, or wines and which derives at least 50 percent of its total annual gross food and beverage sales from the sale of prepared meals or foods. In each county having a population of not less than 153,000 nor more than 165,000 according to the United States decennial census of 1980 or any future such census in which the sale of alcoholic beverages is lawful and in which the sale of alcoholic beverages is lawful, the governing authority of the county or municipality, as appropriate, may authorize the sale of alcoholic beverages on the premises:

(1) At any such time from 11:55 p.m. on Saturdays and the two hours immediately following such time; and

(2) In eating establishments which are located in the unincorporated area of the county, in the case of the county, or which are located in the corporate limits of the municipality, in the case of a municipality, on Sundays from 12:30 p.m. until 12:00 midnight. As used in this paragraph, the term "eating establishment" means an establishment which is licensed to sell distilled spirits, malt beverages, or wines for the consumption on the premises and which derives at least 50 percent of its total annual gross food and beverage sales from the sale of prepared meals or food.

In each county having a population of not less than 100,000 nor more than 150,000 according to the United States decennial census of 1970 or any future such census in which the sale of alcoholic beverages is lawful and in all municipalities in such counties in which the sale of alcoholic beverages is lawful, the governing authority of the county or municipality, as appropriate, may authorize the sale of alcoholic beverages for consumption on the premises in bona fide full-service restaurants at any time from 11:55 p.m. on Saturdays until 2:00 a.m. on Sundays; provided, however, that this subsection shall not apply to any geographic area of any municipal corporation which is located outside of the limits of any county in which the sale of alcoholic beverages is not lawful. As used in this subsection, the term "bona fide full-service restaurant" means an established place of business: (a) which is licensed to sell alcoholic beverages, distilled spirits, malt beverages, or wines for consumption on the premises; (b) where meals with substantial entrees selected by the patron from a full menu are served; (c) which has adequate facilities and sufficient employees for cooking or preparing and serving such meals for consumption at tables in dining rooms on the premises; and (d) which derives at least 50 percent of its gross income from the sale of such meals prepared, served, and consumed on the premises. The governing authority of such a county or municipality, by ordinance, may authorize any other establishment otherwise licensed to sell alcoholic beverages, distilled spirits, malt beverages, or wines for consumption on the premises to engage in such sales at any time from 11:55 p.m. on Saturday until 2:00 a.m. on Sundays; provided, however, that this subsection shall not apply to any geographic area of any municipal corporation which is located outside of the limits of any county in which the sale of alcoholic beverages is not lawful. The governing authority of such a county or municipality may provide for special licenses for and charge a license fee to establishments which engage in sales of such beverages at any time from 11:55 p.m. on Saturdays until 2:00 a.m. on Sundays. The license fee shall be set by the governing body.

In every county having a population of not less than 6,530 nor more than 6,600 according to the United States decennial census of 1970 or any future such census in which the sale of alcoholic beverages was lawful on April 11, 1979, and in all municipalities in such counties in which the sale of alcoholic beverages was lawful on April 11, 1979, the governing authority of the county or municipality, as appropriate, may permit and regulate Sunday sales by licensees if Sunday sales are approved by referendum as provided in this subsection. Any governing authority desiring to permit and regulate Sunday sales shall so provide by proper resolution or ordinance. Not less than ten nor more than 60 days after the date of approval of such resolution or ordinance, it shall be the duty of the election superintendent of the county or municipality to issue the call for an election for the purpose of submitting the question of Sunday sales to the electors of the county or municipality for approval or rejection. The superintendent shall set the date of the election for a day not less than 30 nor more than 60 days after the date of the issuance of the call. The superintendent shall cause the date and purpose of the election to be published in the official organ of the county once a week for two weeks immediately preceding the date thereof. The ballot shall have written or printed thereon the words:

[ ] YES Shall the governing authority of (name of municipality or county) be authorized to permit and regulate Sunday sales of
[ ] NO   distilled spirits or alcoholic beverages for beverage purposes by the drink?

All persons desiring to vote for approval of Sunday sales shall vote "Yes," and those persons desiring to vote for rejection of Sunday sales shall vote "No." If more than one-half of the votes cast on the question are for approval of Sunday sales, the governing authority may by appropriate resolution or ordinance permit and regulate Sunday sales by licensees. The expense of the election shall be borne by the county or municipality in which the election is held. It shall be the duty of the superintendent to hold and conduct the election. It shall be his further duty to certify the result thereof to the secretary of state.

In each county having a population of not less than 69,000 and not more than 75,000 according to the United States decennial census of 1980 or any future such census in which the sale of alcoholic beverages is lawful and in all municipalities in those counties in which the sale of alcoholic beverages is lawful, the governing authority of the county or municipality, as appropriate, may authorize the sale of alcoholic beverages for consumption on the premises at any time from 11:55 p.m. on Saturdays and one hour immediately following that time. This subsection shall not become effective in the unincorporated area of any such county or in any municipality unless the application to the unincorporated area of such county or municipality is approved at a referendum by the voters of the unincorporated area of any such county or municipality. Such referendum shall be held on the date of the first general primary election held after this paragraph first applies to the county or municipality. Not less than 30 nor more than 60 days prior to the date of such primary, it shall be the duty of the election superintendent of the county to issue the call for an election for the purpose of submitting this question to the electors of the unincorporated area of any such county and each affected municipality for approval or rejection. The superintendent shall set the date of such election for the date of said primary. The superintendent shall cause the date and purpose of the election to be published once a week for two weeks immediately preceding the date thereof in the official organ of the county. The ballot shall have written or printed thereon the words:

[ ] YES Shall the law allowing the governing authority of (insert name of the affected political subdivision) to allow the sale of alco-
[ ] NO holic beverages for one hour after 11:55 p.m. on Saturdays be approved?

All persons desiring to vote for approval shall vote "Yes," and those persons desiring to vote for rejection shall vote "No." If more than one half of the votes cast on such question in the unincorporated area of such county are for approval, then this subsection shall become of full force and effect in the unincorporated area of the county. If more than one-half of the votes cast on such questions in any municipality are for approval, then this subsection shall become of full force and effect in such municipality. The expense of such election shall be borne by the county. It shall be the duty of the superintendent to hold and conduct such election. It shall be his further duty to certify the result thereof to the secretary of state.

In all counties having a population of not less than 295,000 nor more than 300,000 according to the United States decennial census of 1980 or any future such census in which the sale of alcoholic beverages is lawful:

(1) The governing authority of the county may authorize the sale of alcoholic beverages for consumption on the premises at any time from 11:55 p.m. on Saturdays and the three hours immediately following such time; and

(2) Alcoholic beverages may be sold and served for consumption on the premises on Sundays from 12:30 p.m. until 12:00 midnight in any licensed establishment which derives at least 50 percent of its total annual gross food and beverage sales from the sale of prepared meals or food in all of the combined retail outlets of the individual establishment where food is served and in any licensed establishment which derives at least 50 percent of its total annual gross income from the rental of rooms for overnight lodging.

In all counties having a population of not less than 54,600 and not more than 56,000 according to the United States decennial census of 1980 or any future such census in which the sale of alcoholic beverages is lawful, and in all municipalities within such counties in which the sale of alcoholic beverages is lawful, the governing authority of the county or municipality, as appropriate, may authorize the sale of alcoholic beverages for consumption on the premises if Sunday sales are approved in a referendum as provided in this subsection. Eating establishments located in the unicorporated area of the county, in the case of the county, or eating establishments located in the corporate limits of the municipality, in the case of a municipality, shall be authorized to sell alcoholic beverages for consumption on the premises on Sundays between the hours of 12:30 p.m. and 12:00 midnight. As used in this paragraph, the term "eating establishment" means an establishment which is licensed to sell distilled spirits, malt beverages, or wines and which derives at least 50 percent of its total annual gross food and beverage sales from the sale of prepared meals or food. Any governing authority desiring to permit and regulate

Sunday sales shall so provide by proper resolution or ordinance. Not less than ten nor more than 20 days after the date of approval of such resolution or ordinance, it shall be the duty of the election superintendent of the county to issue the call for an election for the purpose of submitting the question of Sunday sales to the electors of the county for approval or rejection. The superintendent shall set the date of the election for a day not less than 30 nor more than 45 days after the date of the issuance of the call.

The superintendent shall cause the date and purpose of the election to be published in the official organ of the county once a week for two weeks immediately preceding the date thereof. The ballot shall have written or printed thereon the words:

[ ] YES Shall the governing authority of (name of county) be authorized
            to permit and regulate Sunday sales of distilled spirits for bev-
[ ] NO   erage purposes by the drink?

All persons desiring to vote for approval of Sunday sales shall vote "Yes," and those persons desiring to vote for rejection of Sunday sales shall vote "No." If more than one-half of the votes cast on the question are for approval of Sunday sales, the governing authority of all municipalities within such counties may by appropriate resolution or ordinance permit and regulate Sunday sales by licensees. The expense of the election shall be borne by the county in which the election is held. It shall be the duty of the superintendent to hold and conduct the election. It shall be his further duty to certify the result thereof to the Secretary of State.

In each county having a population of more than 100,000 in any metropolitan statistical area having a population of not less than 250,000 nor more than 1,000,000 according to the United States decennial census of 1980 or any future such census in which the sale of alcoholic beverages is lawful in such a county and in all municipalities within such counties in which the sale of alcoholic beverages is lawful, the governing authority of the county or municipality, as appropriate, may authorize the sale of alcoholic beverages for consumption on the premises if Sunday sales are approved by referendum as provided in this subsection: (A) At any time from 11:55 p.m. on Saturdays until 2:55 a.m. on Sundays; and (B) In eating establishments which are located in the unincorporated area of the county, in the case of the county, or which are located in the corporate limits of the municipality, in the case of a municipality, on Sundays between the hours of 12:30 p.m. and 12:00 midnight. As used in this subparagraph, the term "eating establishment" means an establishment which is licensed to sell distilled spirits, malt beverages, or wines and which derives at least 50 percent of its total annual gross food and beverage sales from the sale of prepared meals or food.

Any governing authority desiring to permit and regulate Sunday sales pursuant to paragraph one of this subsection shall so provide by proper resolution or ordinance. Not less than ten nor more than 60 days after the date of approval of such resolution or ordinance, it shall be the duty of the election superintendent of the county or municipality to issue the call for an election for the purpose of submitting the question of Sunday sales to the electors of the county or municipality for approval or rejection. The superintendent shall set the date of the election for a day not less than 30 nor more than 60 days after the date of the issuance of the call. The superintendent shall cause the date and purpose of the election to be published in the official organ of the county once a week for two weeks immediately preceding the date thereof. The ballot shall have written or printed thereon the words:

[ ] YES Shall the governing authority of (name of municipality or county) be authorized to permit and regulate Sunday sales of
[ ] NO distilled spirits or alcoholic beverages for beverage purposes by the drink?

All persons desiring to vote for approval of Sunday sales shall vote "Yes," and those persons desiring to vote for rejection of Sunday sales shall vote "No." If more than one-half of the votes cast on the question are for approval of Sunday sales, the governing authority may by appropriate resolution or ordinance permit and regulate Sunday sales by licensees. The expense of the election shall be borne by the county or municipality in which the election is held. It shall be the duty of the superintendent to hold and conduct the election. It shall be his further duty to certify the result thereof to the Secretary of State.

Notwithstanding any other provisions of law, in all counties or municipalities in which the sale of alcoholic beverages is lawful for consumption on the premises, the governing authority of the county or municipality may, by resolution or ordinance conditioned on approval in a referendum, authorize the sale of alcoholic beverages for consumption on the premises on Sundays from 12:30 p.m. until 12:00 midnight in any licensed establishment which derives at least 50 percent of its total annual gross sales from the sale of prepared meals or food in all of the combined retail outlets of the individual establishment where food is served and in any licensed establishment which derives at least 50 percent of its total annual gross income from the rental of rooms for overnight lodging. Any governing authority desiring to permit and regulate Sunday sales pursuant to this subsection, but only after a referendum election, shall so provide by proper resolution or ordinance conditioned on a referendum. Not less than ten nor more than 60 days after the date of approval of such resolution or ordinance, it shall be the duty of the election superintendent of the county or municipality to issue the call for an election for the purpose of submitting the question of Sunday sales to the electors of the county or municipality for approval or rejection. The superintendent shall set the date of the election for a day not less than 30 nor more than 60 days after the date of the issuance of the call. The superintendent shall cause the date and purpose of the election to be published in the official organ of the county once a week for two weeks immediately preceding the date thereof. The ballot shall have written or printed thereon the words:

[ ] YES Shall the governing authority of (name of municipality or county) be authorized to permit and regulate Sunday sales of
[ ] NO   distilled spirits or alcoholic beverages for beverage purposes by the drink?

All persons desiring to vote for approval of Sunday sales shall vote "Yes," and those persons desiring to vote for rejection of Sunday sales shall vote "No." If more than one-half of the votes cast on the question are for approval of Sunday sales, the governing authority may by appropriate resolution or ordinance permit and regulate Sunday sales by licensees. Otherwise, such Sunday sales shall not be permitted. The expense of the election shall be borne by the county or municipality in which the election is held. It shall be the duty of the superintendent to hold and conduct the election. It shall be his further duty to certify the result thereof to the Secretary of State.

Notwithstanding this subsection or any other provision of law, all county or municipal resolutions or ordinances enacted prior to April 6, 1984, pursuant to the authorizations granted by the above-listed subsections of this Code section are declared to be valid and shall remain in full force and effect unless affirmatively repealed by the governing authority of the county or municipality.

Notwithstanding other laws, in any county in which one-half of the net revenues collected from the legalizing, controlling, licensing, and taxing of the wholesale and retail sale of alcoholic beverages is paid over to the boards of education in such county, a municipality having an independent school system shall be authorized through its governing authority, either by proper resolution or ordinance approved by a majority of that governing authority or by proper resolution or ordinance so approved and by its terms having its effectiveness being contingent upon referendum approval of the second paragraph of this subsection, to allow: (A) The sale of alcoholic beverages for consumption on the premises at any time from 11:55 p.m. on Saturdays and three hours immediately following such time; and (B) The sale and service by the drink of alcoholic beverages on Sundays from 12:30 p.m. until 12:00 midnight in any licensed establishment which derives at least 50 percent of its total annual gross food and beverage sales from the sales of prepared meals or food in all of the combined retail outlets of the individual establishment where food is served and in any licensed establishment which derives at least 50 percent of its total annual gross income from the rental of rooms for overnight lodging.

If a resolution or ordinance is approved pursuant to the first paragraph of this subsection and by its terms has its effectiveness contingent upon referendum approval pursuant to this paragraph, not less than ten nor more than 60 days after the date of approval of such resolution or ordinance it shall be the duty of the election superintendent of the municipality, whose governing authority approved that resolution or ordinance, to issue the call for an election for the purpose of submitting the question of Sunday sales to the electors of that municipality for approval or rejection. The superintendent shall set the date of the election for a day not less than 30 nor more than 60 days after the date of the issuance of the call. The superintendent shall cause the date and purpose of the election to be published in the official organ of the county in which that municipality is located once a week for two weeks immediately preceding the date thereof. The ballot shall have written thereon the words:

[ ] YES Shall Sunday sales of alcoholic beverages by the drink be authorized in (name of municipality)?
[ ] NO

All persons desiring to vote for approval of Sunday sales shall vote "Yes," and those persons desiring to vote for rejection of Sunday sales shall vote "No." If more than one-half of the votes cast on the question are for the approval of Sunday sales, the resolution or ordinance approving such Sunday sales shall become effective upon the date so specified in that resolution or ordinance. The expense of the election shall be borne by the municipality in which the election is held. It shall be the duty of the superintendent to hold and conduct the election. It shall be his further duty to certify the result to the Secretary of State. OFFICIAL CODE OF GEORGIA ANN., 1985 Cumulative Supplement Vol. 3, Title 3, sec. 3-3-7.

Except as specifically authorized by law, no person knowingly and intentionally shall sell or offer to sell alcoholic beverages on Sunday.

Any person violating the provisions of this paragraph shall be guilty of misdemeanor. OFFICIAL CODE OF GEORGIA ANN., 1985 Cumulative Supplement Vol. 3, Title 3, sec. 3-3-20.

(b) Motor vehicle sales—none.

Delaware

Sunday laws that affect retail sales—none in general.

Exceptions:

(a) Liquor sales—(b) No manufacturer or importer shall sell or deliver alcoholic liquor on any holiday specified in subsection (e) of this section, or at hours other than those prescribed by the rules or regulations of the Commission, except as subsection (g) of this section may apply.

(c) No holder of a license for the sale of spirits, wines or beer in a store shall sell or deliver the same on any holiday specified in subsection (e) of this section or in any territory where an election is held during the hours of the day upon which the polling at such election takes place, or between the hours of 1:00 a.m. and 9:00 a.m. of any other day, except as subsection (g) of this section may apply.

(d) No holder of a license for the sale of alcoholic liquor in a hotel, restaurant, club, tavern taproom, horse racetrack, dining room of a boat, passenger cars of a railroad or caterer shall sell the same between the hours of 1:00 a.m. and 9:00 a.m. The closing hour may be made earlier in any municipality by ordinance of the municipal corporation. The sale of alcoholic liquors shall be permitted in a licensed hotel, restaurant, club, horse racetrack, dining room of a boat, passenger cars of a railroad or caterer on every day of the year; provided, that no such licensee shall be required to be open to sell alcoholic liquors on any of the holidays specified in subsection (e) of this section. Any holder of a license to sell alcoholic liquor in a licensed hotel, restaurant, horse racetrack, dining room of a boat, passenger car of a railroad or caterer who wishes to sell alcoholic liquors on Sundays shall pay a fee of $200 for the issuance of a special license to serve alcoholic liquors on Sundays, which shall be in addition to any other license fees which may be required of the licensee. The sale of alcoholic liquors shall be permitted in a licensed tavern or taproom on every day of the year except the holidays specified in subsection (e) of this section, on which days such licensees shall not be permitted to sell alcoholic liquors.

(g) Notwithstanding subsection (e) of this section, importers or holders of license for the sale of spirits, wines or beer may deliver beer on Sundays in motor vehicles equipped with permanently installed devices for the refrigeration and dispensing of beer to licensed gatherings only; provided, however, that such licensee shall have first given notice of such delivery to the Commission. DEL. CODE ANN., revised 1974, 1984 Cumulative Supplement, Vol. 2.4, section 714.

(b) Motor vehicle sales—none.

Hawaii

Sunday laws that affect retail sales—none in general.

Exceptions:
(a) Liquor sales—none.
(b) Motor vehicle sales—none.

Idaho

Sunday laws that affect retail sales—none in general.

Exceptions:
(a) Liquor sales—It shall be unlawful to transact the sale or delivery of any alcoholic liquor in, on, or from the premises of any state liquor store or distribution station:

1. After the closing hours as established by the dispensary.
2. On any Thanksgiving, Christmas, or Memorial Day.
3. On any Sunday.
4. On any national or state election day.
5. On any municipal election day held in the municipality in which a store or distributing station may be situated during the time the polls are open.
6. During other such periods or days as may be designated by the dispensary. IDAHO CODE, 1985 Cumulative Pocket Supplement, Vol. 5, pt. 1, sec. 23-307.

Hours of sale of liquor—(1) No liquor shall be sold, offered for sale, or given away upon any licensed premises and all liquor not in sealed bottles must be locked in a separate room or cabinet during the following hours:

a. Sunday, Memorial Day, Thanksgiving, and Christmas from 1 o'clock a.m., to 10 o'clock a.m. the following day; provided however, that on any Sunday not otherwise being a prescribed holiday, it shall be lawful for a licensee having banquet area of meeting room facilities, separate and apart from the usual dispensing area (bar room) and separate and apart from a normal public dining room unless such dining room is closed to the public, to therein dispense liquor between the hours of 2 o'clock p.m. and 11 o'clock p.m. to bona fide participants of banquets, receptions or conventions for consumption only within the confines of such banquet area or meeting room facility. IDAHO CODE ANN., Vol. 5, pt. 1, sec. 23-927.

(b) Motor vehicle sales—none.

Illinois

Sunday laws that affect retail sales—none in general.

Exceptions:

(a) Liquor sales—No person shall sell at retail any alcoholic liquor on Sundays unless authorized by general ordinance or resolution by the city council, president and board of trustees or county board, as the case may be; provided, however, that the city council, president and board of trustees or county board, as the case may be, may further restrict the permissable hours for the sale of alcoholic liquors under such licenses in its political subdivision as the public good and convenience may require. IL. ANN. STAT., 1985 Cumulative Annual Pocket Part, Chs. 43ff45, sec. 43-129.

(b) Motor vehicle sales—none.

Indiana

Sunday laws that affect retail sales—none in general.

Exceptions:

(a) Liquor sales (clubs)—(a) the commission may issue the appropriate permit upon the application of a club if the premises to be licensed are situated within the corporate limits of a city or town. (b) A person issued a permit under sections 2,3, or 4 [7.1-3-20-3, 7.1-3-20-4 or this section] of this chapter may sell those alcoholic beverages allowed by that permit one Sunday during each month of the calendar year to members for on-premises consumption only, notwithstanding IC 7.1-3-16.5 [IC 7.1-3-20-2, as added by Acts

1973, P.L. 55, sec. 1; 1975, P.L. 72, sec. 1; 1977, P.L. 95, sec. 1.] Burns IND. STAT. ANN., Title 6, 7, 7.1, 1984 Replacement Volume, sec. 7.1-3-20-2.

It is a class C misdemeanor for a person to deliver or transport an alcoholic beverage to the holder of a retailer's or dealer's permit of any type, except a temporary beer or wine permit, on Sunday. [IC 7.1-5-11-16, as added by Acts 1973, P.L. 55, sec. 1; 1973, P.L. 59, sec. 9; 1978, P.L. 2, sec. 726.]. Burns IND. STAT. ANN., Title 6, 7, 7.1, 1984 Replacement Volume, sec. 7.1-5-11-16.

(b) Motor vehicle sales — none.

Iowa

Sunday laws that affect retail sales — none in general.

Exceptions:
(a) Liquor sales — (6) Any club, hotel, motel, or commercial establishment holding a liquor control license for whom the sale of goods and services other than alcoholic liquor or beer constitutes fifty percent or more of the gross receipts from the licensed premises, subject to the provisions of section 123.49, subsection 2, paragraph "b", may sell and dispense alcoholic liquor to patrons on Sunday for consumption on the premises only, and beer for consumption on or off the premises between the hours of ten a.m. and twelve midnight on Sunday. For the privilege of selling beer and alcoholic liquor on the premises on Sunday the liquor control license fee of the applicant shall be increased by twenty percent of the regular fee prescribed for the license pursuant to this section, and the privilege shall be noted on the liquor control license. The department shall prescribe the nature and the character of the evidence which shall be required of the applicant under this subsection. IA. CODE ANN., Vol. 8, 1985 Cumulative Annual Pocket Part, sec. 123.36.

(b) Motor vehicle sales — (9) No person licensed under this chapter shall, either directly or through an agent, salesman or employee, engage in this state, or represent or advertise that the person is engaged or intends to engage in this state, in the business of buying or selling at retail new or used motor vehicles, other than mobile homes more than eight feet in width or more than thirty-two feet in length as defined in section 321.1, on the first day of the week, commonly known and designated as Sunday. IA. CODE ANN., Vol. 15A, sec. 322C.3.

(8) Except under subsection 9 of this section, a person licensed under section 322C.4 shall not, either directly or through an agent,

salesperson, or employee, engage or represent or advertise that the person is engaged or intends to engage in this state, in the business of buying or selling new or used travel trailers on Sunday. IA. CODE ANN., Vol. 15A, sec. 322C.3.

Kansas

Sunday laws that affect retail sales—none in general.

Exceptions:
(a) Liquor sales—No person shall sell at retail any alcoholic liquor . . . on the first day of the week, commonly called Sunday . . . . KANSAS STAT. ANN., Vol. 3A, sec. 41-712. (b) Except as provided by subsection (g), no cereal malt beverages may be sold . . . on Sunday . . . . KANSAS STAT. ANN., 1985 Cumulative Supplement, Vol. 3A, sec. 41-2704.
(b) Motor vehicle sales—none.

Kentucky

Sunday laws that affect retail sales:

(1) Any person who works on Sundays at his own or at any other occupation or employs any other person, in labor or other business, whether for profit or amusement, unless his work or the employment of others is in the course of ordinary household duties, work of necessity or charity or work required in the maintenance or operation of a public service or public utility plant or system, shall be fined not less than two dollars ($2.00) nor more than fifty dollars ($50.00). The employment of every person employed in violation of this subsection shall be deemed a separate offense.
(2) Persons who are members of a religious society which observes as a Sabbath any other day in the week than Sunday shall not be liable to the penalty prescribed in subsection (1) of this section, if they observe as a Sabbath one (1) day in each seven (7).
(3) Subsection (1) of this section shall not apply to amateur sports, athletic games, or operation of grocery stores whose principal business is the sale of groceries and related-food items, drug stores whose principal business is the sale of drugs and related drug items, gift shops, souvenir shops, fishing tackle shops and bait shops, moving picture shows, chautauqua, filling stations, or opera.
(4) Subsection (1) of this section shall not apply to employers using continuous work scheduling provided that such scheduling

permits at least one (1) day of rest each calendar week for each employee. KY REV. STAT. ANN., Vol. 16, 1985 Replacement, sec. 436.160.

In addition to the provisions of K.R.S. 436.160:

(1) The legislative body of any city, except as to activities permitted under K.R.S. 436.160, shall have the exclusive power to enact ordinances or orders permitting and regulating other retail sales and activities on Sunday within its jurisdictional boundaries, subject to subsection (4) hereof.

(2) The fiscal court of each county, except as to activities permitted under K.R.S. 436.160, shall have exclusive power to enact resolutions or orders permitting and regulating other retail sales and activities on Sunday in that portion of the county which lies outside of the corporate limits of any cities within said county, subject to subsection (4) hereof.

(3) In any city, county, or urban-county government where the legislative body has failed to enact ordinances permitting retail sales and activities on Sunday, the matter may be put to a vote of the people. Upon a petition signed by eligible voters in a number equal to twenty-five percent (25) of the voters who voted in the last general election, a proposition to permit retail sales and activities on Sunday shall be placed before the voters at the next general election. Any such petition shall be submitted to the county clerk of that county for verification of the signatures. The petition shall be submitted at least three (3) months prior to a general election to be eligible for placement of the question before the voters.

(4) Notwithstanding subsections (1), (2) and (3) of this section, any ordinance, resolution or order adopted by the legislative body of any city or the fiscal court of any county pertaining to retail sales and activities on Sunday shall be subject to the following limitations:

(a) No employer shall require as a condition of employment that any employee work on Sunday or on any other day of the week which any such employee may conscientiously wish to observe as a religious Sabbath.

(b) No employer shall in any way discriminate in the hiring or retaining of employees between those who designate a Sabbath as their day of rest and those who do not make such designation, provided, however, that the payment of premium or overtime wage rates for Sunday employment shall not be deemed discriminatory.

(c) No person permitted, under the provisions of this section, to engage in a retail business on Sunday shall be open to the public between the hours of 6:00 a.m. and noon on any Sunday.

(d) Every employer engaged in retail sales on Sunday shall allow each person employed by him in connection with such business or service at least twenty-four (24) consecutive hours of rest in each calendar week in addition to the regular periods of rest normally allowed or legally required in each working day.

(e) No business shall be required to be open on Sunday as part of a lease agreement, franchise agreement or any other contractual agreement. The provisions of this subsection shall not apply to any lease agreement, franchise agreement, or any other contractual arrangement entered into before July 15, 1980. KY REV. STAT. ANN., Vol. 16, 1985 Replacement, sec. 436.165.

Exceptions:

(a) Liquor sales—(1) No premises for which there has been granted a license for the sale of distilled spirits or wine at retail shall be permitted to remain open for any purpose between midnight and 8 a.m., or at any time during the twenty-four hours of a Sunday or during the hours the polls are open on any regular, primary, school or special election day, provided, that if a licensee provides a separate department within his licensed premises capable of being locked and closed off, within which is kept all stocks of distilled spirits and wine, and all fixtures and apparatus connected with his business as a licensee, and said department is kept locked during the times mentioned above, he shall be deemed to have complied with this section; except that the city council, board of aldermen or other municipal legislative body of cities of the first, second, third or fourth class in which traffic in distilled spirits and wine is permitted under K.R.S. Chapter 242 shall have the exclusive right and power, by ordinance duly enacted to establish the hours and times in which distilled spirits and wine may be sold within its jurisdictional boundaries, and except further that the fiscal court of each county in which cities of the first, second, third or fourth class are located shall have the exclusive right and power to establish the hours and times in which distilled spirits and wine may be sold over that portion of the county which lies without the corporate limits of such cities, except any portion in which distilled spirits and wine are prohibited from being sold. Provided, however, that no distilled spirits or wine may be sold in any portion of the counties containing cities of the first, second, third or fourth class during the twenty-four (24) hours between 6 a.m. Sunday and 6 a.m. Monday, except as provided in K.R.S. 243.050 and subsections (2) and (4) of this section, and that no distilled spirits or wine may be sold on any election day while the polls are still open; and provided also that all stocks of distilled spirits and wine must be kept locked during the hours which the licensee is prohibited from selling same.

(2) In any county containing a city of the first or second class in which the sale of distilled spirits and wine is permitted under K.R.S. Chapter 242, an election on the question of permitting the sale of distilled spirits and wine by the drink on Sunday may be held as provided in K.R.S. 242.020 to 242.040 and 242.060 to 242.120. In any election, the form of the proposition shall be, "Are you in favor of the sale of distilled spirits and wine by the drink between the hours of one p.m. and midnight on Sunday in (name of county)?"

(3) In any county containing a city of the first or second class in which the sale of distilled spirits and wine by the drink is permitted on Sunday as provided in subsections (2) and (4) of this section, holders of distilled spirits and wine retail drink licenses may apply to the administrator of the distilled spirits unit for a special Sunday-sale retail drink license. Upon receipt of an application and payment of the prescribed fee, the administrator shall issue a license.

(4) In any county containing a city of the first or second class or in any city located therein in which sale of distilled spirits and wine is permitted under K.R.S. Chapter 242, the respective legislative body of such city or fiscal court, of such areas, shall have the power by duly enacted ordinance, to permit the sale of distilled spirits and wine by the drink on Sunday from 1 p.m. until a closing hour to be established by the legislative body of the area concerned, by hotels, motels, and restaurants which are licensed for the retail sale of distilled spirits and wine by the drink and which have dining facilities with a minimum seating capacity of one hundred (100) people at tables and which receive at least fifty percent (50) or more of their gross annual income from their dining facilities by the sale of food.

(5) Any hotel, motel, restaurant operation, convention center or commercial airport which sells liquor on Sunday shall pay each of its employees wages at a rate of not less than the minimum wage as set forth in K.R.S. 337.275(1), the provisions of K.R.S. 337.275(2) and K.R.S. 337.010(2)(a)(vi) notwithstanding. KY. REV. STAT. ANN., 1984 Cumulative Supplement, Vol. 10, sec. 244.290 (see also sec. 244.295).

(1) Except as provided in subsection (2), no brewer or distributor shall deliver any malt beverages on Sunday or between the hours of 7 p.m. and 6 a.m. on any week day except Saturday, when the hours of deliveries shall be between 6 a.m. and midnight. No retailer shall sell, give away or deliver any malt beverages between midnight and 6 a.m. or at any time during the twenty-four

(24) hours of a Sunday or during the hours the polls are open on an election day. KY. REV. STAT. ANN., 1984 Cumulative Supplement, Vol. 10, sec. 244.480.

Louisiana

Sunday laws that affect retail sales:

> All stores, shops, saloons, and all places of public business, licensed under the law of Louisiana or under any parochial or municipal law and all plantation stores, shall be closed at twelve o'clock on Saturday nights, and remain continuously for twenty-four hours, during which time no proprietor thereof shall give, trade, barter, exchange or sell any of the stock or any article of merchandise kept in his establishment.
>
> Whoever violates this section shall be fined not less than twenty-five dollars nor more than two hundred and fifty dollars, or imprisoned for not less than ten days nor more than thirty days, or both for each offense. LA. STAT. ANN., Vol. 27A, sec. 51:191.
>
> The provisions of R.S. 51:191 shall not apply to the following:
> (1) News dealers.
> (2) The sale of ice.
> (3) Watering places and public parks.
> (4) Places of resort for recreation and health.
> (5) Newspaper offices.
> (6) Keepers of soda fountains.
> (7) Printing offices.
> (8) Book stores.
> (9) Art galleries insofar as sales of original art and prints constitute a substantial portion of their operation.
> (10) Drug stores and other apothecary shops.
> (11) Undertaker shops.
> (12) Public and private markets.
> (13) Bakeries.
> (14) Dairies.
> (15) Livery stables.
> (16) Railroads, whether steam or horse.
> (17) Hotels.
> (18) Boarding houses.
> (19) Steamboats and other vessels.
> (20) Warehouses for receiving and forwarding freights.
> (21) Restaurants.
> (22) Telegraph offices.

(23) Theaters, or any place of amusement, unless intoxicating liquors are sold in the premises.

(24) Sales at a convention and trade show, sponsored by an association and not held more frequently than once a year in a particular locality in this state, held in a public room or rooms of a hotel or at a public convention facility; provided that said public room or rooms of a hotel is at least three times the size of an average room which is rented or leased for sleeping purposes at the hotel.

(25) Sales at the site of the 1984 Louisiana World Exposition, in the city of New Orleans, from May 12, 1984 through and including November 11, 1984 as more particularly described in the Master Plan dated March 1, 1982, registered in Conveyance Office Book 783D, folio 493 of the Conveyance Records of the Parish of Orleans, Notarial Archives Number 482982, and any buildings or portions thereof, that are located on or near the perimeter of said site and leased or operated by Louisiana World Exposition, Inc., its subsidiaries or licensees.

B. Stores may be opened for the purpose of selling anything necessary in sickness and for burial purpose.

C. Hotels or boarding houses may sell wine for table use on Sundays. No alcoholic, vinous, or malt liquors shall be given, traded, bartered, sold, or delivered in any public place on Sundays, except when administered or prescribed by a practicing physician in the discharge of his professional duties, in which case the physicians administering the intoxicating liquors may charge therefore. LA. STAT. ANN., Vol. 27A, 1986 Supplementary Pamphlet, sec. 51:192.

No person shall operate on Sunday a barber shop, tonsorial parlor, or any other place of business where the trades of cutting and clipping hair, shaving, or massaging is carried on. LA. STAT. ANN., ol. 27A, sec. 51:193.

A. On the first day of the week, commonly designated as Sunday, it shall be unlawful for any person, whether at retail, wholesale or by auction, to sell, attempt to sell, offer to sell or engage in the business of selling, or require any employee to sell any clothing or wearing apparel; lumber or building supply materials; furniture, home or business or office furnishings; any household, office or business appliances; new or used automobiles and trucks or parts for and servicing of such motor vehicles in all places or business wherein such motor vehicles are sold. In the case of an emergency, parts and servicing may be sold.

B. Whoever violates any provision of this Section shall be fined not more than one hundred dollars for the first offense. If it is shown upon the trial of a case involving a violation of this Section that the defendant once before has been convicted of the same offense, he shall, upon a second conviction and upon each subsequent conviction, be imprisoned for not more than six months or be fined not more than five hundred dollars, or both.

C. The purpose of this Section being to promote the health, recreation and welfare of the people of this state and to prevent unfair competition among persons, firms or business establishments, the operation of any business, whether by an individual, partnership or corporation, in contravention of the provisions of this Section is declared to be a nuisance, and any person may apply to any court of competent jurisdiction for and may obtain an injunction restraining such violation.

D. A sale of an item falling within the categories enumerated in Subsection A of this Section by persons not engaged in the business of selling such an item shall be exempt from the operation of this Section.

E. The provisions of this Section shall not apply to any sale or sales:

(1) for charitable purposes; or

(2) Of items for funeral or burial purposes; of items sold as part of or in conjunction with the sale of real property or mobile homes; or of drugs, medicines, medical or surgical supplies and appliances;

(3) Of clothing or wearing apparel, new and used furniture, new and used home or business or office furnishings, or any new or used household, office or business appliances in the Vieux Carre section of the city of New Orleans being that section of the city bounded by Iberville Street, North Rampart Street, Esplanade Avenue and the Mississippi River.

(4) Of any merchandise, services, alcoholic beverages, and any other sales authorized by Louisiana World Exposition, Inc. from May 12, 1984 through and including November 11, 1984, in the city of New Orleans, on the site of the 1984 Louisiana World Exposition as more particularly described in the Master Plan dated March 1, 1982, registered in Conveyance Office Book 783D, folio 493 of the Conveyance Records of the Parish of Orleans, Notarial Archives Number 482982, and any buildings, or portions thereof, that are located on or near the perimeter of said site and leased or operated by Louisiana World Exposition, Inc., its subsidiaries, subleasees or licensees.

(5) In retail outlets, each not exceeding one thousand five hundred square feet in area, of wearing apparel, souvenirs, and jewelry, used or antique furniture, or new and used home or office accessories in that certain section of the city of Baton Rouge, which is within a

historical district or part of a historical district, and which is inside the area. . . . This specific exemption shall not be applicable to any one-time auction or liquidation sale held in the Baton Rouge Centroplex, except for those such functions held by non-profit organizations otherwise authorized by law.

(6) In the area of the New Orleans Exhibition Hall bounded by the upriver arcade of the Mississippi River Bridge Authority Canal Street Ferry Terminal, the Mississippi River, the new Mississippi River Bridge right-of-way, and the New Orleans Public Belt Railroad right-of-way. LA. STAT. ANN., Vol. 27A, 1986 Supplementary Pamphlet, sec. 51-194.

The governing authority of each parish and municipality is authorized to waive, suspend, or otherwise delimit or exempt from the effect and operation of the provisions of R.S. 51:191 and 51:192 any and all businesses, persons or firms licensed to and selling, serving or dispensing alcoholic beverages at retail within its respective jurisdiction. In order to take advantage of the foregoing provision, any such governing authority shall adopt an ordinance declaring the extent to which any person, firm, or business selling, serving, or dispensing alcoholic beverages at retail might engage in such business on Sundays. The operation of this provision shall be retroactive and shall recognize and give effect to any such ordinances previously adopted by any such governing authorities within their respective jursidictions prior to the enactment of this Section. LA. STAT. ANN., Vol. 27A, 1986 Supplementary Pamphlet, sec. 51:195.

Municipalities having a population of over twenty-five thousand may regulate or prohibit the opening and closing of butcher shops, meat markets, baker shops, and bakeries within their corporate limits on Sunday. Municipalities of over one hundred thousand may also regulate or prohibit the sale and delivery of bakery products within their corporate limits on Sunday. . . . LA. STAT. ANN., Vol. 20A, sec. 33:4738.

Maine

Sunday laws that affect retail sales:

No person, firm or corporation may, on the Lord's Day. . . . keep open a place of business to the public, except for works of necessity, emergency or charity.

This section shall not apply to: The operation or maintenance of common, contract and private carriers: taxicabs, airplanes; newspapers; radio and television stations; hotels, motels; rooming houses; tourist and trailer camps; restaurants; garages and motor vehicle service stations; retail monument dealers automatic laundries; machines that vend anything of value; including, but not limited to, a product, money or service; a satellite facility approved by the Superintendent of Banking under Title 9-B; or comparable facility approved by the appropriate federal authority; pharmacies; greenhouses; seasonal stands engaged in sale of farm produce, dairy products, sea food or Christmas trees; public utilities; industries normally kept in continuous operations, including, but not limited to, pulp and paper plants and textile plants; processing plants handling agricultural produce or products of the sea; ship chandleries; marinas; establishments primarily selling boats, boating equipment, sporting equipment, souvenirs and novelties; motion picture theatres; public dancing; sports and athletic events; bowling alleys; displaying or exploding fireworks, under Title 8, chapter 9; musical concerts; religious, educational, scientific or philosophical lectures; scenic, historic, recreational and amusement facilities; real estate brokers and real estate salesmen; mobile home brokers and mobile home salesmen; provided that this section shall not exempt the businesses or facilities specified in sections 3205 and 3207 from closing in any municipality until the requirements of those sections have been met; stores wherein no more than five persons, including the proprietor, are employed in the usual and regular conduct of business; stores which have no more than 5,000 square feet of interior customer selling space, excluding back room storage, office and processing space.

Any person, firm or corporation found guilty of violating any of the provisions of this section shall be punished by a fine of not more than $100 or by imprisonment for 30 days, or by both, for the first offense; and by a fine of $500 or by imprisonment for 60 days, or both, for the 2nd offense occurring within one year following the first conviction. Any offense subsequent to the 2nd offense and occurring within 2 years following the 2nd conviction shall be punishable by a fine of not more than $1,000 or by imprisonment for 90 days, or by both. No complaint charging violation of this section shall issue later than 5 days after its alleged commission.

Each separate sale, trade or exchange of property or offer thereof, in violation of this section, and each Lord's Day or one of the aforementioned holidays a person, firm or corporation engages in or employs others to engage in the sale, trade or exchange of property in violation of the law constitutes a separate offense.

In addition to any criminal penalties provided in this section, the Attorney General, district attorney or any resident of a municipality in which a violation is claimed to have occurred may file a complaint with the Superior Court to enjoin any violation of this section. The Superior Court shall have original jurisdiction of such complaints and authority to enjoin such violations. MAINE REV. STAT. ANN., Vol. 9, Titles 16-17, 1985 Cumulative Pocket Supplement, sec. 17-3204.

Any person who shall carry on or engage in the business of buying, selling, exchanging, dealing or trading in new or used motor vehicles; or who shall open any place of business or lot wherein he attempts to or does engage in the business of buying, selling, exchanging, dealing or trading in new or used motor vehicles; or who does buy, sell, exchange, deal or trade in new or used motor vehicles as a business on the first day of the week, commonly known and designated as Sunday, is a disorderly person. Such a disorderly person upon conviction for the first offense shall be punished by a fine of not more than $100 or by imprisonment for not more than 10 days, or by both; and for the 2nd offense shall be punished by a fine of not more than $500 or by imprisonment for not more than 30 days, or by both; and for the 3rd or each subsequent offense shall be punished by a fine of not more than $750 or by imprisonment for not more than 6 months, or by both. If the person is the holder of a dealer or transporter registration plates under Title 29, chapter 5, subchapter III-A, such person shall be subject to the suspension or revocation of said plates, as provided for in Title 29, section 350-A, for the violation of this section. MAINE REVE. STAT. ANN., 1964, Titles 16-17, sec. 17-3203.

No liquor shall be sold in this State in Sundays except as hereafter provided, and no licensee by himself, clerk, servant or agent shall, between the hours of midnight and 6 a.m., sell or deliver any liquors, except no liquors shall be sold or delivered on Saturdays after 11:45 p.m. and except that in restaurants, class A restaurants, taverns, class A taverns, retail stores, hotels and clubs, liquor may, except as provided, be sold to 1 a.m. Liquor may be sold on January 1st of any year from midnight to 2 a.m. If January 1st falls on a Monday, licensees shalll be permitted to sell or deliver any liquors between 9 p.m., Sunday, December 31st and 2 a.m., January 1st. Liquor may be sold in any municipality on the day of holding a general election or statewide primary only after the closing of the polls in such municipality. Except as hereafter provided, no licensee shall permit the consumption of liquors on his premises on Sundays, or after 15 minutes past the hours prohibited for sale thereof, except by bona fide guests in their rooms. . . .

Any person, except an officer in performance of his duties, who purchases liquor on Sunday, in violation of this section shall be guilty of a misdemeanor and shall be subject to the same penalty provided in this section for the illegal sale of liquor on Sunday.

Any licensee by himself, clerk, servant or agent, except as herein provided, who sells liquor on Sunday shall be punished by a fine of not less than $100 nor more than $500, and costs, and a penalty of not less 2 months nor more than 6 months in jail, at the discretion of the court; and in default of fine and costs an additional penalty by imprisonment for 6 months. Any clerk, servant, agent or other person in the employment of a licensee, who violates or in any manner aids or assists in violating the law relating to Sunday sale of liquor, shall suffer like penalties.

Licensed hotels, class A restaurants and clubs, as defined under section 2, shall have the right to sell liquor on Sundays between the hours of 12 noon and midnight and such sales may be made during such time by the licensee himself, a clerk, servant or agent in a municipality or unicorporated place where a majority of votes cast in the municipality or unincorporated place in a state-wide special election shall answer in the affirmative to the following local option question:

Shall this municipality or unincorporated place authorize the sale on Sunday of liquor in those licensed hotels, class A restaurants and clubs where liquor is permitted to be sold during the rest of the week?

and where there was a majority of affirmative votes cast on any local liquor option question voted upon, other than questions 1, 5 and 6, at the last election at which local liquor option questions were on the ballot in the municipality or unincorporated place.

Licensees who are licensed to sell malt liquors in retail stores not to be consumed on the premises shall have the right to sell malt liquors for off-premises consumption on Sunday between the hours of 12 noon and midnight and such sales may be made during such time by the licensee himself, a clerk. servant or agent in a municipality or unincorporated place where a majority of votes cast in the municipality or unincorporated place in a general election shall answer in the affirmative to the following local option question:

Shall this municipality or unincorporated place authorize the sale on Sunday of malt liquor for consumption off the premises by such licensees who are permitted to make such sales during the rest of the week?

and where there was a majority of affirmative votes cast on local option question 6, voted upon at the last election at which local liquor option questions were on the ballot in the municipality or unincorporated place.

Licensees who are licensed to sell table wines in retail stores not to be consumed on the premises shall have the right to sell table wines for off-premises consumption on Sunday between the hours of 12 noon and midnight and such sales may be made during such time by the licensee himself, a clerk, servant or agent in a municipality or unincorporated place where a majority of votes cast in the municipality or unincorporated place in a general election shall answer in the affirmative to the following local option question:

Shall this municipality or unincorporated place authorize the sale on Sunday of table wine for consumption off the premises by such licensees who are permitted to make such sales during the rest of the week?

and where there was a majority of affirmative votes cast on local option question 6-A, voted upon at the last election at which local liquor option questions were on the ballot in the municipality or unicorporated place.

Any violation by a licensee of this section or commission rules and regulations related thereto, upon conviction after hearing before the Hearing Commissioner, shall be grounds for suspension or revocation, or both, of the license or right to sell on Sunday. MAINE REV. STAT. ANN., 1964, Vol. 13A, sec. 28.4.

In any municipality that shall so vote, as provided, it shall be lawful to engage in as a participant, manager, or official, or to attend as a spectator any outdoor recreational or competitive amateur sport or game, except boxing, horse racing, air circuses or wrestling between the hours of 1 p.m. and 7 p.m. on Sunday. . . . MAINE REV. STAT. ANN., 1964, Vol. 9, Titles 16-17, sec. 17-3205.

In any municipality that shall vote as provided, it shall be lawful for any moving picture theater to have an exhibition of moving pictures on Sunday between the hours of 1 p.m. and 11:30 p.m. This section shall not be effective in any city until a majority of the legal voters, present and voting, at any regular election so vote. . . . When a municipality has voted in favor of adopting this section, said section shall remain in effect therein until repealed in the same manner as provided for their adoption. It shall be unlawful for any person, firm or corporation operating any theatrical or motion picture show on Sunday to require or permit any employee of said person, firm or corporation to work or be on duty more than 6 days in any one week. MAINE REV. STAT. ANN., 1964, Vol. 9, Titles 16-17, sec. 17-3207.

No person conscientiously believing that the 7th day of the week ought to be observed as the Sabbath, and is actually refraining from secular business and labor on that day, is liable to said penalties for doing such business or labor on the first day of the week, if he does not disturb other persons. MAINE REV. STAT. ANN., Vol. 9, Titles 16-17, sec. 17-3209.

Maryland

Sunday laws that affect retail sales:

Working on Sunday; permitting children or servants to game, hunt, etc.; certain municipalities excepted. No person whatsoever shall work or do any bodily labor on the Lord's day, commonly called Sunday; and no person having children or servants shall command, or wittingly or unwittingly or willingly suffer any of them to do any manner of work or labor on the Lord's day (works of necessity and charity always excepted), nor shall suffer or permit any children or servants to profane the Lord's day by gaming, fowling hunting, or unlawful pastime or recreation. Every person transgressing this section and being hereof convicted shall forfeit five dollars, which, if the fine is imposed by a circuit court of any county, shall be applied to the use of the county or city as the case may be. Notwithstanding anything to the contrary, the provisions of this section shall not apply:

(1) To Anne Arundel County, Baltimore City, Baltimore County, Prince George's County, Washington County, Harford County, Howard County, Worcester County, Montgomery County, Dorchester County, Charles County, Talbot County; or

(2) To any person who conscientiously believes that the seventh day of the week ought to be observed as the Sabbath and who actually refrains from secular business and labor on that day, and whose business establishment or establishments or employer's business establishment or establishments (whether a sole proprietorship, partnership or corporation) are actually closed on that day; or

(3) To any person who conscientiously believes that the Sabbath begins at sundown on Friday night and ends at sundown on Saturday night and who actually refrains from secular business and labor during such period, and whose business establishment or establishments or employer's business establishment or establishments (whether a sole proprietorship, partnership or corporation) are actually closed during such period. MD. ANN. CODE., Vol. 3A, 1982 Replacement, sec. 492. There are a number of additional exceptions to section 492; see, sections 493, 494, 500, 501, 510, 515, 517, and 519.

Exceptions:

(a) No person in this State shall sell, dispose of, barter, or deal in, or give away any articles of merchandise on Sunday, except retailers, who may sell and deliver on said day tobacco, cigars, cigarettes, candy, sodas and soft drinks, ice, ice cream, ices and other confectionary, milk, bread, fruit, vegetables, gasoline, oils and greases.

(b) In Kent and Queen Anne's counties, in addition to the articles of merchandise hereinbefore mentioned, retailers may sell, barter, deal in, and deliver on Sunday the following articles of merchandise: butter, eggs, cream, soap and other detergents, disinfectants, vegetables, meats, and all other food or foodstuffs prepared or intended for human or household pet consumption, automobile accessories and parts, boating and fishing accessories, artificial and natural flowers and shrubs, toilet goods, hospital supplies, thermometers, camera films, souvenirs, surgical instruments, rubber goods, paper goods, drugs, medicine, patent medicines, and all other articles used for the relief of pain or prescribed by a physician; provided, however, that nothing in this subtitle shall be construed to prevent the operation of any retail establishment on Sunday, the operation of which does not entail the employment of more than one person, not including the owner or proprietor. Every market or department store in which stalls or departments are rented or concessions given to individual merchants or vendors shall be considered as one establishment and each stall or department thereof is not a separate establishment. Nothing in this subsection shall be construed to allow any person or retailer to sell, dispose of, barter, deal in, deliver, give away, show, or offer for sale any motor vehicle or any certificate of title for any motor vehicle on Sunday.

(c) Any person violating any one of the provisions of this section shall be liable to indictment in any court in this State having criminal jurisdiction, and upon conviction thereof shall be fined a sum of not less than twenty nor more than fifty dollars, in the discretion of the court, for the first offense, and if convicted a second time for a violation of this section, the person or persons so offending shall be fined a sum of not less than $50 nor more than $500, and be imprisoned for not less than 10 nor more than 30 days, in the discretion of the court, and his, her, or their license, if any was issued, shall be declared null and void by the judge of said court; and it shall not be lawful for such person or persons to obtain another license for the period of twelve months from the time of such conviction, nor shall a license obtained by any other person or persons to carry on said business on the premises or elsewhere, if the person, so as aforesaid convicted, has any interest whatever therein, or shall derive any profit whatever therefrom; and in the case of being convicted more than twice for a violation of this section, such person or persons on each occasion shall be imprisoned for not less than thirty nor more than sixty days, and fined a sum not less than double that imposed on such person or persons on the last preceding conviction; and his, her, or their license, if any was issued, shall be declared null and void by the court, and no new license shall be issued to such person or persons for a period of two years from the time of such conviction, nor to anyone else to carry on said business wherein he or she is in anywise interested, as before provided for the second violation of the provisions of this section; all the fines to be imposed under this section shall be paid to the State.

Subsections (d) through (1) contain exceptions to sec. 521(a). MD. ANN. CODE., Vol. 3A, 1982 Replacement, sec. 521.

The general restrictions on retail trade enumerated above are not applicable in Prince George's, Harford, Montgomery, Carroll or Frederick Counties (see MD. ANN. CODE., secs. 534G, 534K, 534I, and 534P respectively); alternative regulations for Sunday trade are enumerated in sec. 534H for Prince George's County, in sec. 534R for Harford County, in sec. 534J for Montgomery County and in sec. 534Q for Frederick and Carroll Counties. Sections 534L, 534M, 534N, 534O, 534S&T, 534U, 534V and 534W deal with restriction of retail trade on Sundays in Baltimore County & Baltimore City, Wicomico County, Calvert County & Anne Arundel County, Washington County, Worcester County, Cecil County, Charles County and Howard County, respectively.

A number of additional sections of the Maryland Annotated Code address themselves to particular commodities/behavior that are regulated in specified counties. See secs. 493-4, 500-1, 515, 517, 519, 522, 527, 528, 529, 530, 531, 533, 534, and 534A-F.

Beer, wine and liquor licenses—(a) Class A (off-sale)—the hours during which the privileges conferred by a Class A beer, wine and liquor license may be exercised shall be from 6 o'clock a.m. to 12 o'clock midnight, on every day except Sunday. MD. ANN. CODE., Vol. 1, Art. 2B, sec. 85, 1981 replacement vol.

Sundays—(a) Bar and counter sales—(1) No retail dealer holding a class B or C license shall be permitted to sell any alcoholic beverage at a bar or counter on Sunday. MD. ANN. CODE., Vol. 1, Art. 2B, sec. 90, 1981 replacement vol.

Sections 90((a)(2)-(4) spell out specific exceptions to section 90(a)(1).

(b) In the jurisdictions in which this subsection is applicable, it is unlawful for anyone to sell or for any licensed dealer to deliver, give away or otherwise dispose of any alcoholic beverages on Sunday.

Any person selling or any licensed dealer delivering, giving away or otherwise dispensing of such beverages in such jurisdictions on Sundays is guilty of a misdemeanor and shall be fined not more than $50 for the first offense and not more than $100, or imprisoned in the county jail for not more than 30 days, or both for each succeeding offense. MD. ANN. CODE., Vol. 1, Art. 2B, sec. 90, 1981 replacement vol.

Sections 90(b)(2)-(7) spell out additional exemptions and clarifications to the provisions of 90(b)(1).

Massachusetts

Sunday laws that affect retail sales:

> Sunday shall be a common day of rest. Sections 1 to 11, inclusive, of this chapter may be cited as the Common Day of Rest Law. ANN. LAW. OF MASS., Ch. 136, sec. 1.
>
> Whoever on Sunday is present at or engages in dancing, except folk or square dancing, or any game, sport, fair, exposition, play, entertainment or public diversion for which a charge in the form of the payment or collection of money or other valuable consideration is made for the privilege of being present thereat or engaging therein, and for which a license has not been granted under the provisions of section two of chapter one hundred and twenty-eight A or as provided in section four, shall be punished by a fine of not more than fifty dollars. ANN. LAW. OF MASS., Ch. 136, sec. 2.
>
> Whoever on Sunday offers to view, sets up, establishes or maintains, or attempts to set up, establish or maintain, or promotes or assists in such attempt, or promotes, or aids, abets or participates in offering to view, setting up, establishing or maintaining, or acts as proprietor, manager or person in charge of, dancing or any game, sport, fair, exposition, play, entertainment or public diversion for which a charge in the form of the payment of money or other valuable consideration is made for the privilege of being present thereat or engaging therein, and for which a license has not been granted under the provisions of section two of chapter one hundred and twenty-eight A or as provided in section four, shall be punished by a fine of not more than two thousand dollars. ANN. LAWS OF MASS., Ch. 136, sec. 3.
>
> The mayor of a city or the selectmen of a town, upon written application describing the proposed dancing or game, sport, fair, exposition, play, entertainment or public diversion, except as provided in section one hundred and five of chapter one hundred and

forty-nine, may grant, upon such reasonable terms and conditions as they may prescribe, a license to hold on Sunday dancing or any game, sport, fair, exposition, play, entertainment or public diversion for which a charge in the form of payment or collection of money or other valuable consideration is made for the privilege of being present thereat or engaging therein, except horse racing, dog racing, boxing, wrestling and hunting with firearms; provided, however, that no such license shall be issued for which a charge in the form of the payment or collection of money or other valuable consideration is made for the privilege of engaging therein; and provided further, however, that no license issued under this paragraph shall be granted to permit such activities before one o'clock in the afternoon; and provided further, that such application, except an application to conduct an athletic game or sport, shall be approved by the commissioner of public safety and shall be accompanied by a fee of two dollars, or in the case of an application for the approval of an annual license by a fee of fifty dollars. ANN. LAW OF MASS., Ch. 136, sec. 4(1).

Whoever on Sunday keeps open his shop, warehouse, factory or other place of business, or sells foodstuffs, goods, wares, merchandise or real estate, or does any manner of labor, business or work, except works of necessity and charity, shall be punished by a fine of not less than twenty dollars nor more than one hundred dollars for a first offense, and a fine of not less than fifty dollars nor more than two hundred dollars for each subsequent offense, and each unlawful act or sale shall constitute a separate offense. ANN. LAWS OF MASS., Ch. 136, sec. 5.

Section five shall not prohibit the following:

(1) Any manner of labor, business or work not performed for material compensation; provided, no public nuisance is created thereby.

(2) The opening of a store or shop and the sale at retail of foodstuffs therein; provided, not more than a total of three persons, including the proprietor, are employed therein at any one time on Sunday and throughout the week.

(3) The use or repair of any way or bridge, or the payment and collection of any toll incidental thereto.

(4) The conduct of any public service the continuing operation of which is necessary for the maintenance of life, such as, but not limited to, the operation of municipal water and sewege disposal systems, the operation of hospitals and clinics, or the necessary services of physicians, surgeons, dentists and the like.

(5) The making of emergency repairs for the purposes of imme-

diate and necessary protection of persons, or property including realty, or the towing of any motor vehicle or boat for such purpose.

(6) The manufacture, sale or distribution of steam, electricity, fuel, gas, oxygen, hydrogen, nitrogen, acetylene, carbon dioxide and the calcining of lime, manufacturing processes which for technical reasons require continuous operation, and the processing of checks, items, documents or data by a bank or trust company.

(7) The operation of radio and television stations; the operation of telephone and telegraph systems; or the preparation, printing, publication, sale and delivery of newspapers, or the taking of pictures.

(8) The opening and operation of any secular place of business not otherwise prohibited by law if the natural person in control of the business conscientiously believes that the seventh day of the week, or the period which begins at sundown on Friday night and ends at sundown on Saturday night, should be observed as the Sabbath, and causes all places of business in the commonwealth over which he has control to remain closed for secular business during the entire period of twenty-four consecutive hours which he believes should be observed as the Sabbath, and actually refrains from engaging in secular business and from laboring during that period.

(9) The showing, sale, or rental of noncommercial real property to be used for residential purposes.

(10) The opening of art galleries or the display and sale therein of paintings, objects of art, catalogues and pictures.

(11) The operation of libraries.

(12) The operation of public bathhouses.

(13) The operation of boats for the purposes of noncommercial fishing and recreation, or the sale of bait for fishing.

(14) The catching or gathering of seafood and fresh water fish not otherwise prohibited by law.

(15) The letting of horses, vehicles, boats or aircraft for pleasure.

(16) The sale and rental of sporting equipment and clothing on premises where the sport for which the equipment or clothing to be sold or rented is carried on.

(17) The retail sale of fuel, gasoline and lubricating oil.

(18) The retail sale of tires, batteries and automotive parts for emergency use.

(19) The operation of a pleasure vehicle or the piloting of an aircraft.

(20) The sale at retail or growing plants, trees and bushes, and

articles incidental to the cultivation of such plants, trees or bushes; and the retail sale and delivery of cut flowers.

(21)The cultivation of land, and the raising and harvesting of agricultural products and fruit, and the making of butter and cheese.

(22) The sale, for consumption off the premises, of food prepared by a common victualler licensed under other provisions of law to serve on Sunday.

(23) The selling or delivery of kosher meat or fish by any natural person who observes Saturday as the Sabbath by closing his place of business from sundown Friday to sundown Saturday.

(24) The making and baking of bakery products and the sale thereof in a shop or store.

(25) The retail sale of tobacco products, soft drinks, confectionaries, baby foods, fresh fruit and fresh vegetables, dairy products and eggs, and the retail sale of poultry by the person who raises the same.

(26) The sale and delivery of ice.

(27) The retail sale of drugs and medicines and the retail sale or rental of mechanical appliances prescribed by physicians or surgeons and the retail sale of personal health and sanitary supplies.

(28) The retail sale of greeting cards and photographic films and the processing of photographic films.

(29) The sale, at retail, of gifts, souvenirs, antiques, second-hand furniture, hancrafted goods and art goods, in an establishment primarily engaged in the sale of such merchandise, or on the premises of a licensed common victualler.

(30) The opening of a store or shop primarily engaged in the retail sale of pets, and the sale therein of pets and articles necessary for the keeping, care, and feeding of pets.

(31) The transport of goods in commerce, or for consideration, by motor truck or trailer; or the loading or unloading of the same.

(32) The transport of goods by rail, water or air; or the loading or unloading of the same.

(33) The transport of persons by licensed carriers and all matters incidental thereto, including the operation of all facilities incidental thereto.

(34) The transport or processing of fresh meat, fresh poultry, fresh fish, fresh seafoods, fresh dairy products, fresh bakery products, fresh fruits or fresh vegetables, or ice, bees, or Irish moss, when circumstances require that such work be done on Sunday; or all return trips necessitated thereby.

(35) The transport of livestock, farm commodities and farming equipment for participation in and return from fairs, expositions or sporting events.

(36) The operation of a lodging place, including the letting of rooms and all services necessary and incidental to the letting of rooms.

(37) The carrying on of the business of bootblack before eleven o'clock in the morning provided that such business may be carried on at any time at public airports.

(38) The employment for a consideration of musicians in parades by any post or camp of an incorporated organization of veterans of any war in which the United States of America was engaged, or by any incorporated civic, religious or fraternal organization, or by any company or association of policemen or firemen.

(39) The necessary preparation for, and the conduct of, events licensed under section four, or activities as to which, under the provisions of paragraph (7) of section four, sections two, three and four do not apply.

(40) Any labor, business, or work necessary to the performance of or incidental to any religious exercises, including funerals and burials, the execution of wills or codicils, the preparation of contracts, the execution of federal, state or municipal tax returns or reports, the preparations for trials by lawyers or any other activity not prohibited nor required to be licensed on Sunday.

(41) Work lawfully done by persons working under permits granted under section seven.

(42) The conduct of the business of an innholder or common victualler.

(43) The conduct of any business licensed under chapter one hundred and thirty-eight which may be conducted on Sunday in accordance with said chapter.

(44) The operation of a car-washing business between eight o'clock in the forenoon and one o'clock in the afternoon, provided that such business may be carried on at any time if not more than a total of two persons are employed therein at any one time on a Sunday and throughout the week.

(45) The operation of a coin-operated self-service laundry.

(46) The operation of a coin-operated car-washing business.

(47) The sale of tickets or shares for the state lottery.

(48) The operation of a self-service auto repair center.

(49) The transport of amusement devices, such as carousels, ferris wheels, inclined railways and other similar devices, concessions stands and tents from one location to the next between eight o'clock in the forenoon and one o'clock in the afternoon.

(50) The keeping open of a store or shop and the sale at retail of goods therein, but not including the retail sale of goods subject to chapter one hundred and thirty-eight, and the performance of labor,

business, and work directly connected therewith on Sunday; provided, however, that this exemption shall not apply to any legal holiday as defined in this chapter; and provided, further, that any store or shop which qualifies for exemption under this clause but does not qualify for exemption under any other clause in this section shall not open for business on Sunday prior to the hour of noon.

Any store or shop which qualifies for exemption under this clause or under clause (25) or clause (27) and which employs more than a total of seven persons, including the proprietor, on Sunday or any day throughout the week, shall compensate all employees engaged in the work performed on Sunday pursuant to the provisions of this clause, or clause (25) or clause (27), excepting those bona fide executive or administrative or professional persons earning more than two hundred dollars a week, at a rate not less than one and one-half time the employee's regular rate. No employee engaged in work subject to the provisions of this clause shall be required to perform such work, and refusal to work for any retail establishment on a Sunday shall not be grounds for discrimination, dismissal, discharge, reduction in hours, or any other penalty. The provisions of this paragraph shall be enforced by the department of labor and industries. The provisions of section one hundred and eighty A of chapter one hundred and forty-nine shall apply to any violation of this paragraph. ANN. LAWS OF MASS., Ch. 136, sec. 6.

. . . Except as provided in section thirty-three A, no holder of a tavern license shall sell any alcoholic beverages on Sundays, no other licensee under section twelve shall sell any such beverages on Sundays between one o'clock antemeridian and twelve o'clock noon. . . . ANN LAWS OF MASS., Ch. 138, sec. 33.

Two exceptions to Ch. 138, sec. 33 are noted: see sections 33A and 33B.

Michigan

Sunday laws that affect retail sales—none in general.

Exceptions:
(a) Liquor sales—Sunday liquor transactions; local prohibition of sale on certain days—(1) Except as provided in subsection (2), (3) or (5), a licensee enumerated under section 19 or any other person shall not sell at retail, give away, or furnish and a person shall not knowingly and wilfully buy spirits between the hours of 2 a.m. and 12 midnight on Sunday. If January 1 falls on Sunday the hours may be extended to 4 a.m.

(2) If the legislative body of a county has authorized the sale of spirits for consumption on the premises on Sunday, by resolution approved by a majority of the legislative body voting on that resolution, the spirits may be sold after 12 noon in an establishment licensed under this act in which the gross receipts derived from the sale of food and other goods and services exceed 50% of the total gross receipts. With respect to an action taken by the legislative body, or, if the legislative body fails to act, a petition may be filed with the county clerk requesting the submission of the question of the sale of spirits for consumption on the premises in addition to beer and wine on Sunday. The petition shall be signed by a number of the registered and qualified electors of a county which shall be not less than 8% of the total number of votes cast for all candidates for the office of secretary of state in the county at the last general election held for that purpose. The question shall not be submitted to the electors of a county more than once every 4 years.

The county clerk shall submit the question at the next regular state election held in the county if the petitions are filed not less than 60 days before the election. The question of the sale of spirits for consumption on the premises, in addition to beer and wine, on Sunday shall be submitted by ballot in substantially the following form:

"Shall the sale of spirits for consumption on the premises be permitted on Sunday, in an establishment licensed under the liquor control act in which the gross receipts derived from the sale of food or other goods and services exceed 50% of the total gross receipts within the county of _____ under the provisions of the law governing the sale of spirits for consumption?

> YES _____
> NO _____ "

(3) If the legislative body of a county has authorized the sale of spirits for consumption on the premises on Sunday, by resolution approved by a majority of the legislative body voting on the resolution, spirits may be sold after 12 noon in a retail establishment licensed under this act. With respect to an action taken by the legislative body, or, if the legislative body fails to act, a petition may be filed with the county clerk requesting the submission of the question of the sale of spirits for consumption off the premises, in addition to beer and wine, in a retail establishment licensed under this act on Sunday. The petition shall be signed by a number of the registered and qualified electors of a county which shall be not less than 8% of the total number of votes cast for all candidates for the office of secretary of state in the county in the last general election held for that

purpose. The question shall not be submitted to the electors of a county more than once every 4 years. The county clerk shall submit the question at the next regular state election held in the county if the petitions are filed not less than 60 days before the election. The question of the sale of spirits for consumption off the premises, in addition to beer and wine, in a retail establishment licensed under this act on Sunday shall be submitted by ballot in substantially the following form:

"Shall the sale of spirits for consumption off the premises be permitted, on Sunday, in a retail establishment licensed under the liquor control act within the county of _____ under the provisions of the law governing the sale of spirits for consumption?

> YES _____
> NO _____ "

(4) Votes on a question submitted pursuant to this section shall be taken, counted, and canvassed in the same manner as votes cast in county elections are taken, counted, and canvassed. A ballot shall be furnished by the election commission or similar body of the respective county. If a majority of the electors voting at an election vote in favor of the proposal, spirits may be sold in the county under this act for consumption on the premises or by a retail establishment for consumption off the premises, in addition to beer and wine, on Sunday. The sale shall not be permitted in a city, village, or township in which the sale of spirits is prohibited under this act. A violation of this section is a misdemeanor. . . .

(5) A licensee enumerated under section 19 or any other person shall sell at retail and a person shall not knowingly and wilfully buy, alcoholic liquor between the hours of 9 p.m. on December 24 and 7 a.m. on December 26. If December 26 falls on Sunday, the hours of closing shall be determined pursuant to this act. The legislative body of a city, village or township, by resolution or ordinance, may prohibit the sale of alcoholic liquor on Sunday or a legal holiday, primary election day, general election day, or municipal election day. MI. COMP. LAWS. ANN., Vol. 20A, 1985 Supp., sec. 436.19e.

Spirits; special license for Sunday sales; disposition — Any licensee who elects to sell spirits on Sunday under the provisions of section 19e shall not do so until he first pays to the liquor control commission an additional fee in the amount of 15% of the fee charged for the issuance of his license. The revenue received from this section shall be deposited with the state treasurer in a special fund to be used only by the department of public health in programs for the treatment of alcoholics. Mɪ. Cᴏᴍᴘ. Lᴀᴡs Aɴɴ., Vol. 20A, 1985 Supp., sec. 436.19f.

(b) Motor vehicle sales—Motor Vehicles; sale on Sunday unlawful; exception—It shall be unlawful for any person, firm or corporation to engage in the business of buying, selling, trading or exchanging new, used or second-hand motor vehicles or offering to buy, sell, trade or exchange, or participate in the negotiation thereof, or attempt to buy, sell, trade or exchange any motor vehicle or interest therein, or of any written instrument pertaining thereto, on the first day of the week, commonly called Sunday. Mɪ. Cᴏᴍᴘ. Lᴀᴡs Aɴɴ., Vol. 20A, 1985 Supp., sec. 435.251.

Minnesota

Sunday laws that affect retail sales:

All horse racing, except horse racing at the annual fairs held by the various county agricultural societies of the state, gaming, and shows; all noises disturbing the peace of the day; all trades, manufacturers, and mechanical employments, except works of necessity performed in an orderly manner so as not to interfere with the repose and religious liberty of the community; all public selling or offering for sale of property, and all other labor except works of necessity and charity are prohibited on the Sabbath day.

Meals to be served upon the premises or elsewhere by caterers, prepared tobacco in places other than where intoxicating liquors are kept for sale, fruits, confectionery, newspapers, drugs, medicines and surgical appliances may be sold in a quiet and orderly manner. In works of necessity or charity is included whatever is needful during the day for good order, health, or comfort of the community, including the usual shoe-shining service; but keeping open a barber shop or shaving and hair cutting shall not be deemed works of necessity or charity, and nothing in this section shall be construed to permit the selling of uncooked meats, groceries, clothing, boots, or shoes. The games of baseball, football, hockey, basketball, golf, soccer and other contests of athletic skill when conducted in a quiet and orderly manner so as not to interfere with the peace, repose, and comfort of the community, may be played on the Sabbath day. Mɴ. Sᴛᴀᴛ. Aɴɴ., Vol. 40A, 1961 Amendments, sec. 624.02.

Every person who breaks the Sabbath shall be guilty of a misdemeanor and punished by a fine of not less than $1 nor more than $10 or by imprisonment in the county jail for not more than five days; but it shall be sufficient defense to a prosecution for Sabbath breaking that the defendant uniformly keeps another day of the week as holy time and that the act complained of was done in such manner as not to disturb others in the observance of the Sabbath. MN. STAT. ANN., Vol. 40A, sec. 624.03.

Liquor; Hours and days of sale—Subdivision 1. No sale of nonintoxicating malt liquor may be made between 1:00 a.m. and 8:00 a.m. on the days of Monday through Saturday, nor between 1:00 a.m. and 12:00 noon on Sunday, provided that an establishment located on land owned by the metropolitan sports commission may sell nonintoxicating malt liquor between 10:00 a.m. and 12:00 noon on a Sunday on which a sports or other event is scheduled to begin at that location on or before 1:00 p.m. of that day.

Subdivision 2. No sale of intoxicating liquor for consumption on the licensed premises may be made:

(3) after 1:00 a.m. on Sundays, except as provided by subdivision 3;

Subdivision 3. (a) A restaurant, club or hotel with a seating capacity for at least 30 persons and which holds an on-sale intoxicating liquor license may sell intoxicating liquor for consumption on the premises in conjunction with the sale of food between the hours of 12:00 noon and 12:00 midnight on Sundays.

(b) The governing body of a municipality may after one public hearing by ordinance permit a restaurant, hotel, or club to sell intoxicating liquor for consumption on the premises in conjunction with the sale of food between the hours of 10:00 a.m. and 12:00 midnight on Sundays, provided that the licensee is in conformance with the Minnesota Clean Air Act.

(c) An establishment serving intoxicating liquor on Sundays must obtain a Sunday license. The license must be issued by the governing body of the municipality for a period of one year, and the fee for the license may not exceed $200.

(d) A municipality may issue a Sunday intoxicating liquor license only if authorized to do so by the voters of the municipality voting on the question at a general or special election.

(e) An election conducted in a town on the question of the issuance by the county of Sunday sales licenses to establishments located in the town must be held on the day of the annual election of town officers.

(f) Voter approval is not required for licenses issued by the metropolitan airports commission or common carrier licenses issued by the commissioner. Common carriers serving intoxicating liquor on Sunday must obtain a Sunday license from the commissioner at an annual fee of $50, plus $5 for each duplicate.

Subdivision 4. No sale of intoxicating liquor may be made by an off-sale licensee:

(1) on Sundays;

Subdivision 5. No establishment licensed under section 840A.414, may permit a person to consume or display intoxicating liquor, and no person may consume or display intoxicating liquor between 1:00 a.m. and 12:00 noon on Sundays. . . . MN. STAT. ANN., Vol. 22, 1986 Supplement, sec. 840A.504.

Mississippi

Sunday laws that affect retail sales:

Sunday; violations of Sabbath generally — If any person on the first day of the week, commonly called Sunday, shall himself labor at his own or any other trade, calling or business, or shall employ his apprentice or servant in labor or other business, except it be in the ordinary household offices of daily necessity or other work of necessity or charity, or other activity hereinafter expressly excepted, he shall, on conviction, be fined not more than twenty dollars ($20.00) for every offense.

Nothing in this section shall apply to labor on railroads or steamboats, common and contract carriers by motor vehicles, telegraphs or telephone lines, street railways, newspapers or in the business of a livery stable, garage or gasoline stations, or ice house, or to the manufacturing operation of any person, firm or corporation engaged in a manufacturing activity which for economical operation must engage in a manufacturing process; and in municipalities of less than five thousand (5,000) inhabitants, meat markets. Nothing in this section shall prohibit churches or religious societies or their officers, agents and employees from transacting any business, or performing any action on the first day of the week, commonly called Sunday, which they may transact or do on any other day of the week, including but not limited to, the formation of corporations, the execution of deeds, deeds of trust and notes, oil, gas and mineral leases and the issuance of bonds. All such business and actions heretofore transacted or performed on the first day of the week, commonly called Sunday, by churches, religious societies, and their officers, agents and employees acting as such, shall never be declared invalid because transacted or performed on Sunday. Provided, however, that municipalities may by ordinance prescribe certain hours, said hours not to exceed three (3) hours per Sabbath, that garages and gasoline stations within the limits of said municipality shall remain closed. Ms. CODE ANN., Vol. 21, sec. 97-23-63, 1985 supplement.

The word "person" as used in sections 97-23-65 to 97-23-75 shall be construed to include any natural person, firm, partnership, association, or corporation, acting either as principal, agent or employee. Ms. CODE ANN., Vol. 21, sec. 97-23-65.

On the first day of the week, commonly known as Sunday, it shall be unlawful for any person to sell or to offer for sale, or to employ others to sell or to offer for sale, or to engage in the business of selling or offering for sale, any wares or merchandise, goods or chattels, except the following: drugs, vitamins, medicines, medicinal and surgical supplies and appliances, sickroom supplies and sanitary goods; veterinary supplies and requisites; ice, ice cream, ices, confectionery, food, condiments, refreshments and beverages; newspapers, periodicals, books, maps, and pamphlets; tobacco products and smoker's supplies; films, flash bulbs and batteries; fuses and light bulbs; sunglasses; gasoline, motor fuels, fuel additives, lubricants and antifreeze; replacement parts or equipment when installed in making repairs on motor vehicles, trailers, farm implements, boats and aircraft, and on plumbing, heating, cooking, cooling or electrical devices or equipment; cooking, heating, lighting and industrial oils, gases and other fuels; electricity, water and steam; bait; ammunition; accessories and equipment (other than clothing) designed specifically for golf, tennis, boating, fishing, hunting, or other specific sport or athletic activity; funeral and burial supplies; feeding and sanitary supplies for infants; toiletries and shaving and grooming supplies (except power-operated devices); articles customarily sold as souvenirs and mementos; postcards and correspondence supplies; garden and lawn supplies. Ms. CODE ANN., Vol. 21, sec. 97-23-67.

Nothing in sections 97-23-65 to 97-23-75 shall be construed to prohibit on Sunday:

(1) the sale, or offering for sale, of any goods for charitable or governmental purposes, (2) the sale, or offering for sale, of any goods as part of any bona fide trade show, fair or exhibitions, sponsored by or for the benefit of any non-profit trade, labor, industrial or governmental organization or body, (3) isolated or occasional sales by persons not regularly engaged in the business of selling tangible personal property the sale of which is prohibited by sections 97-23-65 to 97-23-75, or (4) the carrying of advertising on Sunday by communications media. Ms. CODE ANN., Vol. 21, sec. 97-23-69.

Any person violating section 97-23-67 shall be deemed guilty of a misdemeanor, and upon conviction thereof shall be fined not more than two hundred dollars ($200.00), in the case of the first offense, and not less than two hundred dollars ($200.00), nor more than five hundred dollars ($500.00), in the case of each subsequent offense. Each separate sale, or offer to sell, in violation of section 97-23-67 shall constitute a separate offense. Ms. CODE ANN., Vol. 21, sec. 97-23-71.

The purpose of sections 97-23-65 to 97-23-75 being to promote the health, recreation and welfare of the state, the violation of sections 97-23-65 to 97-23-75 is declared to be a public nuisance and any state, county or municipal law enforcement officer or any private person may apply to any court of competent jurisdiction for and may obtain an injunction restraining further violation of said sections. In such proceeding, the court shall, if an injunction be granted, assess in favor of the plaintiff and against the defendant, the costs of the action. Ms. CODE ANN., Vol. 21, sec. 97-23-73.

The governing authorities of municipalities or the boards of supervisors of counties acting within areas outside of municipalities may by local ordinance duly adopted prohibit or limit in whole or in part the sale of items hereinabove detailed, and the said authorities may likewise prescribe the hours within which such sales may be made, or within which said sales may be prohibited within their respective jurisdictions. Ms. CODE ANN., Vol. 21, sec. 97-23-75.

If any person shall engage in, show forth, exhibit, act, represent, perform or cause to be shown forth, acted, represented or performed any tricks, juggling, sleight of hand, or any bear baiting, any bull-fighting, horse-racing or cock-fighting, or any such like show or exhibit on Sunday, every person so offending shall be fined not more than fifty dollars ($50.00). Provided, that this section shall not be construed to prohibit the showing of moving picture shows, and baseball, basketball, tennis and golf games, after 1:00 p.m. on Sunday. Provided further, that this section shall not be construed to prohibit the operation of television on Sunday. Ms. CODE ANN., Vol. 21, sec. 97-23-79.

It shall be unlawful for any holder of a package retailer's permit engaged solely in the business of package retail sales under this chapter to sell any alcoholic beverage before 10:00 a.m. and after 10:00 p.m. It shall also be unlawful for said holder to sell alcoholic beverages on Sunday. . . .

Any person who shall violate any of the provisions of this section shall be guilty of a misdemeanor and, upon conviction, shall be punished by a fine of not more than five hundred dollars ($500.00) or by imprisonment in the county jail for a term of not more than six (6) months or by both such fine and imprisonment, in the discretion of the court. In addition, the commission shall forthwith revoke the permit of any permittee who violates the provisions of this section. Ms. CODE ANN., Vol. 14, sec. 67-1-83(3&4).

Missouri

Sunday laws that affect retail sales:

1. Whoever engages on Sunday in the business of selling or sells or offers for sale on such day, at retail, motor vehicles; clothing and wearing apparel; clothing accessories; furniture; housewares; home, business or office furnishings; household, business and office appliances; hardware; tools; paints; watches; clocks; luggage; musical instruments and recordings or toys; excluding novelties and souvenirs; is guilty of a misdemeanor and shall upon conviction for the first offense be sentenced to pay a fine of not exceeding one hundred dollars, and for the second or any subsequent offense be sentenced to pay a fine of not exceeding two hundred dollars or undergo confinement not exceeding thirty days in the county jail by default thereof.

2. Each separate sale or offer to sell shall constitute a separate offense.

3. Information charging violations of this section shall be brought within five days after the commission of the alleged offense and not thereafter.

4. The operation of any place of business where any goods, wares or merchandise are sold or exposed for sale in violation of this section is hereby declared to be a public and common nuisance.

5. Any county of this state containing all or part of a city with a population of over four hundred thousand may exempt itself from the application of this section by submission of the proposition to the voters of the county at a general election or a special election called for that purpose, and the proposition receiving a majority of the votes cast therein. . . . Mo. STAT. ANN., Vol. 41A, sec. 578.100.

Exemptions from the provisions of section 578.100 are possible; the conditions under which such exemptions are granted are spelled out in sections 578.105, 578.106 and 578.110.

No person may be denied employment or advancement in employment because of his or her refusal to work on his or her normal day of worship. Mo. STAT. ANN., Vol. 41A, sec. 578.115.

Notwithstanding any provision in this chapter to the contrary, no dealer, distributor or manufacturer registered under section 301.251, RSMo, may keep open, operate, or assist in keeping open or operating any established place of business for the purpose of buying, selling, bartering or exchanging, or offering for sale, barter or exchange, any motor vehicle, whether new or used, on Sunday. However, this section does not apply to the sale of manufactured housing, washing, towing, wrecking or repairing operations; the sale of petroleum products, tires, and repair parts and accessories; or new vehicle shows or displays participated in by five or more franchised dealers or in towns or cities with five or fewer dealers, a majority.

No association consisting of motor vehicle dealers, distributors or manufacturers registered under section 301.251, RSMo, shall be in violation of antitrust or restraint of trade statutes under chapter 416, RSMo, or regulation promulgated thereunder solely because it encourages its members not to open or operate on Sunday a place of business for the purpose of buying, selling, bartering or exchanging any motor vehicle.

Any person who violates the provisions of this section shall be guilty of a class C misdemeanor. Mo. STAT. ANN., Vol. 41A, 1986 Supplement, sec. 578.120.

Notwithstanding any other provisions of this chapter to the contrary, any person who possesses the qualifications required by this chapter, and who now or hereafter meets the requirements of and complies with the provisions of this chapter, may apply for, and the supervisor or liquor control may issue, a license to sell intoxicating liquor, as in this chapter defined, between the hours of 12:00 noon on Sunday and midnight on Sunday by the drink at retail for consumption on the premises of any restaurant bar as described in the application. . . .

Any new restaurant bar having been in operation for less than ninety days may be issued a temporary license to sell intoxicating liquor by the drink at retail for consumption on the premises between the hours of 1:00 p.m. and midnight on Sunday for a period not to exceed ninety days. . . .

In counties of the first class having a charter form of government and which contain all or part of a city having a population of at least three hundred fifty thousand, any restaurant bar licensed under the provisions of this section which is located on the grounds of a sports stadium primarily used for professional sporting events may sell intoxicating liquor by the drink at retail for consumption within the premises of the restaurant bar on Sunday between the hours of 11:00 a.m. and 12:00 midnight notwithstanding the hours of limitation set forth in subsection 1 of this section. Mo. STAT. ANN., Vol. 16A, 1986 Supplement, sec. 311.097.

Notwithstanding the provisions of section 311.270, or any other provision of law to the contrary, any person, firm, or corporation holding a license to sell malt liquor only may apply for a special license to sell malt liquor or beer containing not in excess of five percent alcohol by weight on Sunday in sports stadiums primarily used for professional sporting events, in cities not within a county.

The special license shall allow such person, firm, or corporation to sell malt liquor or beer containing not in excess of five percent alcohol by weight, for on-premises consumption only, for a period starting at 11:00 a.m. on Sundays, and ending at 1:30 a.m. on the following Monday. Mo. STAT. ANN., Vol. 16A, 1986 Supplement, sec. 311.273.

When December thirty-first falls on Sunday, any person having a license to sell intoxicating liquor by the drink may be open for business and sell intoxicating liquor by the drink under the provisions of his license on that day after 1:00 p.m. and until the time which would be lawful on another day of the week, notwithstanding any provisions of section 311.290 or any other provision of law to the contrary. Mo. STAT. ANN., Vol. 16A, 1986 Supplement, sec. 311.298.

The drinking or consumption of intoxicating liquor shall not be permitted in, upon, or about the licensed premises by any person under twenty-one years of age, or by any other person between the hours of 1:30 a.m. and 6 a.m. on any weekday, and between the hours of 12:00 midnight Saturday and 12:00 midnight Sunday. . . . The provision of this section regulating the drinking or consumption of intoxicating liquor between certain hours and on election day and Sunday shall apply also to premises licensed under this chapter to sell intoxicating liquor by the drink. . . . Mo. STAT. ANN., Vol. 16A, 1986 Supplement, sec. 311.480.

Montana

Sunday laws that affect retail sales—none in general.

Exceptions:
(a) Liquor sales—16-2-104. Hours. (1) State liquor stores shall be and remain open during such period of the day as the department shall deem advisable. The stores shall be closed for the transaction of business on legal holidays and between the close of normal business Saturday p.m. up to the opening of normal business Tuesday a.m. as set by department rule. (2) No sale or delivery of liquor shall be made on or from the premises of any state liquor store nor shall any store be open for the sale of liquor:

(a) on any holiday recognized by state law; (each Sunday is classified as a holiday, see M.C.A. 1-1-216). MT. CODE ANN., Titles 10•19.

(b) Motor vehicle sales—none.

Nebraska

Sunday laws that affect retail sales—none in general.

Exceptions:

(a) Liquor sales—53-179. Sale at retail; forbidden during certain hours; exceptions: alcoholic liquor in open containers; unlawful after hours.

. . . (2) Except as provided for and allowed by ordinance of a local governing body applicable to area within the corporate limits of a city or village, or by resolution of a county board applicable to area within such county and outside the corporate limits of any city or village, no alcoholic liquors, including beer, shall be sold at retail or dispensed between the hours of 6:00 a.m. Sunday and 1:00 a.m. Monday, or for consumption on the premises between the hours of 6:00 a.m. Sunday and 6:00 p.m. Sunday. This subsection shall not apply after 12:00 noon on Sunday to a licensee which is a nonprofit corporation and the holder of a license issued pursuant to either subdivision (5)C. or (5)H. of section 53-124.

(3) It shall be unlawful on property licensed to sell alcoholic liquor in open containers to remain or be in possession or control of any person for purposes of consumption between the hours of 1:15 a.m. and 6:00 a.m. on any day. Where any city or village provides by ordinance, or any county provides by resolution, for an earlier closing hour, the provisions of this subsection shall become effective fifteen minutes after such closing hour instead of 1:15 a.m. NEB. REV. STAT., Vol. 111A, 1984.

(b) Motor vehicle sales—none.

Nevada

Sunday laws that affect retail sales—none in general.

Exceptions:

(a) Liquor sales—none.

(b) Motor vehicle sales—none.

New Hampshire

Sunday laws that affect retail sales:

No person shall do any work, business, or labor of his secular calling, to the disturbance of others, on the first day of the week, commonly called the Lord's Day, except works of necessity and mercy, and the making of necessary repairs upon mills and factories which could not be made otherwise without loss to operatives; and no person shall engage in any play, game, or sport on that day.

No person shall keep his ship, warehouse, cellar, restaurant or workshop open for the reception of company, or shall sell or expose for sale any merchandise whatever on the Lord's Day; but this section shall not be construed to prevent the entertainment of boarders, nor the sale of milk, bread, and other necessaries of life, nor of drugs and medicines.

No provision of this chapter shall prohibit or authorize the prohibition of running or harness horse racing meets or dog racing meets on Sunday after midday and no action shall be required because of the provisions of this chapter by the selectmen of a town or the city council of a city or a town meeting to permit any such meet.

Nothing in this chapter shall prevent the selectmen of any town, or the city council of any city, from adopting bylaws and ordinances permitting and regulating retail business, plays, games, sports, and exhibitions on the Lord's Day, provided such bylaws and ordinances are approved by a majority vote of the legal voters present and voting at the next regular election. In towns of over 10,000, said approval may be obtained at a special election held before the regular election. But no such bylaws or ordinances shall permit public dancing on the Lord's Day after 1 a.m., or prize fights at any time on the Lord's Day, to the games of baseball, hockey, or football, or any games, sports, or exhibitions of physical skill at which admission is charged or donations accepted, to be held earlier than one o'clock in the afternoon, or the opening of theatrical or vaudeville performances or motion pictures earlier than two o'clock in the afternoon.

Any retail business that is required to be closed on Sunday under the provisions of this chapter may not be opened for business on Memorial Day and Veterans Day until twelve noon.

Notwithstanding the provisions of RSA 332-D:4, public dancing shall be permitted after two p.m. on Sundays in hotels licensed under RSA 178:3 and 178:4, in restaurants licensed under RSA 178:3-a and RSA 178:3-c, and in first class ballrooms licensed under RSA 178:7-a, provided that such dancing shall have the approval of the state liquor commission.

A person who violates any provision of this chapter is guilty of a violation. Nн Rev. Stat., Titles 28-30, secs. 332-D:1-7.

Alcoholic Beverages: Said commission shall have the power to make all necessary and proper rules and regulations for carrying out the provisions hereof, and such rules and regulations shall have the effect of law. No sale of beverages shall be made on Sunday by reason of permits issued to manufacture beverages or to sell beverages to other permittees under the provisions of RSA 181:8 or RSA 181:9. Nн. Rev. Stat. Ann., Vol. 2-A., sec. 176-11.

New Jersey

Sunday laws that affect retail sales:

Any person who shall carry on or engage in the business of buying, selling, exchanging, dealing, or trading in new or used motor vehicles; or who shall open any place of business or lot wherein he attempts to or does engage in the business of buying, selling, exchanging, dealing or trading in new or used motor vehicles; or who does buy, sell, exchange, deal or trade in new or used motor vehicles as a business on the first day of the week, commonly known and designated as Sunday is a disorderly person. Such a disorderly person upon conviction for the first offense shall pay a fine not to exceed $100.00 or be imprisoned for a period of not more than 10 days or both; and for the second offense shall pay a fine not to exceed $500.00 or be imprisoned for a period not more than 30 days or both; and for the third or each subsequent offense shall pay a fine of $750.00 or be imprisoned for a period of 6 months or both. N.J. Stat. Ann., Title 2A, sec. 171-1.1.

On the first day of the week, commonly known and designated as Sunday, it shall be unlawful for any person whether it be at retail, wholesale or by auction, to sell, attempt to sell or offer to sell or to engage in the business of selling, as hereinafter defined, clothing or wearing apparel, building or lumber supply materials, furniture, home or business or office furnishings, household, business or office appliances, except as works of necessity and charity or as isolated transactions not in the usual course of the business of the participants.

Any person who violates any provision of this act is a disorderly person and upon conviction for the first offense shall pay a fine of $250.00; and for the second offense shall pay a fine of not less than $250.00 or more than $1,000.00 to be fixed by the court; and for the third offense, shall pay a fine of not less than $1,000.00 or more than $2,000.00 to be fixed by the court or, in the discretion of the court, may be imprisoned for a period of not more than 30 days, or both; and for the fourth or each subsequent offense, shall pay a fine of not less than $2,000.00 or more than $5,000.00 to be fixed by the court, or, in the discretion of the court, may be imprisoned for a period of not less than 30 days or more than six months, or both. A single sale of an article or articles of merchandise of the character hereinabove set forth to any one customer, or a single offer to sell an article or articles of such merchandise to any one prospective customer, shall be deemed to be and constitute a separate and distinct violation of this act. N.J. STAT. ANN., Vol. 2A, sec. 171-5.8.

Section 171-5.10 defines the terms included in the wording of sec. 171-5.8.

This act shall be construed as an additional remedy to secure proper Sunday observance and the directors, officers, managers, agents or employees or corporations shall be personally liable for the penalties hereinabove provided. N.J. STAT. ANN., Vol. 2A, sec. 171-5.11.

This act shall take effect immediately but shall not become operative in any county unless and until the voters of the county shall determine by referendum held pursuant to this act that the same shall apply therein. N.J. STAT. ANN., Vol. 2A, sec. 171-5.12.

Sections 171-5.13 through 171-5.20 detail the referendum process mentioned in sec. 171-5.12. Title 33, sec. 1-47.1 refers to the referendum procedure regarding hours of retail sales of alcoholic beverages.

The governing board or body of each municipality, may, by ordinance, limit the number of licenses to sell alcoholic beverages at retail, but any such limitation adopted by ordinance or resolution prior to July first, one thousand nine hundred and thirty-seven, shall continue in full force and effect until repealed, amended or otherwise altered by ordinance. The governing board or body of each municipality may, as regards said municipality, by ordinance or resolution, limit the hours between which the sale of alcoholic beverages at retail may be made, prohibit the retail sale of alcoholic beverages on Sunday. . . . N.J. STAT. ANN., Vol. 33, sec. 1-40.

. . . If a municipality has no ordinance or local law that authorizes the sale of alcoholic beverages for consumption on the premises, then such municipality may by ordinance authorize the sale of wine and malt alcoholic beverages in original bottle or can containers by retail distribution licensees any time between the hours of 12:30 p.m. and 6:30 p.m. on Sunday, in addition to such weekday hours as may be authorized by ordinance. N.J. STAT. ANN., Title 33, sec. 1-40.3. 1985 supplement.

New Mexico

Sunday laws that affect retail sales:

Auctions and auctioneers. Jewelry sales not to be held. Prohibition—B. No such sales whether licensed or not shall be held or remain open for business on any day after the hour of six o'clock in the evening and before the hour of eight o'clock in the morning. No such sales shall be held or remain open for business on Sundays or legal holidays. NM STAT. ANN., sec. 61-16-5.

Restaurant license. Alcoholic Beverages—B. After the approval of restaurant licenses by the registered qualified electors of the local option district and upon completion of all requirements in the Liquor Control Act for the issuance of licenses, a restaurant located or to be located within the local option district may receive a restaurant license to sell, serve or allow the consumption of beer and wine subject to the following requirements and restrictions:

(7) if Sunday sales have been approved in the local option district, a restaurant licensee may serve beer and wine on Sundays until the time meals (meal) sales and services cease or 11:00 p.m., whichever time is earlier; . . . NM STAT. ANN., 1985 Supplement, sec. 60-6A-4.

Motor vehicles. Judicial proceedings under motor vehicle code—Sunday actions.—Judicial proceedings under any provision of the Motor Vehicle Code (66-1-1 to 66-8-140 NMSA 1978) are valid when performed on Sunday the same as on other days of the week. NM STAT. ANN., 1985 Supplement, sec. 66-8-8.

New York

Sunday laws that affect retail sales:

The first day of the week being by general consent set apart for rest and religious uses, the law prohibits the doing on that day of certain acts hereinafter specified, which are serious interruptions of the repose and religious liberty of the community. N.Y. CODE OF LEGAL STATUTES, Art. 2, sec. 2.

A violation of the foregoing prohibition is Sabbath breaking. N.Y. CODE OF LEGAL STATUTES., Art. 2, sec. 3.

Sabbath breaking is a misdemeanor, punishable by a fine of not less than five dollars and not more than ten dollars, or by imprisonment in a county jail not exceeding five days, or by both, but for a second or other offense, where the party shall have been previously convicted, it shall be punishable by a fine not less than ten dollars and not more than twenty dollars or by imprisonment in a county jail not less than five nor more than twenty days, or both. N.Y. CODE OF LEGAL STATUTES., Art. 2, sec. 4.

All labor on Sunday is prohibited, excepting the works of necessity and charity. In works of necessity or charity is included whatever is needful during the day for good order, health or comfort of the community. N.Y. CODE OF LEGAL STATUTES., Art. 2, sec. 5.

It is sufficient defense to a prosecution for work or labor on the first day of the week that the defendant uniformly keeps another day of the week as holy time, and does not labor on that day, and that the labor complained of was done in such manner as not to interrupt or disturb other persons observing the first day of the week as holy time. N.Y. CODE OF LEGAL STATUTES., Art. 2, sec. 6.

All public sports, exercises or shows, except professional golf tournaments and games of the XIII winter olympiad conducted in Essex county in nineteen hundred eighty, upon the first day of the week, and all noise unreasonably disturbing the peace of the day are prohibited, except as hereinafter provided.

Notwithstanding the provisions of this section, it shall be lawful to conduct, witness, participate or engage in any form of public sports, exercises or shows which are conducted or engaged in primarily for the entertainment of spectators, not specifically prohibited by any provision of the law, on the first day of the week after five minutes past one o'clock in the afternoon, to witness which the public is invited or an admission fee is charged, either directly or indirectly, in a city, town or village as shall be permitted by local law or ordinance heretofore or hereafter adopted by the common council or other legislative body of the city, town or village permitting such public sports, exercises or shows, on such day and after such hour provided, however, the failure of a city, town or village in which a municipally owned stadium, arena or facility is located, to adopt such a local law or ordinance shall not prohibit such public sports, exercises or shows beginning after five minutes past one o'clock in the afternoon on the first day of the week in any such stadium, arena or facility.

Nothing herein contained shall be deemed to prohibit private sports, games or recreational activities which are engaged in primarily for the personal enjoyment, recreation and health of the participants, on the first day of the week, conducted in a manner which does not constitute a serious interruption of the respose or religious liberty of the community. N.Y. CODE OF LEGAL STATUTES., Art. 2, sec. 7.

All trades, manufacturers, agricultural, or mechanical employments upon the first day of the week are prohibited, except that when the same are works of necessity they may be performed on that day in their usual and orderly manner, so as not to interfere with the repose and religious liberty of the community. N.Y. CODE OF LEGAL STATUTES., Art. 2, sec. 8.

All manner of public selling or offering for sale of any property upon Sunday is prohibited, except as follows:

1. Articles of food may be sold, served, supplied and delivered at any time before ten o'clock in the morning;

2. Meals may be sold to be eaten on the premises where sold at any time of the day;

3. Caterers may serve meals to their patrons at any time of the day;

4. Prepared tobacco, bread, milk, eggs, ice, soda-water, fruit, flowers, confectionery, souvenirs, items of art and antiques, newspapers, magazines, gasoline, oil, tires, cemetery monuments, drugs, medicine and surgical instruments may be sold and delivered at any time of the day.

5. Grocers, delicatessen dealers and bakeries may sell, supply, serve and deliver cooked and prepared foods, between the hours of four o'clock in the afternoon and half past seven o'clock in the evening, in addition to the time provided for in subdivision one hereof, and elsewhere than in cities and villages having a population of forty thousand or more, delicatessen dealers, bakeries and farmers' markets or roadside stands selling fresh vegetables and other farm produce, and fishing tackle and bait stores may sell, supply, serve and deliver merchandise usually sold by them, at any time of the day.

6. Persons, firms or corporations holding licenses and/or permits issued under the provisions of the alcoholic beverage control law permitting the sale of beer at retail, may sell such beverages at retail on Sunday before three antemeridian and after twelve noon for off-premises consumption to persons making purchases at the licensed premises to be taken by them from the licensed premises.

7. Sale at public auction of thoroughbred, standardbred and quarterhorse racehorses.

The provisions of this section, however, shall not be construed to allow or permit the public sale or exposing for sale or delivery of uncooked flesh foods or meats, fresh or salt, at any hour or time of the day. Delicatessen dealers shall not be considered as caterers within subdivision three hereof. N.Y. CODE OF LEGAL STATUTES., Art. 2, sec. 9.

Notwithstanding any other provision of law, it shall be a sufficient defense to a prosecution pursuant to this article, for conducting any trade or business or public selling or offering for sale of any property on Sunday, that the defendant:

(1) as the proprietor of such business, uniformly keeps another day of the week as holy time and keeps his business closed on the seventh day of the week,

(2) does not himself labor, employ others to labor in, by or with another conduct a trade or publicly sell or offer for sale any property on the day he keeps as holy time,

(3) conducts such labor, trade or business in its normal course on Sunday by himself and members of his immediate family, and

(4) so conducts such trade, public selling or offer to sell any property on Sunday in such manner as not to disturb the religious observances of the community.

The term "day of the week" as used in this section shall mean and include the period of time of not less than twenty-four consecutive hours commencing at or before sundown on one day and terminating at or after sundown on the following day. N.Y. CODE OF LEGAL STATUTES., Art. 2, sec. 10.

In addition to the penalty imposed by section four, all property and commodities exposed for sale on the first day of the week in violation of the provisions of this article shall be forfeited. Upon conviction of the offender by a justice of the peace of a county, or by any police justice or magistrate, such officer shall issue a warrant for the seizure of the forfeited articles, which, when seized, shall be sold on one day's notice, and the proceeds paid to the overseers of the poor, for the use of the poor of the town or city. N.Y. CODE OF LEGAL STATUTES., Art. 2, sec. 12.

Article 2, sections 15 and 16 outline specific provisions with respect to processions & parades on Sunday and public entertainment on Sunday, respectively.

Any person who carries on or engages in the business of shaving, hair cutting or other work of a barber on the first day of the week, shall be deemed guilty of a misdemeanor, and upon conviction thereof shall be fined not more than five dollars; and upon a second conviction for a like offense shall be fined not less than ten dollars and not more than twenty-five dollars, or be imprisoned in the county jail for a period of not less than ten days, nor more than twenty-five days, or be punishable by both such fine and imprisonment at the discretion of the court or magistrate. N.Y. CODE OF LEGAL STATUTES., Art. 2, sec. 16.

Days of rest and recreation:

a. One day a week may be set aside for rest and recreation.

b. A day of rest and recreation may be determined by the owners of a business or commercial enterprise, which shall include a sole proprietorship, partnership or corporation.

    c. A retail merchants association or organization shall not have the right to determine a day of rest and recreation for any of its members.

    d. Any person, corporation or association who knowlingly attempts to force or coerce an owner or manager of a business to make a determination in violation of this section shall be fined not less than two hundred fifty dollars and not more than five hundred dollars and for a second or other offense, where the party shall have been previously convicted thereof, it shall be punishable by a fine of not less than one thousand dollars and not more than two thousand dollars.

    e. No provision of this section shall be construed to prohibit any owner from doing business seven days a week, where any other general, special or local law, rule or regulation does not specifically prohibit such activity. N.Y. CODE OF LEGAL STATUTES, 1985 supplement, sec. 17.

    Provisions governing licensees to sell at retail for consumption off the premises:

    14. No premises licensed to sell liquor and/or wine for off-premises consumption shall be permitted to remain open: (a) On Sunday. . . . N.Y. CODE OF LEGAL STATUTES, Art. 8, sec. 105.

    Provisions governing licensees to sell at retail for consumption on the premises:

    5. No alcoholic beverages shall be sold, offered for sale or given away upon any premises licensed to sell alcoholic beverages at retail for on-premises consumption during the following hours:

    (a) Sunday, from four antemeridian to twelve noon. N.Y. CODE OF LEGAL STATUTES, Art. 8, sec. 106.

North Carolina

Sunday laws that affect retail sales:

    Sale of certain articles on Sunday prohibited; counties excepted— Any person, firm, or corporation who engages on Sunday in the business of selling, or sells or offers for sale on such day, clothing and wearing apparel, clothing accessories, furniture, home, business or office furnishings, household, business or office appliances, hardware, tools, paints, building and lumber supply materials, jewelry, silverware, watches, clocks, luggage, musical instruments or recordings, shall be guilty of a misdemeanor punishable by a fine not to exceed five hundred dollars ($500.00), imprisonment for not more than six months, or both. GEN. STAT. OF N.C., Vol. 1B, sec. 14-346.2.

Limitations on enactment of Sunday-closing ordinances—No ordinance regulating or prohibiting business activity on Sundays shall be enacted unless the council shall hold a public hearing on the proposed ordinance. Notice of the hearing shall be published once each week for four successive weeks before the date of the hearing. The notice shall fix the date, hour and place of the public hearing, and shall contain a statement of the council's intent to consider a Sunday-closing ordinance, the purpose for such an ordinance, and one or more reasons for its enactment. No ordinance shall be held invalid for failure to observe the procedural requirements for enactment imposed by this section unless the issue is joined in an appropriate proceeding initiated within 90 days after the date of final enactment. . . . GEN. STAT. OF N.C., Vol. 3D, 1985 Supplement, sec. 160A-191.

Alcoholic beverages—Hours for sale and consumption—

(c) Sunday hours—It shall be unlawful to sell or consume alcoholic beverages on any licensed premises from the time at which sale or consumption must cease on Sunday morning until 1:00 p.m. on that day.

(d) Local option—A city may adopt an ordinance prohibiting in the city the retail sale of malt beverages, unfortified wine, and fortified wine during any or all of the hours from 1:00 p.m. on Sunday until 7:00 a.m. on the following Monday. A county may adopt an ordinance prohibiting in the parts of the county outside any city, the retail sale of malt beverages, unfortified wine and fortified wine during any or all of the hours from 1:00 p.m. on Sunday until 7:00 a.m. on the following Monday. Neither a city nor a county, however, may prohibit those sales in establishments having brown-bagging or mixed beverage permits. GEN. STAT. OF N.C., Ch. 18B, sec. 18B-1004.

North Dakota

Sunday laws that affect retail sales:

12.1-30-01. Business or labor on Sunday—Exemptions—Classification of offenses.

1. Except as otherwise provided in sections 12.1-30-02 and 12.1-30-03, it is a class B misdemeanor for any person on Sunday to do any of the following activities:

a. Engage in or conduct business or labor for profit in the usual manner and location.

b. Operate a place of business open to the public.

c. Authorize or direct that person's employees or agents to take action prohibited under this section.

2. The prohibition in subsection 1 does not apply to a person who in good faith observes a day other than Sunday as the Sabbath, if that person refrains from engaging in or conducting business or labor for profit and closes the place of business to the public on the day observed as the Sabbath.

3. The attorney general, a state's attorney, a mayor, a city manager, or a city attorney may petition a district court, for the district where a violation is occurring, to enjoin a violation of this section.

12.1-30-02. Items prohibited from sale or rental on Sunday.

Except for items sold at hobby shows, craft shows, fairs, exhibits, occasional rummage sales including garage sales or other sales for which a sales tax permit is not required, and tourist attractions that derive at least fifty percent of their annual gross sales from seasonal or tourist customers, the sale or rental of any of the following items on Sunday is prohibited:

1. Clothing other than work gloves and infant supplies.
2. Clothing accessories.
3. Wearing apparel other than that sold to a transient traveler under emergency conditions.
4. Footwear.
5. Headwear.
6. Home, business, office, or outdoor furniture.
7. Kitchenware.
8. Kitchen utensils.
9. China.
10. Home appliances.
11. Stoves.
12. Refrigerators.
13. Air conditioners.
14. Electric fans.
15. Radios.
16. Television sets.
17. Washing machines.
18. Dryers.
19. Cameras.
20. Hardware other than emergency plumbing, heating, cooling, or electrical repair or replacement parts and equipment.

21. Tools other than manually driven hand tools.
22. Jewelry.
23. Precious or semiprecious stones.
24. Silverware.
25. Watches.
26. Clocks.
27. Luggage.
28. Motor vehicles other than the daily rental of vehicles by businesses whose sole activity is automobile rental.
29. Musical instruments.
30. The sale of aural or video recordings, records, or tapes. Rental of these items is permitted.
31. Toys other than those customarily sold as novelties or souvenirs.
32. Mattresses.
33. Bed coverings.
34. Household linens.
35. Floor coverings.
36. Lamps.
37. Draperies.
38. Blinds.
39. Curtains.
40. Mirrors.
41. Cloth piece goods.
42. Lawnmowers.
43. Sporting or recreational goods other than those sold or rented on the premises where sports or recreational activities are conducted.
44. Paint and building and lumber supplies.

12.1-30-03. Businesses allowed to operate on Sunday—Limitations.—Subject to the limitations of this section and section 12.1-30-02, a business specified in this section may operate in the business' usual manner, location, and for its usual purposes. The businesses authorized under this section to operate on Sunday include:

1. Restaurants, cafeterias, or other prepared food service organizations.
2. Hotels, motels, and other lodging facilities.
3. Hospitals and nursing homes, including the sale of giftware on the premises.
4. Dispensaries of drugs and medicines.

5. Ambulance and burial services.
6. Generation and distribution of electric power, water, steam, natural gas, oil, or other fuel used as a necessary utility.
7. Distribution of gas, oil, and other fuels.
8. Telephone, telegraph, and messenger services.
9. Heating, refrigeration, and cooling services.
10. Railroad, bus, trolley, subway, taxi and limousine services.
11. Water, air, and land transportation services and attendant facilities.
12. Cold storage warehouse.
13. Ice manufacturing and distribution facilities and services.
14. Minimal maintenance of equipment and machinery.
15. Plane and industrial protection services.
16. Industries where continuous processing or manufacturing is required by the very nature of the process involved.
17. Newspaper publication and distribution.
18. Newsstands.
19. Radio and television broadcasting.
20. Motion picture, theatrical, and musical performances.
21. Motor vehicle service stations that sell motor fuel and motor oil, and that customarily provide daily repair services or products for any of the following parts of a motor vehicle:
    a. Air conditioning system.
    b. Batteries.
    c. Electrical system.
    d. Engine cooling system.
    e. Exhaust system.
    f. Fuel system.
    g. Tires and tubes.
    h. Emergency work necessary for the safe and lawful operation of the motor vehicle.
22. Athletic and sporting events.
23. Parks, beaches, and recreational facilities.
24. Scenic, historic, and tourist attractions.
25. Amusement centers, fairs, zoos, and museums.
26. Libraries.
27. Educational lectures, forums, and exhibits.
28. Service organizations (USO, YMCA, etc.)
29. Coin-operated laundry and drycleaning facilities.
30. Food stores operated by an owner or manager in addition to not more than six employees working in the store at one time on a Sunday.

31. Bait shops for the sale of live bait and fishing tackle.
32. From April first through June fifteenth, floral nurseries for the sale of bedding plants and nursery stock.
33. From November twentieth through December twenty-fourth, Christmas tree stands.
34. Hobby shows, craft shows, fairs, exhibits.
35. Occasional rummage sales, including garage sales or other sales for which a sales tax permit is not required.
36. Community festivals licensed or authorized by the governing body of a city or the board of county commissioners.
37. Premises licensed to dispense beer and alcoholic beverages within the limits prescribed in sections 5-02-05 and 5-02-05.1. ND CENTURY CODE, Vol. 2B.

Liquor sales—Except as permitted by section 5-02-05.1, any person who dispenses or permits the consumption of alcoholic beverages on licensed premises after one a.m. on Sundays, before eight a.m. on Mondays, or between the hours of one a.m. and eight a.m. on all other days of the week, or who dispenses alcoholic beverages or permits consumption of alcoholic beverages on licensed premises on Good Friday, Thanksgiving Day, Christmas Day, or after six p.m. on Christmas Eve, or between the hours of one a.m. and eight p.m. on the day of any statewide special, primary, or general election is guilty of a class A misdemeanor. ND CENTURY CODE, Vol. 1, 1985 Supplement, sec. 5-02-05.

Special Sunday convention alcoholic beverage permit—Penalty:

1. Any city or county may issue a special Sunday convention alcoholic beverage permit to a private club, lodge, motel, or hotel, as defined under city ordinances or county resolutions, and licensed as a retail alcoholic beverage establishment pursuant to chapter 5-02, or to a civic center, which serves as the headquarters for a state, multistate, or national convention of a bona fide organization recognized by the governing body of the city or county in which the convention is held. A county may not issue a permit under this section to a private club, lodge, motel or hotel located within the geographical boundaries of a city.

2. The authority for issuing such special permit shall rest solely with the governing body of the city or county. A special permit shall be granted only upon proper application to and approval by the governing body, and shall include payment of a fee determined by such governing body.

A special permit granted by the city or county shall be effective for one Sunday only.

3. Under the special permit, alcoholic beverages may be distributed and dancing may be permitted in those rooms of the private

club, lodge, motel, hotel, or civic center which have been specifically reserved for convention activities, but may not be permitted in bar and lounge areas containing the permanent bar fixtures and normally open to the public.

A city or county may permit dancing and the distribution of alcoholic beverages between the hours of twelve noon on the specified Sunday and one a.m. on Monday. Under no circumstances may the general public be permitted to participate in the consumption of alcoholic beverages distributed under the authority and conditions of the special permit. It is the duty of the private club, lodge, motel, hotel, or civic center granted the special permit to enforce the requirements of this section and the conditions established by the city or county under the permit.

4. The special Sunday convention alcoholic beverage permit shall not be granted to allow the distribution of alcoholic beverages at gatherings or meetings which, in the opinion of the governing body of the city or county, are primarily local in nature.

5. Any person who dispenses, sells, or permits the consumption of alcoholic beverages in violation of this section or the conditions of a special permit, or who furnishes information required by this section which is false or misleading, shall be guilty of a class A misdemeanor. ND CENTURY CODE, Vol. 1, 1985 Supplement, sec. 5-02-05.1.

Ohio

Sunday laws that affect retail sales—none in general.

Exceptions:
(a) Liquor sales—Sunday sale election; expenses; form of ballot.—If a petition is for submission of the question of whether the sale of intoxicating liquor shall be permitted on Sunday; a special election shall be held in the precinct at the time fixed as provided in section 4301.33 of the Revised Code. The expenses of holding the election shall be charged to the municipal corporation or township of which the precinct is a part.

At the election, one or more of the following questions, as designated in a valid petition, shall be submitted to the electors of the precinct:
(A) "Shall the sale of intoxicating liquor, of the same types as may be legally sold in this on other days of the week, be permitted in this precinct for consumption on the premises where sold, between the hours of one p.m. and midnight on Sunday?"
(B) "Shall the sale of intoxicating liquor, of the same types as

may be legally sold in this on other days of the week, be permitted in this precinct for consumption on the premises where sold, between the hours of one p.m. and midnight on Sunday; at licensed premises where the sale of food and other goods and services exceeds fifty percent of the total gross receipts of the permit holder at the premises?"

(C) "Shall the sale of wine and mixed beverages of the same type as may legally be sold in this on other days of the week, be permitted in this precinct for consumption off the premises where sold, between the hours of one p.m. and midnight on Sunday?"

No C or D permit holder who first applied for his permit after April 15, 1982, shall sell beer on Sunday unless the sale of intoxicating liquor is authorized in the precinct at an election on question (A), (B), or (C) of this section. No D-6 permit is required for the sale of beer on Sunday. OH REV. CODE., 1985 Supplement, sec. 4301.35.1.

Effect of election concerning Sunday sales—If a majority of the electors voting on questions set forth in section 4301.35.1 of the Revised Code in a precinct vote "yes" on question (A), or, if both questions (A) and (B) are submitted, "yes" on both questions or "yes" on question (A) but "no" on question (B), sales of intoxicating liquor shall be allowed in the manner and under the conditions specified in question (A), under a D-6 permit, within the precinct concerned, during the period the election is in effect as defined in section 4301.37 of the Revised Code.

If only question (B) is submitted to the voters or if questions (B) and (C) are submitted and a majority of the electors voting in a precinct vote "yes" on question (B) as set forth in section 4301.35.1 of the Revised Code, sales of intoxicating liquor shall be allowed in the manner and under the conditions specified in question (B), under a D-6 permit, within the precinct concerned, during the period the election is in effect as defined in section 4301.37 of the Revised Code, even if question (A) was also submitted and a majority of the electors voting in the precinct voted "no."

If question (C) was submitted and a majority of electors voting on the question (C) set forth in section 4301.35.1 of the Revised Code in a precinct vote "yes," sales of wine and mixed beverages shall be allowed in the manner and under the conditions specified in question (C), under a D-6 permit, within the precinct concerned, during the period the election is in effect as defined in section 4301.37 of the Revised Code.

If questions (A), (B), and (C), as set forth in section 4301.35.1 of the Revised Code, are all submitted and a majority of the electors voting in such precinct vote "no" on all three questions, no sales of intoxicating liquor shall be made within the precinct concerned after two-thirty a.m. on Sunday; during the period the election is in effect as defined in section 4301.37 of the Revised Code. OH REV. CODE., 1985 Supplement, sec. 4301.36.1.

D-6 permit—Except as otherwise provided in this section, permit D-6 shall be issued to the holder of an A-1-A, A-2, C-2, D-2, D-3, D-4, D-4a, D-5, D-5a, D-5b, D-5c, or D-7 permit to allow sale under such permit between the hours of one p.m. and midnight on Sunday; if such sale has been authorized under section 4301.36.1 of the Revised Code and under the restrictions of such authorization. . . OH. REV. CODE., 1985 Supplement, sec. 4303.18.2.

(b) Motor vehicle sales—none.

Oklahoma

Sunday laws that affect retail sales:

Sunday to be observed—The first day of the week being by very general consent set apart for rest and religious uses, the law forbids to be done on that day certain acts deemed useless and serious interruptions of the repose and religious liberty of the community. Any violation of this prohibition is Sabbath-breaking. OK. STAT. ANN., Crimes and Punishments, sec. 907.

Sabbath-breaking defined—The following are the acts forbidden to be done on the first day of the week, the doing of which is Sabbath-breaking:

First. Servile labor, except works of necessity or charity.

Second. Trades, manufactures and mechanical employment.

Third. All shooting, horse racing or gaming.

Fourth. All manner of public selling, or offering or exposing for sale publicly, of any commodities, except that meats, bread, fish and all other foods may be sold at anytime, and except that food and drink may be sold to be eaten and drank upon the premises where sold, and drugs, medicines, milk, ice and surgical appliances and burial appliances and all other necessities may be sold at anytime of the day. OK. STAT. ANN., Crimes and Punishments, sec. 908.

Persons observing other day as holy—It is a sufficient defense in preceedings for servile labor on the first day of the week, to show that the accused uniformly keeps another day of the week as holy time, and does not labor upon that day, and that that labor complained of was done in such manner as not to interrupt or disturb other persons in observing the first day of the week as holy time. OK. STAT. ANN., Crimes and Punishments, sec. 909.

Punishment for Sabbath-breaking—Every person guilty of

Sabbath-breaking is punishable by a fine of not more than Twenty-five Dollars ($25.00) for each offense. OK. STAT. ANN., Crimes and Punishments, sec. 911.

Hours during which sale prohibited — From and after the effective date of this act it shall be unlawful for any place licensed to sell beverages containing more than one-half of one percent (1/2 of 1) of alcohol by volume and not more than three and two tenths percent (3.2) of alcohol by weight to sell such beverages for consumption on the premises between the hours of two o'clock a.m. and seven o'clock a.m. excepting Saturday nights when such beverages may not be sold between the hours of two o'clock a.m. and twelve o'clock noon on Sundays; provided, the governing body of any city or town is hereby authorized to prohibit, by ordinance regularly enacted, the sale of such beverages between the hours of two o'clock a.m. on Sunday and seven o'clock a.m. of the following Monday. OK. STAT. ANN., Intoxicating Liquors, 1985 Supplement, sec. 213.

Sales, barter or exchange of motor vehicles on Sunday prohibited. Activities exempt. No person, firm or corporation, whether owner, proprietor, agent or employee, shall keep open, operate or assist in keeping open or operating any place or premises or residences whether open or closed, for the purpose of selling, bartering, or exchanging, or offering for sale, barter or exchange, any motor vehicle or motor vehicles, whether new, used or secondhand, on the first day of the week, commonly called Sunday, except as otherwise provided in this section; and provided, however, that this act shall not apply to the opening of an establishment or place of business on the said first day of the week for other purposes, such as the sale of petroleum products, tires, automobile accessories, or for the purpose of operating and conducting a motor vehicle repair shop, or for the purpose of supplying such services as towing or wrecking. Antique, classic, or special interest automobiles sold, bartered, auctioned, or exchanged by any person, firm, or corporation are exempt from the provisions of this section. OK. STAT., ANN., Crimes and Punishments, 1985 Supplement, sec. 918.

Penalties — Any person, firm, partnership, or corporation who violates any of the provisions of this act shall be guilty of a misdemeanor, and upon each conviction thereof, shall be punished by a fine of not less than Seventy-five Dollars ($75.00) nor more than Five Hundred Dollars ($500.00), or by imprisonment in the county jail for a period not to exceed six (6) months, or the court, in its discretion, may suspend or revoke the Oklahoma motor vehicle dealer's license issued under the provisions of 47 O.S.1951, sec. 22.15, or by such fine and imprisonment and suspension or revocation. OK. STAT. ANN., Crimes and Punishments, sec. 919.

Oregon

Sunday laws that affect retail sales—none.

Exceptions:
(a) Liquor sales—none.
(b) Motor vehicle sales—none.

Pennsylvania

Sunday laws that affect retail sales:

No part of any act of assembly heretofore passed shall be construed to require any canal or railroad company to attend their works on the Sabbath days, for the purpose of expediting or aiding the passage of any boat, craft or vehicle along the same; any clause or clauses in their respective charters, imposing a penalty for not aiding boats, crafts or vehicles to pass within a certain time, to the contrary notwithstanding. 15 PA. STAT., sec. 4163.

Sales of liquor; restrictions—(2) Hotel and restaurant liquor licensees, airport liquor licensees, municipal golf course restaurant liquor licensees and privately-owned public golf course restaurant licensees may sell liquor and malt or brewed beverages only after seven o'clock antemeridian of any day until two o'clock antemeridian of the following day, except Sunday, and except as hereinafter provided, may sell liquor and malt or brewed beverages on Sunday between the hours of twelve o'clock midnight and two o'clock antemeridian. 47 PA. STAT., sec. 4-406, 1985 supplement.

Rhode Island

Sunday laws that affect retail sales:

Work or recreation on Sunday prohibited—Except as provided in sections 5-22-6 to 5-22-11, inclusive, every person who shall do or exercise any labor or business or work of his ordinary calling, or use any game, sport, play or recreation on the first day of the week, or suffer the same to be done or used by his children, servants or apprentices, works of necessity and charity only excepted, shall be fined not exceeding five dollars ($5.00) for the first offense and ten dollars ($10.00) for the second and every subsequent offense; provided, further, however, that the above prohibitions shall not apply to any person or persons operating or functioning under a valid permit or license. GEN. LAWS OF R.I., Vol. 3, sec. 11-40-1.

Employment of servants of others on Sunday—Every person who shall employ, improve, set to work or encourage the servant of any other person to commit any act named in sec. 11-40-1 shall suffer the like punishment. GEN. LAWS OF R.I., Vol. 3, sec. 11-40-2.

Time of filing complaints—All complaints for violations of the provisions of sections 11-40-1 and 11-40-2 shall be made within ten (10) days after the committing thereof and not afterwards. GEN. LAWS OF R.I., Vol. 3, sec. 11-40-3.

Faiths observing other days as Sabbath—Every professor of the Sabbatarian faith or of the Jewish religion, and such others as shall be owned or acknowledged by any church or society of said respective professions as members of or as belonging to such church or society, shall be permitted to labor in their respective professions or vocations on the first day of the week, but the exception in this section contained shall not confer the liberty of opening shops or stores on the said day for the purpose of trade and merchandise, or lading, unlading, or of fitting out vessels, or of working at the smith's business or any other mechanical trade in any compact place, except the compact villages in Westerly and Hopkinton, or of drawing seines or fishing or fowling in any manner in public places and out of their own possessions. . . . GEN. LAWS OF R.I., Vol. 3, sec. 11-40-4.

Sundays and holidays, sales to underage persons, intoxicated persons and persons of intemperate habits—Licenses issued under the provisions of this title shall not authorize the sale or service of beverages on Sunday, nor on Christmas day excepting licensed taverns, clubs, victualing houses and retailer's class F licensed places when served with food to guests, and except in places operated under a retailer's class E license described above and except in cars or on passenger-carrying marine vessels operated by holders of class G licenses. . . GEN. LAWS OF R.I., Vol. 1, sec. 3-8-1.

Sunday business prohibited—No dealer shall have open for the conduct of business any display room or outside display lot where motor vehicles are exhibited on the first day of the week, commonly called Sunday. . . . GEN. LAWS OF R.I., Vol. 5A, sec. 31-5-19.

South Carolina

Sunday laws that affect retail sales:

On the first day of the week, commonly called Sunday, it shall be unlawful for any person to engage in worldly work, labor, business of his ordinary calling or the selling or offering to sell, publicly or privately or by telephone, at retail or at wholesale to the consumer any goods, wares or merchandise or to employ others to engage in work, labor, business or selling or offering to sell any goods, wares or merchandise, excepting work of necessity or charity.

Provided, that in Charleston County the foregoing shall not apply to any person who conscientiously believes, because of his religion, that the seventh day of the week ought to be observed as the Sabbath and who actually refrains from secular business or labor on that day. CODE OF LAWS OF SOUTH CAROLINA, Vol. 17, sec. 53-1-40.

Section 53-1-40 does not apply to the following:

(1) The sale of food needs, ice, or soft drinks.

(2) The sale of tobacco and related products.

(3) The operation of radio or television stations nor to the printing, publication, and distribution of newspapers or weekly magazines, nor to the sale of newspapers, books, and magazines.

(4) The operation of public utilities or sales usual or incidental thereto.

(5) The transportation by air, land, or water of persons or property, not to the sale or delivery of heating, cooling, refrigerating, or motor fuels, oils, or gases, or the purchase or installation of repair parts or accessories for immediate use in cases of emergency in connection with motor vehicles, boats, bicycles, aircrafts, or heating, cooling, or refrigerating systems, nor to the cleaning of motor vehicles.

(6) The providing of medical services and supplies, nor to the sale of drugs, medicine, hygenic supplies, surgical supplies, and all other services and supplies related thereto.

(7) The operation of public lodging or eating places, including food caterers.

(8) Janitorial, custodial, and like services.

(9) Funeral homes and cemeteries.

(10) The sale of novelties, souvenirs, paper products, educational supplies, cameras, film, flash bulbs and cubes, batteries, baby supplies, hosiery and undergarments, flowers, plants, seeds, and shrubs.

(11) The sale of art and craft objects at arts or craft exhibitions held pursuant to sec. 53-1-10 provided that each art or craft object shown or sold has been designed by and is the original work of artisans present at the exhibition.

(12) Exhibition of noncommercial real property and mobile homes.

(13) The providing of any service, product, or other thing by means of a mechanical device not requiring the labor of any person.

(14) The sale or rental of swimming, fishing, and boating equipment.

(15) Any farming operations necessary for the preservation of agricultural commodities.

16. Light bulbs or flourescent tubes. CODE OF LAWS OF SOUTH CAROLINA, Vol. 17, sec. 53-1-50, 1985 supplement.

The sale or offer to sell the following items on Sunday is prohibited: Clothing, and clothing accessories (except those which qualify as swimwear, novelties, souvenirs, hosiery, or undergarments); housewares, china, glassware, and kitchenware; home, business and office furnishings, and appliances; tools, paints, hardware, building supplies, and lumber; jewelry, silverware, watches, clocks, luggage, musical instruments, recorders, recordings, radios, television sets, phonographs, record players or so-called hi-fi or stereo sets, or equipment; sporting goods (except when sold on premises where sporting events and recreational facilities are permitted); yard or piece goods; automobiles, trucks and trailers. No inference shall arise from the foregoing enumeration that either the sale or the offering for sale on Sunday of items or articles not mentioned is permitted. CODE OF LAWS OF SOUTH CAROLINA, Vol. 17, sec. 53-1-60, 1985 supplement.

A violation of any of the provisions of sec. 53-1-40 shall be punished by a fine of not less than fifty dollars nor more than two hundred fifty dollars in the case of the first offense, and by a fine of not less than one hundred dollars nor more than five hundred dollars for each and every subsequent offense. Each separate sale, offer or attempt to sell on Sunday, and each Sunday a person is engaged in other work, labor or business in violation of sec. 53-1-40, or employs others to be so engaged, shall constitute a separate offense. CODE OF LAWS OF SOUTH CAROLINA, Vol. 17, sec. 53-1-70.

The doing of any worldly work or labor, business of his ordinary calling, or the selling or offering for sale of any goods, wares or merchandise contrary to sec. 53-1-40 is declared to be a public nuisance and any State, county or municipal law-enforcement officer may apply to any court of competent jurisdiction for and may obtain an injunction restraining such operation, work, labor, sale, or offering for sale. *Provided,* that any employee in a retail store where there are more than three employees shall upon request of said employee be granted time off to attend service allowing one hour for preparing to go and traveling to church and one hour after service for returning therefrom. CODE OF LAWS OF SOUTH CAROLINA, Vol. 17, sec. 53-1-80.

The provisions of sections 53-1-40 to 53-1-80 shall not be applicable to or affect the carrying on of any business or the rendering of any service which was lawful on April 7, 1962. CODE OF LAWS OF SOUTH CAROLINA, Vol. 17, sec. 53-1-90.

Notwithstanding any other provision of law, the operation of machine shops and rubber molding and plastic injection molding facilities shall be exempt from the provisions of this chapter.

No person shall be required to work on a Sunday who is conscientiously opposed to Sunday work. If any person refuses to work on Sunday because of conscientious or physical objections, he shall not jeopardize his seniority rights by such refusal or be discriminated against in any manner. Sunday work shall be compensated at a rate no less than that required by the Fair Labor Standards Act. CODE OF LAWS OF SOUTH CAROLINA, Vol. 17, sec. 53-1-100, 1985 supplement.

Notwithstanding any other provision of law, the manufacture and finishing of textile products shall be exempt from the provisions of Chapter 1, Title 53, as amended. *Provided,* however, that no person shall be required to work on Sunday who is conscientiously opposed to Sunday work. If any person refuses to work on Sunday because of conscientious or physical objections, he shall not jeopardize his seniority rights by such refusal or be discriminated against in any manner. Sunday work shall be compensated at a rate no less than that required by the Fair Labor Standards Act. CODE OF LAWS OF SOUTH CAROLINA, Vol. 17, sec. 53-1-110.

It shall be unlawful for any person to employ, require or permit the employment of children to work or labor in any mercantile establishment or manufacturing establishment on Sunday. . . . CODE OF LAWS OF SOUTH CAROLINA, Vol. 17, sec. 53-1-120.

The provisions of sections 53-1-5 through 53-1-120 do not apply to manufacturing establishments or to research and development operations of any person, including the support services necessary for these operations, or to the employees of these operations when these establishments in the nature of their business involve manufacturing processes requiring continuous and uninterrupted operation or which for economical operation must engage in a continuous process nor do the provisions apply to maintenance, repair, and other service personnel of any manufacturing establishment. CODE OF LAWS OF SOUTH CAROLINA, Vol. 17, sec. 53-1-130.

(A) The General Assembly finds that certain areas of the State would benefit greatly from a complete exemption from Chapter 1, Title 53, of the 1976 Code. This benefit would be a result of an expanded tax base thereby reducing the burden placed on property owners through the property tax. Allowing the operation of establishments on Sunday in these areas would also reduce the property tax burden through additional accommodation tax revenue which allows these areas to provide necessary governmental service from these revenues.

(B) The provisions of Chapter 1, Title 53, of the 1976 Code do not apply to any county area, as defined in sec. 12-35-730 of the 1976 Code, which collects more than nine hundred thousand dollars in revenues from the tax imposed in sec. 12-35-710 of the 1976 Code.

(C) Any employee of any business which operates on Sunday under the provisions of this section has the option of refusing to work in accordance with provisions of sec. 53-1-100 of the 1976 Code. Any employer who dismisses or demotes an employee because he is a conscientious objector to Sunday work is subject to a civil penalty of triple the damages found by the court or jury plus court costs and the employee's attorney's fees. The court may order the employer to rehire or reinstate the employee in the same position he was in before the dismissal or demotion without forfeiture of compensation, rank or grade.

No proprietor of a retail establishment who is opposed to working on Sunday may be forced by his lessor or franchisor to open his establishment on Sunday nor may there be discrimination against persons whose regular day of worship is Saturday. CODE OF LAWS OF SOUTH CAROLINA, Vol. 17, sec. 53-1-150.

The provisions of this chapter do not apply after the hour of 1:30 p.m. on Sunday. Any employee of any business which operates on Sunday under the provisions of this section has the option of refusing to work in accordance with provisions of sec. 53-1-100. Any employer who dismisses or demotes an employee because he is a conscientious objector to Sunday work is subject to a civil penalty of triple the damages found by the court or the jury plus court costs and the employee's attorney's fees. The court may order the employer to rehire or reinstate the employee in the same position he was in before dismissal or demotion without forfeiture of compensation, rank, or grade.

No proprietor of a retail establishment who is opposed to working on Sunday may be forced by his lessor or franchisor to open his establishment on Sunday nor may there be discrimination against persons whose regular day of worship is Saturday. CODE OF LAWS OF SOUTH CAROLINA, Vol. 17, sec. 53-1-5, 1985 supplement.

It shall be unlawful to sell any alcoholic liquors on Sunday. . . . CODE OF LAWS OF SOUTH CAROLINA, Vol. 20, sec. 61-13-380. 1985 supplement.

South Dakota

Sunday laws that affect retail sales:

> The state fair commission as such shall have the power to hold state fairs at the city of Huron at such times as it may determine, provided, however, that if held on a Sunday, no concession operations will be open to the public, prior to twelve o'clock noon on said Sunday. . . . SOUTH DAKOTA CODE OF LAW, Vol. 2, sec. 1-21-10.
>
> Alcoholic beverages; license for sale—(12) On-sale dealers in light wines containing not more than fourteen percent by weight for Sunday - five hundred dollars. SOUTH DAKOTA CODE OF LAW, Vol. 11A, sec. 35-4-2(12), 1984 supplement.
>
> Additional regulations governing the sale of alcoholic beverages by on-sale and off-sale licensees are set forth in sections 35-4-2.1, 35-4-2.2, 35-4-81 and 35-4-81.1. SOUTH DAKOTA CODE OF LAW, Vol. 11A.

Tennessee

Sunday laws that affect retail sales:

> Repeal of blue laws by referendum—(a) Any municipality having an ordinance prohibiting retail sales or deliveries of merchandise on Sunday may repeal the same by a referendum election for the ratification or rejection of the ordinance. The mayor and council by resolution may request the county election commission to hold a special or regular referendum election for the ratification or rejection of the Sunday ordinance, provided the county election commission receives the necessary resolution requesting the election at least thirty (30) days before the date on which the election is scheduled to be held.
>
> (b) At any such election, the only question submitted to the voters shall be in the following form:
>
> "For ordinance prohibiting sale or delivery of retail merchandise on Sunday.
>
> Against ordinance prohibiting sale or delivery of retail merchandise on Sunday."
>
> (c) The election commission shall certify the result to the mayor and council of the municipality. If a majority of those voting in the referendum favor repeal, the ordinance thereby shall be repealed. If a majority of those voting in the referendum oppose repeal, the ordinance shall continue in effect until legally amended or repealed.

(d) A referendum on this subject shall not be held more than once every twelve (12) months from the date of election. Tn. CODE ANN., Vol. 2B, sec. 6-32-208, 1985 replacement.

Texas

Sunday laws that affect retail sales—none in general.

Exceptions:
(a) Liquor sales—none.
(b) Motor vehicle sales—none.

Utah

Sunday laws that affect retail sales—none in general.

Exceptions:
(a) Liquor sales—none.
(b) Motor vehicle sales—none.

Vermont

Sunday laws that affect retail sales—none in general.

Exceptions:
(a) Liquor sales—A person, partnership, association or corporation shall not sell any malt or vinous beverages or spiritous liquors on Sundays, except that such beverages and liquors may be sold on Sundays by holders of first and third class licenses, including hotels, inns, holders of a caterer's permit and duly licensed clubs, and by druggists holding permits on prescriptions only at the times and under the conditions the liquor control board determines to be reasonably necessary in the public interest. The liquor control board may issue regulations controlling the hours of Sunday sales under this section, except that spiritous liquors may not be sold by persons holding druggist permits between the hours of 1:00 a.m. and 12:00 noon on Sundays. Malt and vinous beverages or spiritous liquors may not be sold by first and third class licensees between the hours of 1:00 a.m. and 10:00 a.m. on Sundays. Licensees of the second class may sell malt and vinous beverages on Sundays between the hours of eight a.m. and ten o'clock in the evening in accordance with the law relating to those licenses. The provisions of chapter 74 of Title 13 shall not apply to licenses of the first, second or third class, or to

clubs, operating on Sunday in accordance with this section and the regulations of the liquor control board. A person, partnership, association or corporation who violates a provision of this section shall be imprisoned not more than twelve months nor less than three months or fined not more than $1,000.00 nor less than $100.00 or both, and for a subsequent conviction thereof within one year, shall be imprisoned not more than three years nor less than six months or fined not more than $2,000.00 nor less than $300.00, or both. Notwithstanding any other provisions of this section, the board may extend the hours of sale by first and third class licensees on New Year's Day when it falls on Sunday. VT. STAT. ANN., Vol. 7, sec. 62.

(b) Motor vehicle sales—none.

Virginia

Sunday laws that affect retail sales:

Working or transacting business on Sunday—(a) On the first day of the week, commonly known and designated as Sunday, no person shall engage in work, labor or business or employ others to engage in work, labor or business except in the following industries and businesses:

(1) Transportation by whatever means and supporting facilities;

(2) Public services and utilities, manufacturing, processing and plant operation of all types;

(3) Publishing, including the distribution and sale of products thereof;

(4) Servicing, fueling and repair of motor vehicles, boats and aircraft, and the selling of parts and supplies therefor;

(5) Operation of motion picture theaters and the production of radio and television programs;

(6) Medical services; and other services on an emergency basis;

(7) Sports, athletic events and the operation of historic, entertainment and recreational facilities, and the sale or rental of boats, and swimming, fishing and boating equipment;

(8) Agriculture, including the operation of nurseries and florist establishments;

(9) Preparation and sale of prescription and nonprescription drugs and the sale of medical and hygenic supplies and baby supplies;

(10) Wholesale food warehouses and ship chandleries;

(11) Restaurants and delicatessens;

(12) Janitorial, custodial and like services.

(13) Operation of hotels and motels and funeral homes and cemeteries;

(14) Mining and supporting facilities;

(15) Sale of food, ice and beverages;

(16) Sale of tobacco and related products;

(17) A drugstore, a majority of the sales receipts of which consist of prescription and nonprescription drugs, health and beauty aids;

(18) Sale of novelties, cameras, photographic supplies (including film and flash bulbs), antiques, pictures, paintings, art supplies; souvenirs, animals as pets, including tropical fish, and pet supplies;

(19) Sale or leasing of noncommercial real property, mobile homes, and the sale of residential modular, panelized or prefabricated houses, notwithstanding that such houses are not then erected or constructed on a site;

(20) Providing of any service, product or other thing by means of a mechanical device not requiring the labor of any person;

(21) Sale of any item, providing such sale takes place on publicly owned property or property designated by the governing body of any county, city or town, on a case-by-case basis, as the site of a festival, trade show, convention, festival market place or other type of public celebration or gathering. The governing body of a county, city or town may extend such a designation to nonpublicly owned property only when more than fifty percent of the area in which sales are made is used for otherwise exempt activities.

This section shall not be applicable to works of charity conducted solely for charitable purposes by any person or organization not organized or engaged in business for a profit.

(b) Any person violating the provisions of this section shall be guilty of a misdemeanor.

(c) Nothing contained herein shall be construed to permit any fine or penalty against any employee or agent who has been caused, directed or authorized by his employer to violate any provisions of this section, in which case the employer shall be subject to the sanctions prescribed by this section. VA. CODE, Vol. 4, sec. 18.2-341, 1985 supplement.

The provisions of sec. 18.2-341 shall have no force or effect within any county or city in the Commonwealth which has by ordinance expressed the sense of its citizens, as provided in sec. 15.1-29.5, that such laws are not necessary. VA. CODE, Vol. 4, sec. 18.2-342.

The penalties imposed by sec. 18.1-363.1 or sec. 18.2-341 shall not be incurred by any person who conscientiously believes that the seventh day of the week ought to be observed as a Sabbath, and actually refrains from all secular business and labor on that day, provided he does not compel an apprentice or servant, not of his belief, to do secular work or business on a Sunday. VA. CODE, Vol. 4, sec. 18.2-343.

When government stores closed—No sale or delivery of alcoholic beverages shall be made at any government store, nor shall any such store be kept open for the sale of alcoholic beverages:

(a) on Sunday;

(b) on legal holidays;

(c) during such other periods and on such other days as the Commission may direct. VA. CODE, Vol. 10, sec. 4-19.

Hours and days of sale of wine and beer are determined by referendum and/or ordinance as provided by sections 4-96.3, 4-97 and 4-114.1.

Washington

Sunday laws that affect retail sales—none in general.

Exceptions:

(a) Liquor sales—no sale or delivery of liquor shall be made on or from the premises of any state liquor store, nor shall any store be open for the sale of liquor, on Sunday, REV. CODE OF WASH., Vol. 6, sec. 66.16.080.

(b) Motor vehicle sales—none.

West Virginia

Sunday laws that affect retail sales:

Engaging in work, labor or business, etc., on Sunday—Prohibited. On the first day of the week, commonly known and designated as Sunday, it shall be unlawful for any person to engage in work, labor or business, or to employ any person to engage in work, labor or business, except in household or other work of necessity or charity. Except as hereinafter provided the exemption for works of necessity or charity contained in the preceding sentence shall not be deemed to include selling at retail or wholesale or by auction, or offering or attempting to sell on Sunday any of the following: Jewelry, precious and semiprecious stones; silverware, watches, clocks; luggage; musical instruments; recordings; toys; clothing and wearing apparel; clothing accessories; footwear; textile yard goods; housewares; china; kitchenware; home, business, office or outdoor furniture, furnishings and appliances; sporting goods (excluding sales or rental of bathing, boating and fishing paraphernalia and equipment, and sales or rental on the premises where sports, athletic games and events or recreational facilities are located or conducted of equipment essential to the normal use or operation of such premises for the purposes specified); pets, pet equipment or supplies; photographic supplies (excluding cameras, film and flash bulbs); hardware (excluding light bulbs, batteries and electrical fuses); tools; paints, building and lumber supplies and materials; motor vehicles; and farm implements.

Also, said exemption shall not be deemed to include the redemption of trading stamps. No inference shall arise from the foregoing enumeration of classes of personal property that sales or offers or attempts to sell other classes of personal property not mentioned are included within the above exemptions for works of necessity or charity. W. VA. CODE ANN., Vol. 17, sec. 61-10-25 [1964].

Specific activities exempted from sec. 61-10-25 are enumerated in sec. 61-10-26.

Penalties: Any person violating the provisions of section twenty-five of this article shall, for the first offense, be guilty of a misdemeanor and, upon conviction thereof, shall be fined not less than twenty-five nor more than one hundred dollars. Any person violating the provisions of section twenty-five of this article shall, for the second offense occurring within one year of the first offense, be guilty of a misdemeanor and, upon conviction thereof, shall be fined not less than two hundred and fifty dollars nor more than five hundred dollars and, in the discretion of the court, may be confined in jail for a period not exceeding thirty days. Any person violating the provisions of section twenty-five of this article shall, for the third or any subsequent offense occurring within two years of the previous offense, be guilty of a misdemeanor and, upon conviction thereof, shall be fined not less than five hundred nor more than one thousand dollars and, in the discretion of the court, may be confined in jail for a period not exceeding six months.

Each Sunday a person is engaged in work, labor or business or employs others to be so engaged, in violation of section twenty-five of this article, shall constitute a separate offense.

The penalties imposed by this section shall not be incurred by any person who conscientiously believes that Saturday ought to be observed as a Sabbath, and who actually refrains from all secular business and labor on that day, provided he does not compel an apprentice or servant or employee, not of his belief, to do secular work or business on a Sunday. W. VA. CODE ANN., Vol. 17, sec. 61-10-27.

The provisions of section 61-10-25 are continued in effect in each county by local county option. See sec. 61-10-28 for specific procedures with respect to the local option elections.

Other unlawful acts: (b) For a distributor, his agents, servants or employees to transport or deliver wine to any retail licensee or to any licensee under article seven of this chapter on Sunday. . . . W. VA. CODE ANN., Vol. 17, sec. 60-8-31.

Intoxicating liquors; When retail sales prohibited: It shall be unlawful for a retailer, his servants, agents or employees to sell or deliver wine on any general or primary election day, or on any special election day in the locality where such special election is held, or prior to one o'clock p.m., or after midnight on Sundays, or between the hours of midnight and nine o'clock a.m. on weekdays and Saturdays. W. VA. CODE ANN., Vol. 17, sec. 60-8-34, 1983.

The commission [commissioner] shall fix the days on which state stores shall be open and the hours of opening and closing, and the hours during which agencies may sell alcoholic liquors.

Stores shall not be open nor shall agencies sell alcoholic liquors on:

1. Sundays.
2. any general election day. W. VA. CODE ANN., Vol. 17, sec. 60-3-12, 1935.

Wisconsin

Sunday laws that affect retail sales—none in general.

Exceptions:
  (a) Liquor sales—none.
  (b) Motor vehicle sales—none.

Wyoming

Sunday laws that affect retail sales—none in general.

Exceptions:
  (a) Liquor sales—none.
  (b) Motor vehicle sales—none.

Enforcement

With respect to Sunday-closing laws there may be, and frequently is, a significant difference between what the law says and what the law does. Not only do the statutes vary from one state to the next, the pattern of enforcement differs as well. Thus, two states may have highly similar laws relating to retail trade on Sunday but substantially different patterns of enforcement. The net impact on human behavior ought predictably to differ between the states as a result. In addition, it is not unusual for a state to maintain Sunday-closing statutes, with the lightest of penalties for violation of the law. Not surprisingly, the law does not necessarily serve as a reliable predictor of individual behavior, since people do not feel bound to adhere to it carefully.

Formally, there are two aspects to the enforcement of blue laws; support of legislative statute by the state court system and apprehension and prosecution of violators by the state or local police, or both. Recent experience in Louisiana demonstrates that a state's court system does not unambiguously uphold that state's Sunday-closing statutes. Moreover, the courts have been used to enjoin law enforcement authorities from enforcing the law.

The extent to which Sunday-closing laws are enforced is largely dependent upon local attitude. Most police departments around the country do not send out officers with specific intent of policing blue laws. They do not check to make sure that certain department stores are closed and that drug and grocery stores are not selling prohibited items. Says Jefferson Parish (Louisiana) Sheriff Harry Lee, "I just respond to complaints. I'm not going to send my guys out and say check every Schwegmann (grocery) store and K&B (drug) store. It's something I can't get excited about."

Identification of lawbreakers generally results from complaint from a private citizen, not infrequently from a competitor of the outlet in question. The *Baltimore Sun* ran a story on February 3, 1986 regarding a decision by the state's attorney office to disallow Sunday rental of video cassettes; identification of violators was clearly accomplished via competitors who did not wish to open on Sunday.

It is clear that enforcement of Sunday-closing laws is not a top priority item for the authorities. Adherence to the law is perhaps more a function of social custom than anticipated penalty. Certainly enforcement would be terribly difficult to ensure under the circumstance of widespread violation. As states and localities with restrictions on commercial activity on Sunday feel the increasing economic pinch from businesses located in nearby, but unrestricted, localities, implicit or explicit violation of the law, or both, will become an increasing occurrence. Law enforcement officials, sympathetic to the plight of local businessmen, may simply choose to not enforce the law. Paradoxically, strict enforcement of the law may serve to catapult the forces favoring repeal of blue laws.

Notes

1. Much of the information in this section can be found in a research monograph on blue laws published by the Legislative Research Division of the State of Oregon in 1980 and prepared by Ken Elverum, legislative analyst.

2. Although local governments have no inherent authority to make laws or adopt regulations with respect to Sunday behavior, the state may delegate such powers to localities. The premise for this delegation of authority is that the appropriate governing body for defining Sunday activity is a local authority that is "in touch" with the popular sentiment within its jurisdiction.

3. KENTUCKY REV. STAT., sec. 436.160.

4. All states, for example, permit the sale of gasoline on Sundays to facilitate recreational or religious activity, or both. It is illegal to sell cameras and film projectors on Sunday in Arkansas, whereas sales of film, flash bulbs, and batteries are permitted (ARK. STAT., sec. 41-3813).

4

The Public Policy Debate

There are two fundamentally different approaches to explaining why governments regulate markets. Each reflects a very different view of the role of government in society. The first, which we shall call the "public interest view," holds that governments function as benevolent guardians of the public interest by protecting community members from undesirable effects of the otherwise unfettered working of markets. In regulating markets, governments are considered to have objectives whose aim is the improvement of society. For example, regulation of workplace safety is believed necessary to achieve a socially desired level of job safety that will not be provided by the free interplay between employers and employees in labor markets.

According to this view of government, restriction of retail trade on Sunday would be imposed by a state in order to make that political jurisdiction a "better" place to live. While there can be no doubt that the restrictions on Sunday shopping provide benefits for certain individuals, the question of whether they promote the general public interest depends on the magnitude of such benefits relative to the detrimental effects imposed on others, especially consumers.

Does concern for the public interest really underlie the reluctance of state governments to relax restrictions on Sunday trading? The *prima facie* evidence suggests not. In particular, inconsistencies in the application of the law argue against such an interpretation. For example, governments apparently perceive little need to protect the families of employees and self-employed proprietors who provide the "essentials" of weekend living (e.g., gasoline, airline travel, movies, newspapers, etc.). Why, one might ask, is family unity threatened by sales of hammers on Sunday but not by sales of gardening tools? Moreover, why does the citizenry of certain states need regulation of Sunday trading whereas the citizenry of other states does not? Why, for that matter, is it more socially desirable for an item to be sold in a small shop as opposed to a large department store on Sunday?

Even if we grant the argument that governments should intervene in markets for purposes they believe will promote the public interest, it is by no means clear that that is what they will do in fact. Governments are, as the Virginia school of political economy has argued so forcefully over the past twenty years, comprised of private utility-maximizing individuals whose interests frequently conflict with the public interest.

The second approach to explaining why governments are in the business of regulating markets is termed the "private interest theory of politics." Investigators in this tradition question the validity of the assumption that "government" is the benevolent guardian of the public interest. Instead, there is a recognition that political decisions are motivated by the interaction of the self interest of politicians and members of the community.

Those individuals who constitute the governmental authority within the boundaries of a specific political jurisdiction have the power to confer benefits on selected individuals or groups, by using regulatory devices such as protective tariffs, occupational licensing, production subsidies, minimum wages. Members of the community recognize that the power of politicians to implement regulations that influence market outcomes can be exploited to create profit opportunities. The desire for economic gain by private citizens coupled with the desire of politicians for electoral success and their ability to define, or redefine, market structures generates the conditions for mutually advantageous trade between politicians and those who seek to gain from economic regulation. Members of the community supply campaign contributions and votes to politicians in exchange for the various benefits politicians can bestow. Individuals or groups, or both, will rationally invest time and money in pursuit of benefits provided by the political authority. This type of behavior is now recognized widely in America as special-interest group lobbying for political favors.

The special interest approach casts doubt on claims that restriction of Sunday trade serves the public interest. It leads instead to a suspicion that politically well-organized vested-interest groups in the community derive benefits at the expense of the less well-organized but much larger group of consumers. Legal change in America is effectuated either through the judicial system or the legislative system. Courts have been reluctant to consider the economic motivations and special interests that may have an intimate association with blue laws. The position of the courts is clearly stated by the case of *New York v. Abrahams* 386 N.Y.S. 2d. 661, 667 n.4 (1976): "It is beyond the province of the judiciary to hypothesize about the motives of legislators and whether or not portions of a statute are attributable to the efforts of so-called special interests." Since the public policy debate as regards competing special-interest groups (including the large, diffuse group of consumers) must be fought out in the state legislatures, it is of critical importance that we attempt to assess whether the benefits conferred on particular groups contribute to the overall welfare of the community and to balance any such benefits against the costs such restrictions may impose on others.

Consumers

As has been noted previously in this volume, there is evidence of strong popular support for removal of all restrictions on Sunday shopping. Recent surveys conducted in America and abroad indicate that popular sentiment favors a complete repeal of such restrictions by a consistent, roughly two-to-one, margin. The data suggest that Sunday shopping would be very popular, if permitted.

Although the potential benefits for consumers from more opportunities to shop cannot be expressed in monetary terms, it does not follow that those benefits are trivial. Admittedly, the benefits of a wider choice of shopping days (or hours) may be small for any particular individual. However, because the number of consumers who would benefit is enormous, total benefits to the community as a whole from repeal of blue laws would also be very large.

The changing pattern of family involvement in the workplace suggests that the benefits to consumers from permitting Sunday shopping may have risen substantially since the 1960s. Since that time the proportion of all families with both parents working as well as the percentage of single parent (working, almost by definition) households has risen dramatically. With less opportunity to shop during the week these individuals shift their buying to weekends; as more and more people focus their shopping attention on the weekend period so must the opportunity to shop on Sunday become more valuable.

This is not to say that Sunday shopping is supported by all consumers. Although the opportunity to shop constitutes a benefit to consumers, the increased traffic and congestion that would result from legalized Sunday trading would constitute a real cost to residents of communities located near major shopping areas. Moreover, it has been argued that the opportunity to shop on Sunday is detrimental to the well-being of the family unit because it would encourage individuals to spend time outside of the home on Sunday. Proponents of Sunday shopping respond that shopping can be (and often is) a family-oriented activity, and that for families in which one or both parents work outside of the home during the week, Sunday shopping would actually encourage family togetherness.

Finally, there are individuals who believe that Sunday is, and should be, a day of rest. Although Sunday trading does not prohibit these persons from taking Sunday as a day of rest *for themselves,* some argue that society as a whole benefits from mandating that all individuals observe a day of rest on

Sunday. The exact benefits conferred are, of course, somewhat obscure, but they arise consistently in discussions of the blue laws issue. Again, we note that even though these benefits nominally weigh heavily in the decision to enact or retain Blue laws, or both, the fact that so many exemptions and special exceptions exist suggests that state legislatures, in fact, are willing to seriously compromise the net value of these social benefits, perhaps because they are of doubtful significance.

Employers

Pressures to relax or eliminate restrictions on Sunday trading have come most vociferously from certain elements of the business community. We can presume that this is so because these proprietors expect to gain profits from Sunday sales. In order for such profits to be made, consumers must patronize their shops on Sundays. This suggests that efforts by businessmen to persuade the political authority to ease restrictions against retail sales on Sunday are founded upon a belief that there is a strong underlying consumer demand for the additional shopping time.

Paradoxically, the protests of those (primarily small) retailers opposed to Sunday trading imply a similar belief that Sunday shopping would prove to be popular with consumers. If retailers believed that consumers did not want additional time to shop they would not be concerned about easing of restrictions, because they would have no reason to fear loss of sales and profits to stores that did decide to open for business on Sundays.

The bottom line is that if consumers did not want an additional day of the week to be used for shopping it would not be profitable for stores to open on that day, and all arguments on either side of the blue laws issue would be absolutely irrelevant. Stores would not open with or without restrictions. All parties concerned with blue laws argue unambiguously that they expect a significant shift by consumers into shopping during currently prohibited days. The freedom-of-shopping choice for consumers is the argument that is not championed frequently or loudly, because it concerns benefits expected by the not-politically well-organized silent majority. It is, however, the argument most likely to sway an individual concerned about the maximization of social welfare.

Owners of relatively small shops oppose repeal of Sunday-closing statutes on two grounds. First, they fear the competition offered by larger, more efficient stores. For example, if large department stores were permitted to open on Sundays they would attract customers away from the small shops, because of their lower prices. The owners of larger establishments argue that this savings will benefit millions of consumers, even though it may harm a few small retailers. The small retailers respond by noting that the quality of the seller/buyer interaction is much better in small shops than in large establishments, and that consumers really are losers in the broader sense. The final response to that line of reasoning is that consumers can be trusted to demand shopping conditions to their best advantage; if they prefer low prices to service, then society is best served by stores that respond to those demands.

Small proprietors additionally dislike Sunday trading for labor supply reasons. Much or all of the labor supply that keeps a small shop open is provided by the owner-manager and his or her family. They may not be able to afford to hire outside help to provide themselves with a day's rest each week, whereas the large department stores are run by managers who can be induced to work on Sunday by high wages. Blue laws provide small proprietors a guaranteed day of rest from their labors, without fear of losing much of their business to competitors. Repeal of blue laws would force many small proprietors to work seven days per week without rest. One might argue that such a work schedule comes with the territory of being a self-employed proprietor. On the other hand, these individuals decided to start their businesses under the protection of Sunday-closing legislation. To remove that protection after the fact is, in some sense, unfair. Repeal of blue laws would certainly be costly to those small businessmen who do not want to open on Sundays, possibly in terms of profits, most certainly in terms of time.

The retailers who do not wish to open on Sundays support their position by claiming the following. They cannot afford the additional overhead that Sunday openings would cause, especially in terms of payroll. Sunday is the traditional day of rest and that their employees don't want to work on that day. Sunday sales do not add to profitability.

There is only so much spendable income, it is argued, so Sunday sales would not mean an added day of revenue but rather six days of sales spread over seven days. Clarence G. Adamy, president of the National Association of Food Chains, disagreed with this assessment. He suggested stores that do operate on Sunday find that it becomes the second or third largest shopping day of the week.[3]

Notwithstanding the large numbers of small businessmen who are opposed to any easing of restrictions on Sunday trading by larger retailers (or by any retailers), it should be pointed out that there are, in fact, small proprietors who would like to open on Sundays. The example that surfaces occasionally in newspaper articles concerns the owners of small shops located in large shopping malls. Normally speaking, these malls are "anchored" by two or three of the largest, most recognizable department stores in the area. These chain stores attract a considerable population of shoppers to the mall, these shoppers then browse through the smaller shops for ancillary needs or wants. The forced closure of the large chain stores on Sunday has the side effect of forcing the smaller shops located in the mall to close as well, because the normal complement of patrons is discouraged from coming to the mall in the first place. Smaller shops that are legally permitted to open suffer lost sales and lost profits due to Sunday closing laws that target large department stores.

Employees

Understandably, there is a strong split in opinion among workers with respect to the desirability of blue laws. As mentioned previously, the small proprietor who must himself provide the labor to operate his shop is generally opposed to any easing of restrictions on Sunday trading. Similarly, many employees are opposed to any repeal of blue laws because they fear that their employers would force them to work on Sundays, which they are loathe to do. A number of points can be, and should be, made at this juncture.

There is no question that if workers can be forced to work undesirable hours, then society would suffer a loss, in terms of employees' utility, from repeal of blue laws. The typical employee will tell you that his or her employer can force him or her to engage in certain types of behavior that the employee would prefer not to engage in. The apparently widespread and recurring pattern of sexual harassment of female employees by male employers or bosses is the most obvious example of this. Employees agree to compromise their own concept of fair terms and conditions of employment in favor of their bosses' for fear of losing their jobs.

The most visible employers, large department stores, respond to this charge by arguing that they will not, indeed cannot, force any employee to work on Sundays and that additional hiring needs will be met via the hiring of part-time personnel, not by asking current employees to work longer hours or extra days. Indeed, the creation of new jobs has long been a standard argument by large businesses in favor of blue laws repeal.

Despite such assurances, employees remain wary of employer response to free trade on Sunday. This wariness is partially reflected in the fact that virtually every state that seeks to repeal its Sunday-trading restrictions includes a passage in the repeal bill that guarantees job security and tenure to employees who do not wish to work on Sundays. Nonetheless, the possibility that employers could subtly force employees to work on Sundays remains, since firms could simply refuse to hire new workers unless they expressed a willingness to accept Sunday work assignments. Of course, the employer had better not indicate that reason as being the critical factor in *not* hiring a particular individual. Such a hiring policy would ultimately put pressure on all workers to accept Sunday employment, at the risk of having no job otherwise.

The situation with smaller firms is somewhat different. The small businessman who employs only one or two additional workers may find it very difficult to hire any additional staff, even on a part-time basis. If he or she is to open on Sunday in order to remain competitive with other outlets, the additional labor required must be supplied personally or by asking the current employees to work some, or all, of that day. Again, competitive pressures would exert subtle pressure on small-businessowners as well as large ones to hire workers who were willing to accept hours on Sundays.

The extension to this argument is that however additional hiring needs are met, either by asking current employees to work an extra day of the week or by hiring new personnel, the resulting increase in employment on Sundays will have a detrimental impact on the family. If both parents are required to work on Sunday, child care would have to be provided by day-care centers or other non-family babysitting arrangements. Thus, the sheer volume of time that the family has available together would be restricted. Even if only one parent was required to work there would be an adverse effect on the amount of time both parents together could spend with their children. This, it is argued, can only have a detrimental effect on the family unit.

The magnitude of any losses implied by the foregoing arguments from any easing of restrictions on Sunday selling are critically dependent upon the question of whether or not an employer is able to force an employee to work when he or she does not wish to. This issue is analyzed in some detail in the following chapter. In addition, any losses in quality of family life due to parental absence must be balanced off against potential gains in the quality of family life that are forthcoming due to the potential gains in family income.

This brings us to the issue of fairness; it is an issue that intertwines throughout virtually all of the arguments on both sides of the blue laws issue. Small stores claim that competing with large stores on Sundays gives the large stores an unfair advantage. Large stores claim that it is unfair to permit small stores to open on Sundays if large stores must remain closed. Employees feel that it is unfair that they should be made to work on Sundays in addition to the other days of the week that they are required to work. We are not in a position to validate claims of fairness. However, it is even less clear that politicians are able to render decisions on issues of fairness in an unbiased manner. Again, one can justifiably raise the issue of why certain items or shops are permitted to open on Sundays while others are not, given the aforementioned perils to workers and their families. Apparently, fairness is not applied equally by state legislatures in the regulation of Sunday trading. This raises the distinct possibility that fairness is a criterion that is given lip service but otherwise ignored by legislators.

The Church

There is little disagreement over the original intent behind Sunday closing laws in America. Such laws were designed to force individuals to devote their time on Sundays to worship rather than to commerce.[1] Over the ensuing three hundred or so years, blue laws have proven to be remarkably enduring, although the basis for regulation has long since ceased to be religious. This is not to say that religious organizations are silent on the issue; religious leaders, private citizens, and politicians continue to support Sunday-closing laws on the grounds that the Sabbath day is sacred, deserving of the encouragement of the state. Of course, the church as an organization has a legitimate, secular interest in blue laws—they restrict competing ways of spending one's Sunday time. New Orleans attorney Harvey Koch, who has defended clients charged with violations of Louisiana's blue laws, is one critic who believe's in this cartel theory of blue laws. He argues that the basic purpose of the Louisiana statute—although any direct expression of this purpose was carefully avoided—was to permit people to attend Sunday church service without being subject to the business competition of those who were non-Christians or not practicing Christians.[2]

Opponents have attacked blue laws on the grounds that they violate the constitutional separation of church and state. In addition, they point out that the church is not floundering in states without protective Sunday-closing legislation, which implies that the church has nothing major to fear from repeal.

We note, finally, that strong, consistent opposition to blue laws has come from members of religious organizations that consider Saturday or some other day of the week as the Sabbath. The language of the law in many states has evolved to reflect this opposition and virtually all states with enforced blue laws on the books exempt individuals who actively keep a day other than Sunday as the Sabbath.

Other Arguments and Considerations

Proponents of blue laws have always argued that the state has a legitimate interest in promoting the well-being of persons living within its boundaries. This justification was firmly upheld by the United States Supreme Court in *McGowan vs. Maryland* [1960] and continues to form the basis for Sunday closing laws in the 1980s. Opponents of blue laws respond that the proponents are hypocrites because the laws only apply to about one-sixth of the work force and are filled with dozens, perhaps hundreds, of exceptions and exemptions. For example, in Louisiana drug and grocery stores can open on Sundays and sell non-drug and non-food items while hardware stores with the same or similar merchandise cannot. The arbitrariness with which the law has been applied or enforced, or both, seems to indicate that although the state legislatures claim to have the well-being of society in mind in keeping blue laws on the books, the pattern of the law makes a lie out of that consideration.

The obvious response to this charge is that the well-being of society is best served by permitting only certain types of business operations to open on Sundays. This does not, of course, placate would-be repealers, who insist on the arbitrariness of the law. There are numerous examples of items that can be purchased from one type of retailer on Sunday, but not from a different seller. Similarly, one can purchase certain items from a given shop, but not other items, and it is difficult to argue that the public welfare is best served by the distinction being made. Finally, the fact that only a minority of states have Sunday-closing statutes at the present time while the majority do not suggests that public welfare is not harmed in the slightest by repeal. In fact, proponents of repeal argue more forcefully than that: not only will repeal not be socially deleterious, it will be socially beneficial.

An additional argument in favor of Sunday-closing laws surfaced during the so-called "energy crunch" of the late 1970s and early 1980s. It has been suggested that closing down business operations on Sundays helps to conserve America's energy resources, both by saving on energy used by firms that open for business and by saving on the fuel used by shoppers. Of course, with the price of oil taking a nosedive in the mid-1980s, the argument has become outdated. Nonetheless, earlier opponents of blue laws took issue with the energy-savings claim, arguing that many firms use energy even when they are not officially open for business and that opening the shops would not lead to a significant reduction in energy supplies. Moreover, if the Sunday-shopping option were not available, individuals would find some other means of occupying their time, probably involving some expenditure of energy (e.g., driving their automobile, turning up the thermostat at home and watching television, etc.). In fact, Sunday shopping may have become of increased importance during the energy crisis, according to the International Council of Shopping Centers, because Sunday provided a time when one shopping trip could fulfill the needs of all members of the family and saved energy by reducing the number of trips previously taken during the week.[4]

The Public Policy Debate

A flavor of the public-policy debate and the arguments employed by individuals both pro and con can be gleaned from a variety of sources. Herewith, a sampling of editorial comment from interested parties on both sides of the issue. The sentiments expressed convey the nature and power of the arguments far more eloquently than can any recap.

From the *Baltimore Sun,* January 14, 1986:

> Editor:
> In this legislative session, blue laws will again be an issue. But if our legislators run true to form, they will again refuse to repeal the blue laws for Baltimore City and the surrounding counties.

If the blue laws are not repealed, then let us make them fairer.

Since not all residents of the region are Christians, and since non-Christians are in no way protected from being required to work on their days of rest, and since non-Christians are not given the same sort of encouragement to attend to their religious duties as is given to Christians, let us extend the blue laws to include both the Muslim and the Jewish days of rest.

The current blue laws are riddled with exceptions. Small stores may open; big ones may not. Baseball players may work; salespeople in package goods stores may not. While the blue laws apply, no stores or businesses other than emergency ones such as hospitals should be open. This means no restaurants, no baseball stadiums, no movie theaters, and no collection plates should be permitted to operate on Friday, Saturday, or Sunday.

In short, if our legislators are not willing to get rid of the blue laws, then they should be willing to end the hypocrisy of the current blue laws. And Delegate Wendell Phillips, the chairperson of the Baltimore City delegation, who announced last year that blue-law repeal was dead and who is a Christian minister, ought to be willing to amend laws that currently grant special favors to his religion and that currently permit him to pass around a church collection plate while others are not allowed to engage in commerce.

From the *Baltimore Sun,* December 27, 1985:

Editor:

I have heard enough about shopping on Sunday. As a retail employee, I think it is time for greedy retailers and selfish consumers to stop thinking of themselves and start thinking of the people who bend over backwards six days a week to keep them happy.

Sunday shopping at Christmastime is fine with most employees but the idea of shopping on Sunday year-round is an obscene injustice to us counter-clerks.

Full-time employees already only get a one-day weekend, that day being Sunday. To eliminate that would be an outrage.

If the blue laws are repealed, the next step would be to eliminate pay benefits for working on Sundays, and then holidays.

Why not let the stores stay open twenty-four hours, seven days, so that everyone can pick up a Gucci bag on the way home from a bar at 2:00 a.m.?

Retail employees are already expected to give up Memorial Day, July 4, Labor Day and New Year's Day. Next, maybe we'll be forced to work on Thanksgiving Day and Christmas.

Roger Simon (see chapter 1) suggests that staying open that extra day will cause retail stores to hire poor unfortunate folks in the unemployment lines. How can anyone be so blind? Retailers, being good capitalists, will just push their part-timers one more day.

Most part-timers are college students who already have five days of classes and maybe three days during the week to work plus Saturdays. To expect them to push themselves seven days a week is absurd. Already schoolwork suffers, and since fall semester exams fall around Christmas, they work until 11:00 p.m. or midnight, and next day take a final exam at 8:00 a.m.

Next time you are sitting in your chair watching football, just think about how much you would rather be at work. Or maybe you should apply to a department store to see how fun it is to work there.

From a position paper put out by the group, Marylanders for Blue Law Repeal, Fall 1985:

In Montgomery and Prince Georges Counties (suburban Washington), the blue laws governing Sunday shopping have been abandoned altogether. Yet for Baltimore City, Baltimore County, Anne Arundel County and Howard County the blue law restrictions are perhaps even more curious than the original blue laws enacted in the 1600s.

The traditional concept of setting Sunday aside as a day of rest is no longer an issue under the laws. In the Baltimore–Annapolis metropolitan area, any business may open on Sunday, but only so long as an arbitrarily decided six or fewer employees work on each shift.

Supermarkets and drug stores generally open on Sunday. The law exempts them from restrictions. Drugstores and supermarkets sell hundreds of items ranging from socks to hardware that might be more competitively purchased in larger non-food, non-drug stores that must remain closed on Sunday.

Movie theaters, ballparks, racetracks, restaurants, boating and other recreational facilities, and many tourist attractions all fall outside the purview of the blue laws. Among the many other exceptions are bakeries, delicatessens, and gasoline stations.

Thousands of people work on Sunday in commercial facilities that are permitted to do business. Thousands more work in factories, warehouses, health-care facilities and other seven-day-a-week operations.

Sunday shopping is not the issue at all. Sunday shopping is a fact of life in Baltimore City, Baltimore County, and Anne Arundel County. What's left in the law is a narrow restriction that effectively cripples large stores such as department stores, and, as a side effect, shopping malls.

In the end, what is really restricted is the freedom of shoppers to shop in a large retail store or, in most cases, a shopping mall, on Sunday.

A department store, for example, simply cannot operate under the six employees rule. Thus, since customer traffic in a shopping mall is largely dependent on the large anchor stores, dozens of small shops that could open under the rule of six generally remain closed as well. Some larger stores do try to open under the rule of six. While the opening is a service to their customers, the store must sacrifice customer convenience, speedy checkouts, and personal assistance in order to do so.

Under yet another exception, the legislature has "okayed" Sunday opening for all merchants during the Thanksgiving to Christmas season—four Sundays, or five in some years—allowing commercial concerns to carry more weight during the holiday season than during other times of the year.

If Sunday shopping is not the issue, what is? A number of issues arise whenever blue laws are debated. These are religion, protectionism, family values, convenience, economic progress and fairness.

Religion? Certainly, no one questions the motivation of those who, as a matter of religious principle, oppose all commerce on Sunday. However, there are those who observe a period other than Sunday as their Sabbath and who might prefer to do all their shopping on Sunday rather than Saturday. Under current Maryland law, employees may choose a Sabbath on which they may not be required to work. Some of those who oppose Sunday shopping at large retail stores or shopping centers on religious grounds have doubtless opposed other exceptions to the original blue laws, and likely do not, themselves, engage in any unnecessary commerce on Sunday. While no one would quarrel with motives of those who oppose blue law reform on religious grounds, it should be noted that imposing that view on those who do not share the same beliefs is not necessarily in the best interests of the community as a whole.

Protectionism? A limited number of small-business owners actively oppose repeal of the blue laws. For this special-interest group the motivation appears to be less grounded in moral principle than in economics. These opponents of blue-law reform either are open on Sunday and want to avoid the same competition they meet the other six days of the week, or are themselves closed on Sunday and do not want to lose potential customers to other retailers. As these small business owners press for retention of the blue laws, they penalize other small businesses, particularly those located in malls. The protectionists, while few in number, have been very vocal with state legislators and have consistently shown support for legislators who favor the protectionist umbrella the blue laws now provide. Sunday shopping is not the issue. Restriction of competition is, in fact, the issue.

Family values? Some opponents of blue-law reform say families need Sunday as a day to be together and propose that having department stores and shopping malls open on Sunday would do harm to that togetherness. Family togetherness is conceded to be a valuable goal, but those who espouse this argument ignore the fact that no family member would be compelled to dissolve that togetherness by shopping at the local mall on any given Sunday. In fact, it can be argued that local shopping malls, given their variety of facilities and entertainment, can and do serve as the focal point for a family outing. Some argue that individuals will have to work on Sundays when they would prefer to be with their families. In fact, given the dramatic changes in our society, many people already work on Sundays now, and many others would welcome the opportunity to earn extra income or make more flexible use of their time.

Convenience? Sunday is the only day when many people can do their shopping or the day when they prefer to shop. Requiring department stores and shopping malls to close on Sunday severely restricts freedom of choice for these shoppers. In many cases, department stores and mall shops in nearby counties—such as Montgomery and Prince Georges—benefit economically from dollars spent in their counties. For many shoppers, Delaware and Pennsylvania malls are equally accessible and dollars—and sales tax revenues that might be used for the benefit of Marylanders—flow out of state.

Economic progress? Major retailers and shopping malls offer expanded employment opportunities for current employees and create part-time employment opportunities for young people who, because of school schedules, cannot work during weekdays or evenings. Additionally, the Baltimore area will be a more attractive area in which to locate shopping malls or departments stores if out-of-date restrictions no longer limit commerce.

Fairness? The measure of any law must be in terms of fairness and equity. The blue laws governing commerce in the Baltimore and Anne Arundel areas fail miserably by that measure. What began as a very restrictive, all-encompassing law has become a law almost solely targeted at large retailers.

The following two essays, published in *Liberty,* a magazine of religious freedom, in 1975, cut to the heart of the religious position in favor of blue laws, and the arguments advanced by opponents of such, respectively.

From A. Graham Maxwell, director, division of religion, Loma Linda University, "The Day of Freedom" is a chapter from his book *I Want to be Free:*

Of all the laws that God has given, perhaps none has been so misunderstood as His commandment to observe the Sabbath.

When the sun goes down next Friday evening, I expect to join 2.5 million other Seventh-day Adventists the world around in acknowledging the continuing authority and meaning of that ancient law, "Remember the Sabbath day, to keep it holy" (Exodus 20:8). Moreover, I expect to do this in the highest sense of freedom.

Admittedly, this puzzles Christians who understand that the truth has set them free from the necessity of Sabbath observance, and particularly the observance of Sabbath on the seventh day. They wonder whether Sabbath-keeping might suggest a lingering trace of legalism, a failure to see the truth that would enable us Seventy-day Adventists to share their freedom.

In the first place, let it be reaffirmed that the truth about God and His gracious ways will indeed set a man free from all that is meaningless, arbitrary, and superstitious.

This truth includes the good news that in our relationship with God we are not under law but under grace (see Romans 6:14). How thankful we should be. For were we under law, we would be reaping the legal consequences of having violated the law. And "the wages of sin is death" (Romans 6:23). But our relationship with God is not on a legal basis.

The Bible makes it clear, too, that what God desires most is our faith, and that the sinner can find righteousness by faith and not by the works of law. For Christ is the end of law as a means of salvation, the termination of legalism as a way of being saved. "Christ means the end of the struggle for righteousness-by-the-Law for everyone who believes in Him" (Romans 10:4, Phillips).

It is clear, too, that real obediance to the law is love (see Romans 13:8). And we should gladly submit to Jesus' *new* commandment that we love one another as He has loved us (see John 15:12).

But if what God is looking for is faith and love, and if, by telling us the truth about our gracious God, Christ is seeking to free us from the empty requirements of legalism, what justification could there be for continuing to recognize so apparently arbitrary a regulation as keeping holy one day in seven? Yet Jesus said that the Sabbath was made *for* us (see Mark 2:27). It was not to be a mere test of obedience but rather to be a help.

I believe that the great purpose of the Sabbath is to remind us of the truth that is the basis of our faith, the very truth that sets us free.

In the first place, the Bible tells us in Exodus 20 and 31 that the Sabbath is designed to serve as a reminder that God created us, that we are His creatures. But to be more specific, according to Colossians 1:13–16, the One who created us was none other than Christ Himself.

The seventh-day Sabbath reminds us that the One who came to save us is also the One who made us in the beginning. The gentle Jesus who died on Calvary is also the supreme, all-powerful Creator of the universe. God did not send some subordinate person to die for us. The Creator came Himself, One who is equal with God, for He is God. By keeping holy the seventh-day Sabbath we acknowledge our faith in Jesus as not only our Saviour but also our Creator and our God.

What kind of person, then, is our God? Could He be as gracious and respectful of our freedom as is the Son? The reply comes every Sabbath: God is just like Christ, for Christ is God.

Some Christians prefer to observe the first day of the week as a memorial of Christ's resurrection. Surely it is a good thought on a Sunday morning to reflect. This is the day on which Christ rose from the grave. And on Friday would it not be well to reflect. This is the day on which Christ was crucified? And on Thursday evening. This is the time when Christ met with His disciples in the upper room?

But the only weekly Sabbath of which the Bible speaks is the one set apart to remind us that the Person who gave His life for us, the One who said, "If you have seen Me, you have seen the Father," is Himself the One who made us, for He too is God.

A second way in which the seventh-day Sabbath serves to strengthen our faith is mentioned in Exodus 31:13 and Ezekiel 20:12,20. There we are told that the Sabbath is designed to remind us that God is the One who sanctifies us.

Our sanctification includes not just forgiveness but the healing of damage sin has done. It means the harmonious development of our physical, mental, and spiritual powers, until the image of God in which we were originally created is perfectly restored.

The observance of the seventh-day Sabbath is an acknowledgement that only the Creator can perform such a marvelous work of transformation. Just as He created us in the beginning, so He has the power to re-create us now.

It is no less a miracle of Creation to restore fallen human beings than it was to create them perfect in the beginning. No wonder David prayed as he did after his sad experience with Bathsheba, "Create in me a clean heart, O God" (Psalm 51:10).

Some seek to accomplish this transformation by themselves, by rigorous obedience, self-discipline, self-denial. But the Sabbath comes each week to remind us that only by faith in our Creator can the healing work be done. Strange that Sabbathkeeping should be thought a legalistic act, a denial of true faith!

A third way in which the Sabbath serves to remind us of the truth and to strengthen our faith in God is mentioned in Hebrews, chapter 4, where the Sabbath is described as a type and foretaste of the final rest and restoration to come. Just as God rested from His labors at the end of Creation week, so there remains a Sabbathlike rest for the people of God.

When the children of Israel marched into the land of Canaan, they failed to enter into God's rest because of lack of faith. They possessed the Promised Land but did not enjoy the Sabbath-like rest that faith brings. But those who maintain their faith in Christ may begin to enjoy this rest even in this life. And they will enter into it fully when they are admitted to the heavenly Canaan, and Eden is restored.

By keeping holy the seventh-day Sabbath we acknowledge our anticipation of this Sabbathlike rest to come, our faith in the second coming of Christ and the re-creation of all things.

These three purposes of the Sabbath answer the three great questions that have stirred the minds of thinking people, the so-called three great quests of philosophy: Where have we come from? Why are we here? And where do we go after we die?

Where have we come from?

The seventh-day Sabbath has always reminded us that "in the beginning God created the heaven and the earth."

Why are we here? What is the great purpose of life? How do we attain to the greatest good in life?

The seventh-day Sabbath has always reminded us that the great purpose of life is our sanctification, our restoration to the image of God by faith in the One who made us perfect in the beginning. This is the purpose of life, and this is how we may attain to it.

Where do we go after we die?

The seventh-day Sabbath points forward to the second coming of Christ, the final rest and restoration to come.

Since the Sabbath is so important, it was only natural that the great adversary would seek to destroy it. Satan's purpose is to destroy faith in Christ, to undermine our confidence in Him as the Creator. But this he could hardly hope to accomplish so long as men continued to recognize all that is represented by the Sabbath. Therefore, he lent his influence to the neglect or perversion of the Sabbath, or to the substitution of another day.

It was a day cleverly chosen. The first day of the week had long been observed as a pagan holiday, the great and holy day of the sun. Besides, many early Christians were eager to dissociate themselves from the Jews.

There was no more conspicuous mark of Judaism than the observance of the seventh day, and the substitution of the first day of the week was regarded by some as evidence that the Christian had made his break with the legalistic practice of the Jews.

Many devout Christians who do not observe the seventh-day Sabbath have a faith that is an example to us all. They have rightly rejected legalism, and they have considered the keeping of the seventh-day Sabbath as its chief example.

But mankind has paid a heavy price for neglecting the Sabbath or substituting another day. For without the Sabbath to provide the answers to the three great questions of life, other solutions have been substituted.

Where have we come from?

Without the seventh-day Sabbath to remind us that in the beginning Christ created us, room has been left to substitute the theory of the evolutionary origin of the human race. Or, as others say more scientifically, We don't know where we come from.

Why are we here? How do we attain to the greatest good in life? Without the seventh-day Sabbath to remind us that righteousness and salvation come by faith in Jesus Christ, room has been left for the substitution of the fundamental error of righteousness by works. Or, as others have said more carelessly, we don't know why we're here. So let's eat, drink, and be merry, for tomorrow we die.

Where do we go after we die?

Without the seventh-day Sabbath to point forward to the Second Coming, to the rewards of faith and the results of sin, room has been left for the substitution of the belief in the natural immortality of the soul. Or, as others prefer to say, we don't know where to go after we die. So again, let's eat, drink, and be merry.

This is why the seventh-day Sabbath is so vital a part of God's last message to the world. The main difference between the many religions in the world and true Christianity lies in the answer to these three great quests.

I like the way Moffatt has interpreted Ezekiel 20:12: "I gave them my Sabbath, to mark the tie between me and them, to teach them that it is I, the Eternal, who sets them apart."

Most of the world has broken this tie, the seventh-day Sabbath. God's last message to the world is the restoration of this tie. It is not a message of legalism, it is much more than a warning to people that they must keep the Sabbath and the other commandments of God lest they be destroyed. On the contrary, it is a message of love and faith.

We preach Christ as the One who created us in the beginning, as the One who is working to re-create us now, and as the One who is coming again to restore all things. And when we preach this, we are preaching the seventh-day Sabbath.

If the Sabbath means so much, what is the proper way to keep it holy?

Many of the Jews of Christ's day tried hard to live up to every requirement of the Sabbath commandment. As a safeguard, they multiplied rules for its correct observance. Yet, when Jesus came to live among them, He had to tell them that in spite of their efforts, their way of spending the Sabbath hours was in error. The trouble was that they had forgotten what the Sabbath represents. They were simply obeying an arbitrary command to refrain from work.

They had lost sight of the fact that the Sabbath speaks of God, of His goodness and creative power, or they would have trusted Him more and would have recognized His Son.

They failed to realize that the Sabbath speaks of God's original purposes for man, of the peace in the Garden of Eden, and the rest that was offered in Canaan, of the Sabbathlike rest yet to come when our world is restored. Instead, they were looking for an earthly kingdom to be set up by force.

Above all, they had forgotten that the Sabbath speaks of the Creator's power to heal, that a sinner cannot heal himself, that salvation comes by faith and not by works of law, however good those works may be.

So confused were some of them as to the purpose of the Sabbath, that on crucifixion Friday they nailed their Creator to the cross and hurried to prepare for sundown worship. They cleaned their sandals, they tidied their homes, and how they wished that He would hurry up and die so they could bury Him before the sun went down.

Sabbathkeepers today may make the same grave mistake if unthinkingly they merely obey a command not to work from sundown Friday to sundown Saturday. For no matter how careful they may be, they do not really keep the Sabbath holy, and they miss all the benefits of its true observance.

It is significant to notice that when Moses repeated the Ten Commandments in the book of Deuteronomy, he mentioned the Exodus rather than Creation as the reason for Sabbath observance: "Remember that you were slaves in Egypt and the Lord your God brought you out with a strong hand and an outstretched arm, and for that reason the Lord your God commanded you to keep the sabbath day" (Deuteronomy 5:15, N.E.B.).

This is no discrepancy in Scripture, nor a lapse of the great leader's memory. The purpose of the seventh-day Sabbath is to remind us of the truth about God. He is not only our Creator but our Saviour and Redeemer as well. The One who created us free is now exercising His creative power to release us from any kind of bondage and give us back our freedom once again.

How strange that the Sabbath should ever become a symbol of subjection to legalism, when from beginning to end it is identified in the Scriptures with freedom!

As God designed it, the Sabbath is to strengthen our faith in Him and in Jesus Christ. It answers our questions about God and the meaning of life. It sums up the truth that sets us free.

From Mr. Roland P. Hegstad, editor, *Liberty,* a magazine of religious freedom:

I once debated Melvin Forney, head of the Lord's Day Alliance, on the Steve Allison program in Washington, D.C. The subject: Sunday laws. "I'm willing to bet," he said, "that you would approve of Sabbath laws if they protected the seventh-day Sabbath."

He was wrong. I oppose seventh-day Sabbath laws, Sunday laws—all religious legislation. I support separation of church and state. I've seen what happens when the state dominates the church. I've seen what happens when the church turns to the state for laws to protect its institutions.

Though I oppose legislated religion, I speak as a man sympathetic to many of the objectives of those citizens who support enactment of Sunday laws.

I believe it is well for a man to have a day of repose with his family each week—but Sunday laws generally do not provide that.

I want to see every man have the opportunity to go to church on the day of his choice, and to go without penalty. And not even in America is that always possible.

Recently a woman was being fined every fourth Sunday by her labor union because she chose to attend church rather than a union meeting.

A member of the Reformed Church lost his post-office job in New Jersey because he refused to work on Sunday. And during recent years a score of seventh-day Sabbathkeepers have been discharged from their post-office jobs for refusing to work on the seventh-day Sabbath—Saturday.

I am concerned for spiritual values. I'm concerned for my country, for its growing secularism, its declining morality, its delinquency and crime.

I'm concerned for the church, for its witness, that it be vital; for its voice, that it be prophetic; for its freedoms, that they be preserved. And I'm concerned for the Sabbath, observance of which is a sign of a man's devotion to his God. But there is a lot of difference between regard for the Sabbath and regard for Sunday laws.

Here are five reasons why I oppose Sunday laws:

First, Sunday laws have a bad record.

The great-grandpappy of all civil Sunday laws dates to March of A.D. 321. It was enacted by the Roman Emporer Constantine as part of his new "togetherness" policy. He thought it would be nice to have everyone resting on the same day. Why not set aside the day on which pagans as well as some Christians worshipped—Sunday?

That first civil Sunday law commanded all men to rest on the "venerable day" of the sun—*EXCEPT* those engaged in agricultural pursuits.

Here was the first step down that tortuous exemption trail, with all its irrational turnings.

Though Constantine's law was civil—as our Sunday laws of today are presumed to be—it became, within a few decades, an instrument of persecution on behalf of the church.

The English Reformation produced the law that is the direct forebear of many found on our statute books. It was brought here by the Puritans, who proceeded to focus it on their fellows with all the zeal of the rookie cop homing in his radar set on the neighborhood hot rodder. And those early laws packed a real sting. The Virginia law of 1610 provided that "those who violated the Sabbath or failed to attend church services, morning and afternoon, should on the first offense lose their provisions and allowance of the whole week following; for the second, lose their allowance and be publicly whipped; and for the third, suffer death."

Keep that Virginia statute in mind when next you hear that Sunday laws are part of the great American heritage—and that we must return to the "faith of our fathers."

Those early Sunday laws had a whole host of offspring. In 1646 church attendance was made compulsory. (Next time you read the comics at ten on Sunday morning, remember that!) In 1647 banishment or death was made the penalty for denying the Bible. Think what they would have done to today's "death of God" theologians!

Early America was no great exercise in brotherhood. Our forefathers fled to this country to escape their neighbors' religion, but it took a while for them to grant their New World neighbors what they asked for themselves.

Roger Williams is another exhibit of their bigotry. He was forced to flee Massachusetts because of his belief that church and state should be separate, because of his belief that Sunday laws did not belong in America, because of his belief that Baptist, Jew, Roman Catholic, and Methodist could live together in harmony if church and state were separated. But his hope was not to be achieved overnight. Indeed, we struggle for it yet.

As late as the 1890's scores of seventh-day Sabbathkeepers were imprisoned on chain gangs because they performed little chores in Sunday—after having rested on the Biblical Sabbath—Saturday.

And still today good men are arrested, fined, given criminal treatment for buying or selling on Sunday.

I think of Robert Gibson, clergyman, arrested on a Sunday afternoon in Austin, Texas, for purchasing a pair of shoes. His own had gotten soaked, so he dashed into a store, purchased an inexpensive pair, in order that he might continue making missionary visits. After he was arrested, he told the city council: "I sent my son to Vietnam and I told him, 'Son, love your country and serve it as a good citizen should.' Now," he said, "I am to be hailed into court and made a criminal because I sought to continue my Christian visiting on Sunday."

Second, Sunday laws are bad laws.

Consider lawn mowing. In my home State, Maryland, a few years ago, the Attorney General's office ruled that Baltimore residents may cut their lawns with a power mower on Sunday if it makes no loud and unseemly noises and if Baltimoreans don't have to push the mower hard enough to exert bodily labor.

Think of some of the complications this ruling raises. Take that phrase "loud and unseemly noises." Do you suppose two magistrates can be found with the same sensitivity to Noise? And what does "bodily labor" mean?

And a while back in New York City, an employee of a religious telecast was arrested and convicted for printing religious Bible lessons on Sunday. Among the lessons was one entitled, "Why men Ought to Keep the Sabbath."

Can you imagine legislators and police and judges in 49 States wrestling with such profound samples of bad law?

People may be arrested, fined, and jailed in one state for doing acts on Sunday that have no penalty in many other States. Worse, sometimes they can do things in one county but not in another. Sometimes the laws vary from town to town.

Exemptions to many State and local Sunday laws are a rogue's gallery of special interests. No wonder such "taste statutes," as many lawyers call them, leave a bad taste in so many mouths.

Do you think it coincidental that a man who swore out complaints against three Middletown, New York, businessmen, testified he was encouraged to make the rounds by his pastor?

I have investigated Sunday laws in many States. Most are on the books today for one reason: powerful churches want them there. Sunday laws have their roots in religion. They are bad laws.

Third, Sunday laws do not achieve even the civil objectives their backers cite.

Family togetherness? A day of rest? Who is kidding whom? Under New York State Sunday laws Mother may work six days a week in a laundry and then serve as a waitress in a local restaurant on Sunday, or as a maid in a local motel.

And Dad can supplement his regular job by calling balls and strikes for the local semipro team, or sell cigars, or fill mail orders at a local department store.

The hard truth is that nationwide only about 17 percent of the labor force comes under the protection of Sunday laws. The rest are either not covered, or exempted. If you are really concerned for that other 83 percent, you are going to have to write a far more stringent code than is on the books now.

But don't feel too bad. Labor unions have put most American workers on a 40-hour (or less) week, with both Saturday and Sunday off. Most Sunday laws do not guarantee a man Sunday rest. They only ensure that he cannot sell certain items on Sunday.

There is a law that will guarantee a man rest: A one-day-in-seven law, which ensures that a man cannot work seven consecutive days. A few States have it, but it doesn't satisfy quite a number of clergymen, because it gives no special status to Sunday.

And in a community where men have rested on Saturday, does it contribute to their health and welfare to be forced to rest also on Sunday? I am aware, of course, of exemption clauses in many Sunday laws—exemptions for those who keep the seventh-day Sabbath. But these exemptions are hardly equitable. For example, many say, "He may work, if he disturbs no other person thereby." A man in New York cannot close his business on Saturday and open it on Sunday if he employs more than three people. Is that fair? But, you say, the man who wants Sunday off must be protected. I believe he should have protection—the same protection the man has who wishes Saturday off.

I think of Adell Sherbert of South Carolina, a grandmother, ruled ineligible for unemployment compensation because she would not take a job forcing her to work on Saturday, her Sabbath. Carolina law said a Sunday-keeper *could* draw his unemployment compensation while refusing employment on his rest day. The Supreme Court of the United States ruled in her favor: 7-2.

The Sundaykeeper must be protected? He is. Under new Federal Civil Rights statutes employers must give a man his day of worship off, if he wishes it, or prove to the government's satisfaction that accomodation is unduly burdensome.

Fourth, Sunday laws are not in the best interests of the church.

Now let me make something clear. I do not regard Sunday as the Sabbath, although I am sometimes found in church on that day in the company of friends, and even speaking from the pulpit. I honor the millions of honest-hearted men and women who worship on Sunday.

I believe that my Lord honors convictions honestly arrived at. Therefore, I honor my neighbor's belief, though it differs from mine. I would not force him to bow at my altar or at any altar. My Lord did not say, "Go, coerce all men." He said, "Go, teach all men." I support laws that guarantee my neighbor the same freedoms I ask for myself.

Sunday laws are not in the church's best interest for several reasons.

First, they rob the church of spiritual vigor and vision. The church has always prospered best when its doctrine have been enshrined, not in state law, not in legal codes, but in the hearts of its members.

Consider, for a moment, the experience of Lyman Beecher, great preachers and champion of the church in New England a century and a half ago, who believed in church–state alliance. On that day in May, 1818, when the church in Connecticut was disestablished, he called it as "dark a day as ever I saw." He sat in one of those old-fashioned, rush-bottomed chairs, his head drooping on his breast, his arms hanging down. His son entered the room and asked, "Father, what are you thinking of?"

He answered solemnly, "The church of God."

Ten years later Lyman Beecher was able to say that loss of establishment was the "best thing that ever happened to the State of Connecticut. It cut the churches loose from dependence on State support. It threw them wholly on their own resources and on God."

Said Beecher in later life: "They say ministers have lost their influence: the fact is, they have gained. By voluntary efforts, societies, missions and revivals, they exert a deeper influence than ever they could by queues, and buckles, and cocked hats, and gold-headed canes. . . . We were thrown on God and on ourselves, and this created that moral coercion which makes men work. . . . Then," said Beecher, "there came such a time of revival as never before in the State."

Thomas Jefferson said, "Compulsion in religion is distinguished peculiarly from compulsion in every other thing. I may grow rich by art I am compelled to follow, I may recover health by medicine I am compelled to take against my judgment; but I cannot be saved by a worship I disbelieve and abhor."—Notes on Religion, 1776.

And second, Sunday laws are bad for the church because they advertise to the non-Christian the church's weakness, its dependence on the arm of flesh. I've thought often of the words of Ezra, returning to Jerusalem from captivity in Babylon: "For I was ashamed to require of the king a band of soldiers and horsemen to help us against the enemy in the way" (Ezra 8:22).

What a tinge of shame should touch the cheeks of clerics who trot to the State capitol for soldiers and horsemen and money to support their institutions, for Sunday laws to fill their pews.

Our Lord did not say, "Tarry ye in Washington, D.C., until ye get support from the Government." He said, "Tarry ye in. . . . Jerusalem, until ye. . . . [get] power from on high" (Luke 24:49).

He did not say, "Ye shall receive power after ye have gained control of the legislature," but "Ye shall receive power, after that the Holy Ghost is come upon you" (Acts 1:18).

He did not say, "Without the help of the laws of the State ye can do nothing," but "Without me ye can do nothing" (John 15:5).

We need not so much to pull legislative wires for the cause of God as to clear the channels through to the throne of grace. Legislated religious conformity is legislated religious hypocrisy.

Not one government can set one soul free from the bondage of sin or plant renewing grace in one sinful heart. All the church organizations of the world, allied with all the kingdoms of this world can never force faith into any man's heart. You can ride a man, dig your legal spurs into him, force him to the altar, and when you get him there, the Lord won't accept him, or you, for God accepts only voluntary submission, heart holiness.

It is when men forget the nature of Christ's kingdom and lose their hold on the power of the living God that they turn to carnal weapons and seek to advance the cause of religion by human legislation.

I like the report of the Special Committee on the Church and State of the 174th General Assembly of the United Presbyterian Church in the U.S.A.:

"The church itself bears sole and vital responsibility for securing from its members a voluntary observance of the Lord's Day. The church should not seek, or even appear to seek, the coercive power of the state in order to facilitate Christians' observance of the Lord's Day."

On Saturday, the biggest business day of the week, the Seventh-day Adventist Church holds services. Nearly 2.5 million seventh-day Sabbath-keeping Christians make it to church each Saturday morning. Past open stores. Past sales. Past ball games and gold courses.

If they can make it on the Sabbath day, why can't others make it without help on Sunday? But sometimes a Seventh-day Adventist doesn't make it. Do you know what happens then? The minister calls on him. And in the spirit of Christ, he admonishes him to keep the Sabbath day holy. He reminds him of the words of Christ: "If you love me, keep my commandments."

If the man does not find his way to church, if he finds his way week after week to the sale at the neighborhood department store, the church board, as a last resort, will meet and discipline him, perhaps even remove his name from the church rolls. Here, in the church, is where God placed disciplinary powers. In the church, not in the State legislature.

Never forget that the best way to destroy the church is to enshrine its dogmas in civil law. The best way to prosper the church is to enshrine its principles in the heart. Sundays laws are bad for the church.

And fifth, Sunday laws do not protect the Sabbath.

The point was made dramatically a while back in Houston, Texas, at a Sunday-law hearing. Before some 100 clergymen and others who crowded his office the mayor stated his position:

He said he must support Sunday laws because, after all, the fourth commandment said, "Remember the sabbath day, to keep it holy. Six days thou shalt labour, and do all thy work: but the seventh day is the sabbath of the Lord thy God" (Exodus 20:8–10).

At which point, a layman arose and said, "But, Mr. Mayor, if you will consult the calendar behind you, you will see that the Sabbath of God comes on Saturday, the seventh day of the week, not Sunday, the first day of the week."

The Mayor swiveled around, looked at the calendar, and finally he turned back with a beseeching look at the clergymen present as if to say, "Help me, fellows, please . . . "

Not one of them said a word. Had they, they could only have confirmed what the layman had observed:

The fourth commandment should not be used to support either Sunday laws or Sundaykeeping. Go to church any day you wish: If you feel you can please God by worshipping on Sunday in honor of Christ's resurrection, as millions of earnest Christians do—and as I once did—do so; but do so knowing that the Bible commands men to honor God by keeping only one day holy—the day He set aside at Creation to meet with His people—the seventh-day Sabbath.

Could it be that Sunday law controversies are one way God seeks to open mens' thinking to themes of eternal consequence?

Why did He place in the Bible this solemn warning—"In vain do they worship me, teaching for doctrines the commandments of men" (Mark 7:7)?

Why did He emphasize, "One jot or one tittle"—one dotting of an i, one crossing of a t—"shall in no wise pass from the law, till all [things] be fulfilled," that is, "till heaven and earth pass away" (Matthew 5:18), which is to say, Never?

Could it be that our allegiance to God is shown by our willingness to follow His commandments?

You'll remember that a few years back Premier Khrushchev visited America. What if he had said in an address to our nation, "Forget that your Congress asks you to celebrate Independence Day on the Fourth of July. Celebrate it with us from now on, on the fifth."

Would it matter if we followed his suggestion?

Would we not say that the very integrity of our commitment to America and what it stands for was at stake? Would not the real question be, To whom do we give allegiance?

Could it be that the same issue is at stake in the Sabbath question? God said, "Remember." Somewhere back in history, men said, "Forget."

Now, no legalistic observance of either Saturday or Sunday is going to avail us one whit. Christ said, "If you love me, keep my commandments."

God will accept worship only when it is motivated by love. We do not keep God's commandments to be saved, do we? But rather, we keep them because we are saved.

Next time you hear a legislator or a city official talking about needing Sunday laws to protect the Sabbath, set him straight, won't you? "Remember the sabbath. . . . "

The Demise of Blue Laws

In 1970, twenty-five states had statewide blue laws, with enforcement of varying intensity. By 1984, twelve of these states had repealed their Sunday-closing legislation, and others were threatening to modify or repeal their respective restrictions. In one of the very few examples of formal economic analysis of blue laws (that we are aware of), Price and Yandle [forthcoming, 1987] attempt to explain the decline of blue laws over this time period. The investigative task is doubly difficult: not only must one identify factors that are associated with the successful repeal of the laws, one must explain why these factors were particularly virulent (vis-à-vis blue laws) during the 1970s and 1980s, whereas they were not inimical to survival of the law theretofore.

Price and Yandle approach the problem from an interest-group perspective. They argue that in order for regulations to endure through time they must have special-interest support. By that same logic, of course, erosion of that support implies the eventual demise of those regulations. The heart of their argument is that fundamental changes in labor markets, particularly those that relate to unions and female workers, were instrumental in engineering the repeal of blue laws.

They begin their analysis by noting that the occurrence of blue laws has not increased in recent years, and that states organized later in America's heritage might have avoided any experience with blue laws altogether. The citizenry of older states, in which blue laws were passed on some moral or religious principles, may find it difficult to repeal such laws. The citizenry of newer states would never pass such laws in the first place. Therefore, they control for the date of statehood in their model, which seeks to explain, both in 1970 and in 1984, the presence or absence of Sunday-closing legislation in a state.

Price and Yandle then indicate that blue laws have enjoyed historical support by Southern Baptists, and therefore expect the probability of a state with Sunday-closing legislation to be a positive function of the fraction of the state population that is identified as belonging to the Southern Baptist denomination.

The degree to which one party has strong control over the state legislature may also affect the ease of blue law repeal. Posner [1974] argued that legislative dominance by one political party leads to a weaker legislative response to demands by the citizenry for regulatory reform. As Price and Yandle put it: "Like their counterparts in the private sector, political monopolists tend to reduce output and raise price." They suggest that in states in which the legislature is dominated by one political party, the legislature will be slower to respond to calls for repeal of blue laws than in states characterized by a greater degree of legislative competition.

Price and Yandle argue that the changing composition of the workforce is the critical force motivating repeal of blue laws. There are two aspects to the change in the workforce over this time period: the decline of blue-collar unionism and the tremendous influx of women into the labor force. The net impact of the former influence is a reduction of one of the special interest groups supportive of blue laws, while at the same time the net effect of the latter influence is to increase opposition to blue laws. According to the 'transitional gains trap' argument put forth by Tullock [1980], restrictive Sunday-trading laws permit producers to earn higher profits. Those profits can, in part, be appropriated by strong unions. As blue-collar unions declined over the period in question, the strength of union support for blue laws would have eroded correspondingly. While blue-collar unions were experiencing their decline during the 1970s and 1980s, women were entering the labor force in ever-increasing numbers. The inevitable result was an increase in the opportunity cost of shopping, which led, also inevitably, to an increasing demand for additional time to shop, that is, repeal of restrictive Sunday-shopping laws. They therefore expected to observe a negative relationship between blue laws and percentage of the labor force that was female in those years.

In the empirical results they report, Price and Yandle estimate the influence of the aforementioned variables on the probability of a particular state having a statewide blue law in effect in 1970 and again (in separate regressions) in 1984. Their findings suggest that over that fifteen-year period general support for blue laws declined markedly, while the focused opposition of women increased significantly. The impact of states whose legislature was dominated by one political party became a highly significant force in the thwarting of repeal efforts. Women and the households represented by them, according to the authors, faced the problem in 1984 of "influencing legislative bodies that were dominated by one party, and therefore less sensitive to political demands."

Notes

1. This is, of course, ironic since the European colonizers of America were fleeing religious persecution in their homelands.

2. As taken from Kit Gorman, "The Assault on Louisiana's Blue Law Continues," *Citibusiness,* May 2, 1983, p. 10.

3. John Novotney, "The Energy Crisis and Sunday-Closing Laws," *Liberty,* January/February 1975, p. 5.

4. Id., p. 7.

5
An Empirical Examination of the Impact of Blue Laws

Having discussed the nominal arguments employed by those interests in favor of, and those opposed to, Sunday-closing laws, it is time to get down to the serious business of determining the validity of those arguments. This chapter presents our findings with respect to a wide-ranging examination of social, religious, and economic indicators that potentially support the arguments put forth by the proponents and opponents of blue laws.

In brief, the highlights of these findings follow.

1. Church membership and per capita church contributions do not appear to be adversely affected in states with no Sunday-closing laws.

2. Residential energy consumption, on a per capita basis, is virtually identical in those states with and without blue laws.

3. Commercial and industrial energy consumption, on a per capita basis, is actually higher in blue law states than in non-blue law states, counter to what proponents of blue laws argue.

4. Per capita income is higher and the percent of individuals (and families) that fall below the official U.S. poverty line is lower in states with no blue laws than in those with such laws.

5. In terms of recreation, state appropriations for the arts are substantially greater in blue law states than non-blue law states. On the other hand, there is apparently a greater propensity to recreate in the latter states than in the former, judging by visits to state parks and recreation areas.

6. The labor force participation rate in non-blue law states exceeds that for blue law states. In spite of this fact, the unemployment rate and average number of hours worked per week appear to be slightly lower in the former states than in the latter.

7. In terms of general indices of happiness, or unhappiness, we find that marriage rates are almost identical between the two categories of states, but that the divorce/annulment rate, the suicide rate, and the rate of vio-

lent crime commission appear to be slightly higher in non-blue law states than in blue law states. Nevertheless, over the decade of the 1970s, blue law states were characterized by net outmigration whereas non-blue law states experienced a net inmigration of considerable strength.

8. Total economic activity, as reflected in per capita sales by firms, is greater in non-blue law states than in blue law states. This indicates that repeal of Sunday-closing laws results in an overall increase in commercial activity, not simply a redistribution of sales from six days per week to seven days.

9. The number of business establishments per capita is greater in states that do not regulate business activity on Sundays. Moreover, the average size of a business establishment, measured by the number of employees or by value added, is larger in unregulated states than in regulated states.

Analysis

Much of the ensuing analysis focuses on data gathered for twenty states, ten of which were identified as restricting commercial activity on Sundays during the period 1970 to 1980, ten of which did not restrict commercial activity on Sundays over that same time period. The states and their relative categories are listed in table 5–1.

Table 5–1
States with Regulated and Unregulated Commercial Activity on Sundays during the 1970s

Commercial Activity Restricted on Sundays	Commercial Activity Not Restricted on Sundays
Louisiana	Arkansas
Maryland	California
Mississippi	Connecticut
Missouri	Idaho
New York	Illinois
North Dakota	Oregon
Oklahoma	Pennsylvania
Rhode Island	Tennessee
Texas	Vermont
West Virginia	Washington

Church Membership and Per Member Contributions

As reported in chapter 4, there is a concern among leaders of the various religious organizations in America that repeal of blue laws will ultimately have a negative impact on popular observance of Sunday as a day of worship. If, for example, one is legally permitted to shop on Sunday, might one not occasionally use this time for shopping rather than religious worship? The deletory effects upon church membership, church attendance, and church contributions, as anticipated by church officials, are obvious.

This is, in some sense, an awkward argument for the church to champion. In theory, God's message is attractive enough to out-compete any secular competition, without resort to secular restriction of alternative time-uses. The admission of that failure places religion on a par with all other goods — namely, one's time and money investment are a function of relative (anticipated) costs and benefits, properly discounted. For the church to want the state to restrict individuals from using Sunday for activities valued higher than religious worship in a formal church setting is to admit, albeit indirectly, that one's product is not very attractive, on its own, to potential customers.

From a more formal economic perspective, restriction of competition necessarily results in a reduced choice set for would-be consumers, and therefore lowers societal welfare, for several reasons. First, alternative choices may be valued per se, that is, there may be positive value placed by society on the ability to choose from among alternative uses of one's time. This implies, of course, that social welfare increases as the size of the choice set increases, and vice versa. Second, competition invariably forces producers to produce efficiently. Sellers must pay close attention to the needs and wants of their prospective clientele in a competitive environment; to not do so invites competitors to take away business by providing that attentiveness. Such attentiveness is, of course, a valuable commodity to consumers and is lost to a society under a protectionist regime. Third, it is well-known that sellers insulated from competitors are potentially able to raise the implicit, or explicit, prices they charge for their products or services above those that would prevail in a competitive environment. These higher prices represent a wealth transfer from consumers to the seller and are responsible for creating a new loss to society. This so-called "deadweight loss' is depicted in figure 5–1.

In an unrestricted environment, churches would have to compete with sports teams, shopping malls, and other activities for the patronage of individuals. A general equilibrium average "price" (p^*) for pleasurable or meaningful (i.e., valuable) Sunday activities emerges from the interplay of demanders of suppliers of those activities, with a total quantity of q^* consumed. Laws that prohibit stores from doing business on Sundays effectively

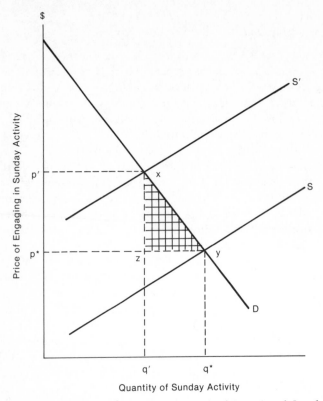

Quantity of Sunday Activity

Figure 5–1. The Deadweight Loss to Society of Restricted Sunday Shopping

reduce the supply of Sunday activities (from S to S′), which results in a new average equilibrium price (p′) that is higher than the old price, p*. Total wealth equal to the rectangle p*p′yx is transferred from consumers to producers and, since certain consumers of secular activities like shopping refuse to engage in religious worship on Sunday when shopping is banned, there is an additional loss to society equal to the triangle xyz.

It is possible to examine the question of whether patterns of church membership or contributions, or both, differ between blue law states and non-blue law states. We can therefore test the validity of the claim that removal of Sunday restrictions on economic activity will adversely affect churches. Data on church membership and per capita contributions, by denomination, are reported in recent editions of the *Statistical Abstract of the United States* and in Quinn et al., *Churches and Church Membership in the United States—1980*. Tables 5–2 and 5–3 include reproduced and generated statistics across twenty-nine denominations in our twenty sample states, in 1971 and 1980, respectively.[1]

Table 5–2
Church Membership and Church Contributions—1971

State	Blue Law States Adherents* State Pop.	Per Member Contributions	Per Capita Contributions
Louisiana	.2256	$84.17	$18.99
Maryland	.1912	88.63	16.94
Mississippi	.4361	82.38	35.92
Missouri	.3089	88.52	27.35
New York	.0809	94.86	7.67
North Dakota	.4639	82.17	38.12
Oklahoma	.4578	86.20	39.46
Rhode Island	.0375	96.78	3.63
Texas	.3326	80.38	26.73
West Virginia	.2005	97.50	19.55
Average	.2217	$85.66	$18.99

State	Non-Blue Law States Adherents* State Pop.	Per Member Contributions	Per Capita Contributions
Arkansas	.3654	84.58	30.91
California	.0907	114.83	10.41
Connecticut	.0930	91.69	8.61
Idaho	.1376	119.41	16.43
Illinois	.2001	91.72	18.35
Oregon	.1411	121.10	17.08
Pennsylvania	.2301	91.10	20.96
Tennessee	.4384	85.53	37.49
Vermont	.1282	91.36	11.71
Washington	.0503	79.71	4.01
Average	.1725	$95.08	$16.40

*For specific definitions of adherents by each religion included in the sample, see Quinn et al. [1982], pp. 311–15.

The data reported are consistent across both years. Church membership as a percent of the total state population is lower in states that do not restrict economic activity on Sundays than in those that do. On the other hand, per member contributions are actually higher in the former group of states than in the latter. On a per capita basis, however, contributions in states with blue laws exceed those in states without such laws. During the decade of the 1970s, for which we have data on church membership and contributions,

Table 5–3
Church Membership and Church Contributions—1980

State	Blue Law States Adherents* State Pop.	Per Member Contributions	Per Capita Contributions
Louisiana	.2134	$173.97	$37.13
Maryland	.1750	177.04	30.97
Mississippi	.4249	170.12	72.29
Missouri	.3024	181.17	54.79
New York	.0759	194.19	14.74
North Dakota	.4301	172.52	74.20
Oklahoma	.4604	168.55	77.60
Rhode Island	,0335	188.92	6.33
Texas	.2989	172.16	51.46
West Virginia	.1981	201.60	39.93
Average	.2191	$176.60	38.69

State	Non-Blue Law States Adherents* State Pop.	Per Member Contributions	Per Capita Contributions
Arkansas	.1565	$185.01	$28.95
California	.0757	243.57	18.43
Connecticut	.0875	173.99	15.22
Idaho	.1108	245.44	27.19
Illinois	.1771	184.97	32.76
Oregon	.1073	224.67	24.11
Pennsylvania	.2213	181.72	40.21
Tennessee	.5294	171.69	90.89
Vermont	.1234	199.68	24.65
Washington	.1274	228.26	29.08
Average	.1607	$194.78	$31.29

*For specific definitions of adherents by each religion included in the sample, refer to Quinn et al. [1982], pp. 311–15.

two states repealed their Sunday-closing laws: Ohio in 1973 and Georgia in 1975. For these two states it is possible to examine the impact of the altered legal environment on church membership and contributions by comparing the 1971 (before repeal) figures with the 1980 (post repeal) figures. This comparison is presented in table 5–4.

Over the ten-year period under scrutiny, the percentage change in adherents as a percent of state population declined faster in non-blue law states

Table 5–4
The Impact of Repeal on Church Membership and Church Contributions

Georgia	Year Blue Law Was Repealed—1973		
	1971	1980	% Change
Adherents/State Population	.3993	.3729	– 6.61
Per Adherent Contributions	$82.83	$173.10	108.98
Per Capita Contributions	$33.07	$64.54	95.16

Ohio	Year Blue Law Was Repealed—1975		
	1971	1980	% Change
Adherents/State Population	.2170	.1984	– 8.57
Per Adherent Contributions	$95.29	$144.22	51.35
Per Capita Contributions	$20.68	$28.62	38.39

	Percent Change 1971–1980	
	Blue Law States	Non-Blue Law States
Adherents/State Population	– 1.17	– 6.84
Per Adherent Contributions	106.16	104.86
Per Capita Contributions	103.74	90

than in blue law states (– 6.84 percent vs. – 1.17 percent, respectively). The rate of decline in Georgia over this period is close to the average, – 6.61 percent, while the rate of decline in Ohio is considerably above the average, at – 8.57 percent. The non-inflation-adjusted rate of increase in per adherent contributions during the 1970s was almost identical across the two categories of states—106.16 percent in blue law states versus 104.86 percent in non-blue law states. In Georgia, the rate of increase in per adherent contributions (108.98 percent) over this period was slightly above either of these averages, despite the mid-decade change in the law, but the rate of increase in Ohio (51.35 percent) fell far below the averages. The figures for the rate of change in per capita contributions mirror this dichotomy.

Church membership, as a fraction of total state population, is somewhat greater in blue law states. However, per member contributions are noticeably higher in non-blue law states. Per capita contributions average more than sixteen percent higher in non-blue law states than in blue law states. As reported previously, per capita income is higher in non-blue law states; if a constant fraction of income is donated to the church, this income differential alone would imply the observed differences in contributions. The ultimate impact on total contributions by denomination in each state will depend, of course, upon a number of additional factors that we have not examined. We are unable to report consistent results across the two states that repealed their blue laws in the mid-1970s—there is no evidence that either church membership or contributions are unambiguously affected adversely by repeal.

Energy Consumption

Proponents of Sunday-closing laws have argued that one benefit of such laws is reduced energy consumption relative to states with no restriction at all on Sunday commercial activity. This generates a public good in the form of reduced demand for energy, which is (in theory) reflected in lower energy prices and perhaps a reduced dependence upon foreign producers of energy, particularly oil.

Available data on energy consumption permit us to examine the validity of the proposition that energy consumption in blue law states is lower than the energy consumption in non-blue law states. Collected statistics on energy use, by type of energy as well as by type of user, are disaggregated by state in the *Statistical Abstract of the United States—1982–83,* 103rd ed., table 977, p. 574. Tables 5–5 and 5–6 report residential, commercial, industrial, and transportation energy usage by state and total energy consumption per state. Total energy consumption and per capita energy consumption are reported.

The data reported in tables 5–5 and 5–6 lead us to reject the notion that energy consumption is lower in states with Sunday-closing laws. In terms of residential energy consumption, there is essentially no difference between blue law states and non-blue law states. On the other hand, commercial, industrial, and transportation energy usage, and, not surprisingly, total energy consumption, is actually greater, on a per capita basis, in states that restrict Sunday activity than in those that do not restrict such activity.

One possible reason for the observed differences in commercial, industrial, and residential energy usage between blue law and non-blue law states is that commercial activity in blue law states takes place in the evening and nighttime hours to a greater extent than in non-blue law states. Since their activity is prohibited on Sundays, businessmen in blue law states may adjust their establishment's working schedules to operate longer hours on days which are not subject to restrictions. This implies greater energy consumption per unit of output produced compared to identical establishments that are permitted to open on Sundays, since energy at night exceeds that by day, due to greater lighting and heating requirements for nighttime operation than for daytime operation, all other things being equal. We do not have the data to prove or disprove the validity of this hypothesized explanation. In fairness to both proponents and opponents of blue laws, we note that if this differential time-of-operation pattern results from restriction of normal economic activity on Sundays, there is some implication that workers are forced to work hours that they would perhaps prefer to not work. This is one of the

Table 5–5
Energy Consumption in Trillions of BTU—1980

| State | Blue Law States | | | | |
	Residential	Commercial	Industrial	Transport	Total
Louisiana	278	281	2101	647	3307
Maryland	259	172	404	318	1154
Mississippi	163	106	282	261	811
Missouri	407	248	390	411	1456
New York	942	915	990	1009	3856
North Dakota	52	34	88	73	247
Oklahoma	244	160	516	306	1227
Rhode Island	56	34	47	52	189
Texas	945	761	4918	1808	8432
West Virginia	138	70	409	146	764
Average	348	277	1017	506	2143

| State | Non-Blue Law States | | | | |
	Residential	Commercial	Industrial	Transport	Total
Arkansas	183	101	369	206	858
California	1166	1081	1811	2375	6433
Connecticut	211	129	213	185	738
Idaho	72	60	140	83	355
Illinois	898	646	1425	820	3789
Oregon	190	156	311	239	896
Pennsylvania	869	442	1792	815	3918
Tennessee	368	225	697	408	1699
Vermont	38	18	28	34	119
Washington	340	206	586	419	1551
Average	434	306	737	558	2036

Source: *Statistical Abstract of the United States—1982–83,* p. 427.

blue laws proponents' most loudly voiced arguments against repeal of such laws—that workers will be forced to work undesirable Sunday shifts. From an economic perspective, undesirable hours are undesirable hours, irrespective of when they must be worked. It is therefore possible that workers are hurt as much by Sunday-closing laws as they would theoretically be by repeal. One could make the further argument, with no current data to support or reject the hypothesis, that workers might actually prefer to work the Sunday hours to the late-night hours.

Table 5–6
Energy Consumption in Millions of BTU per Capita—1980

| State | Blue Law States | | | | |
	Residential	Commercial	Industrial	Transport	Total
Louisiana	66	67	498	153	783
Maryland	61	41	96	75	273
Mississippi	65	42	112	103	321
Missouri	83	50	79	83	296
New York	54	52	56	57	219
North Dakota	80	52	135	112	378
Oklahoma	80	53	170	101	404
Rhode Island	59	36	50	55	199
Texas	66	53	343	126	589
West Virginia	71	36	210	75	392
Average	64	51	187	93	394

| State | Non-Blue Law States | | | | |
	Residential	Commercial	Industrial	Transport	Total
Arkansas	80	44	161	90	373
California	49	45	76	100	271
Connecticut	68	41	68	59	237
Idaho	76	63	148	88	375
Illinois	79	57	125	72	331
Oregon	72	59	118	91	340
Pennsylvania	73	37	151	69	330
Tennessee	80	49	152	89	370
Vermont	75	35	55	66	232
Washington	82	50	141	101	374
Average	66	47	113	85	334

Per Capita Income

One would predict that states with no restrictions on Sunday activities have higher per capita incomes than states that do impose some sort of restraint on Sunday activities, for at least two reasons. First, restriction of economic activity at a minimum raises the real cost of creating added-value in the economy. The reasoning is straightforward. Let us suppose that a proprietor wishes to be open for business a total of fifty-six hours per week and that the least cost arrangement for doing so is to operate for eight hours per day during each of the seven days of the week. A regulation that prohibits Sunday sales forces the owner or manager to re-deploy his hired help during less desirable times—he or she must now stay open for, say, nine and a half hours each day, Monday through Friday and eight and a half hours on Saturday. This requires having the hired help work more hours per day, at an added cost of overtime wages or reduced employee productivity, or it requires hiring additional labor that may not be wanted. It is, after all, costly to hire new employees—costly in terms of finding the workers, training them to do their required tasks, and costly in terms of risk. Evening hours may be additionally costly compared to Sunday hours in terms of reduced customer traffic, higher heating and other overhead expenses, and greater risk due to nighttime operation.

Second, there may be a positive relationship between per capita state income and lack of restriction on Sunday activity because freedom of choice is an income-elastic good. That is to say, as individuals become wealthier they place an increasingly positive value on alternative uses of their time. One might predict, therefore, that people with higher per capita incomes would be less tolerant of restrictions on Sunday activities than individuals with lower per capita incomes.

Although the exact reasons for the positive association between income and unrestricted Sunday activity are unclear, the data reveal a strong relationship in the expected direction. Per capita income statistics across our sample states are reported in table 5–7 and the percent of each state's population officially classified as living below the legally defined poverty line is reported in table 5–8. The tables provide consistent evidence: per capita income is lower in blue law states than in non-blue law states, and the percent of individuals and families with incomes below the officially designated poverty line is higher in blue law states than in non-blue law states.

Recreation

The state has a legitimate and legal interest in regulating Sunday activity in order to promote the well-being of individuals living within its jurisdiction. That was the finding of the United States Supreme Court in the case of *McGowan v. Maryland* (1960), perhaps the most famous court decision regarding Sunday-closing legislation. This decision forms the legal basis for much of the state regulation that occurs in the 1980s.

"Well-being" of the population can, of course, be interpreted in different fashions. The state may have an interest in furthering the economic well-being of inhabitants or in enhancing the more general, less definable social well-being (i.e., quality of life) of its population, or both. The statistics on per capita income and percent of the population living below the officially defined poverty line, discussed previously, indicate that economic well-being is not measurably improved through restriction of economic activity on Sundays. If anything, the aforecited statistics suggest that a state's citizenry is

Table 5–7
Per Capita Income in Constant 1972 Dollars

State	Blue Law States 1970	1980	Percent Change
Louisiana	3288	4727	43.77
Maryland	4672	5856	25.34
Mississippi	2763	3665	32.65
Missouri	4006	4955	23.69
New York	5076	5731	12.90
North Dakota	3477	4822	38.68
Oklahoma	3608	5068	40.47
Rhode Island	4242	5271	24.26
Texas	3823	5326	39.31
West Virginia	3290	4368	32.77
Average	3824.5	4978.9	30.18

State	Non-Blue Law States 1970	1980	Percent Change
Arkansas	2998	4016	33.96
California	4875	6109	25.31
Connecticut	5311	6535	23.05
Idaho	3584	4570	27.51
Illinois	4881	5857	19.96
Oregon	4012	5196	29.51
Pennsylvania	4246	5269	24.09
Tennessee	3348	4305	28.58
Vermont	3816	4366	14.41
Washington	4374	5788	32.33
Average	4144.5	5201.1	25.49

adversely affected, economically, by blue laws. We turn our attention now to the question of whether or not Sunday-closing laws seem to have a positive impact on a state's population in terms of the quality of life, as best as we can measure such an ill-defined concept. It has been argued that Sunday-closing laws encourage citizens to engage in more recreational activity than they would engage in in an unrestricted environment. This type of substitution effect is familiar to economists and necessarily implies that the citizen is not permitted by the state to maximize his or her utility. Consider the unrestricted, utility-maximizing choice of recreation and shopping per week ($r^* s^*$) for a typical individual, as depicted in figures 5–2 and 5–3.

Table 5–8
Percent of Persons and Families Living below the Poverty Line

| | Blue Law States | | | |
| | Persons | | Families | |
State	1969	1979	1969	1979
Louisiana	26.3	18.6	21.5	15.1
Maryland	10.1	9.8	7.7	7.5
Mississippi	35.4	23.9	28.9	18.7
Missouri	14.7	12.2	11.5	9.1
New York	11.1	13.4	8.5	10.8
North Dakota	15.7	12.6	12.4	9.8
Oklahoma	18.8	13.4	15.0	10.3
Rhode Island	11.0	10.3	8.5	7.7
Texas	18.8	14.7	14.6	11.2
West Virginia	22.2	15.0	18.0	11.7
Average	18.41	14.39	14.66	11.19

| | Non-Blue Law States | | | |
| | Persons | | Families | |
State	1969	1979	1969	1979
Arkansas	27.8	19.0	22.8	14.9
California	11.1	11.4	8.4	8.7
Connecticut	7.2	8.0	5.3	6.2
Idaho	13.2	12.6	10.9	9.6
Illinois	10.2	11.0	7.7	8.4
Oregon	11.5	10.7	8.6	7.7
Pennsylvania	10.6	10.5	7.9	7.8
Tennessee	21.8	16.4	18.2	13.1
Vermont	12.1	12.1	9.1	8.9
Washington	10.2	9.8	7.6	7.2
Average	13.57	12.15	10.65	9.25

Source: *Statistical Abstract of the United States—1982–83,* p. 443.

The boundaries of the individual's budget constraints are defined by

r = the amount of recreation purchasable at a price of P_r if all of his income were devoted to recreation, and

s = the quantity of goods and services purchasable at a price of P_s if all of his income were allocated to shopping.

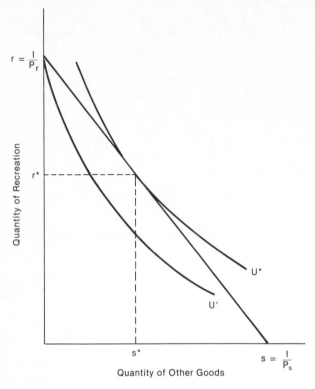

Figure 5–2. The Impact of Sunday Shopping Restrictions on Consumer Choice—Consumer Is Unable to Purchase Certain Items

The mere fact that the individual chooses in an unrestricted environment to do some of that shopping on Sunday indicates that the real cost of shopping is lower on Sundays, for certain items or for certain individuals irrespective of items purchased, than it is on other days of the week.[2] Restriction of economic activity on Sundays has the unambiguous effect of raising the price the consumer pays for goods and services. It might be that the individual is not legally permitted to purchase specific items on Sunday and must therefore arrange to purchase them on some other day that is less suitable from his or her perspective. If stores are restricted by the number of employees permitted on Sundays, both the curtailment of customer services offered and the less timely handling of customers constitute a rise in the real price that the would-be consumer pays for items purchased on Sunday (see note 2). Finally, the individual may not be able to take advantage of economies of scale in combining many shopping errands on one day, if he or she is forced to re-deploy shopping effort to days other than Sunday.

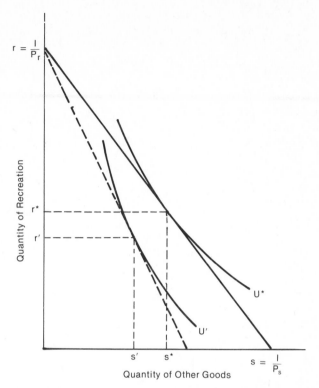

Figure 5–3. The Impact of Sunday Shopping Restrictions on Consumer Choice — Consumer Is Able to Purchase Certain Items

This increase in the implicit price of goods and services may affect the buyer in one of two ways. First, the individual may simply be unable to purchase an item on Sunday (s = 0). Under the circumstances (figure 5–2), the utility-maximizing combination of recreation and shopping is (r,0), where r = I/Pr. The level of utility achieved by the individual in the restricted environment is clearly lower than that achievable in an unrestricted regime. Second, if, as argued above, the real price paid for goods and services (Ps) is higher in blue law states than in non-blue law states, the budget set of an individual in the former category of states is effectively reduced from rs to rs' (figure 5–3). If both shopping and recreation are normal goods, the reduced budget set implies lower consumption of both items in blue law states compared to non-blue law states. The new optimal combination of recreation and shopping is (r', s') with an associated level of consumer utility that falls short of that attainable in a state with no restrictions on Sunday activity (r*, s*).

Any attempt by the state legislature to encourage substitution by individuals of recreation for shopping suggests, at least implicitly, that such recreational activity is desirable. It is, of course, of dubious merit to suggest that politicians have a better awareness than individuals do of what constitutes their utility-maximizing level of recreational activity. Passing by this argument, the available evidence suggests that legislatures in blue-law states are consistent with respect to their belief in the desirability of recreation. Table 5–9 reports legislative appropriations for state arts agencies, on a per capita basis, for the years 1975 and 1980–82.

Table 5–9
State Legislative Appropriations for State Arts Agencies in Current Dollars (per capita)

| | Blue Law States | | | |
State	1970	1980	1981	1982
Louisiana	.015	.203	.465	.480
Maryland	.108	.318	.367	.310
Mississippi	.047	.122	.150	.180
Missouri	.260	.514	.504	.480
New York	1.977	1.894	1.885	2.020
North Dakota	.008	.154	.152	.220
Oklahoma	.034	.182	.282	.390
Rhode Island	.282	.378	.423	.420
Texas	.013	.085	.083	.100
West Virginia	.196	.802	.838	1.030
Average	.294	.465	.515	.560

| | Non-Blue Law States | | | |
State	1970	1980	1981	1982
Arkansas	.077	.368	.373	.330
California	.046	.332	.439	.440
Connecticut	.128	.419	.365	.280
Idaho	.028	.091	.122	.110
Illinois	.082	.196	.276	.250
Oregon	.023	.127	.132	.140
Pennsylvania	.125	.218	.258	.340
Tennessee	.097	.113	.111	.110
Vermont	.014	.211	.266	.320
Washington	.068	.140	.190	.140
Average	.078	.222	.253	.250

Source: *Statistical Abstract of the United States—1982–83,* 103rd edition, table 404, p. 237.

Legislatures is states with intact blue laws appropriate substantially greater revenues per capita to state arts agencies than do legislatures in non-blue law states. The pattern of differences is consistent across the entire period for which data were available and, if anything, the disparity is increasing over time.

Of course, the level of appropriations for the arts by state governments sheds no light whatsoever on the degree to which the inhabitants of the state actually patronize the arts. Available data on actual recreational activity indicate that state parks are utilized more intensively in non-blue law states than in blue law states (see table 5–10).

Table 5–10
Visitors to State Parks and Recreation Areas—1980

State	Blue Law States Total (× 1000)	Percent of 1980 State Population
Louisiana	4211	99.74
Maryland	5240	124.02
Mississippi	4065	161.12
Missouri	9283	188.53
New York	39729	226.05
North Dakota	1013	154.89
Oklahoma	18294	602.17
Rhode Island	7703	811.70
Texas	14022	97.91
West Virginia	8206	420.82
Average	11176.6	288.70

State	Non-Blue Law States Total (× 1000)	Percent of 1980 State Population
Arkansas	5786	251.67
California	58024	244.10
Connecticut	7300	234.43
Idaho	2049	216.37
Illinois	32314	282.64
Oregon	34455	1306.10
Pennsylvania	15613	131.42
Tennessee	14989	326.20
Vermont	1211	236.52
Washington	37154	895.71
Average	20889.5	412.52

Source: Statistical Abstract of the United States—1982–83, p. 232.

The figures in table 5–10 reveal that visitors to state parks and recreation areas in 1980, as a percent of 1980 state population, is considerably greater in non-blue law states than in blue law states. Despite what may be an intent on the part of legislators in the latter states to encourage recreational activity via imposition of restrictions on Sunday commercial activity, actual recreational behavior of individuals in non-blue law states is not adversely affected by the unrestricted economic environment—quite the contrary.

The available statistics on various general measures of social well-being or quality of life provide mixed results with respect to the possible benefits of restricted commercial activity on Sundays. The least ambiguous results are based on crime rates in the late 1970s and early 1980s, as reported in the *Statistical Abstract of the United States—1982–83,* 103rd edition, table 289, p. 175. These data are reported in table 5–11 and discussed below.

Across the four-year period, 1978–81, crime rates per 100,000 population were uniformly lower in blue law states than in non-blue law states, by a factor of 10 percent. To the extent that crime rates can be taken as a useful reflection of the general well-being of the population, these results offer the first potential justification for blue laws. Low crime rates are a public good and are under-provided by private markets, because there is an incentive for individuals to let others provide circumstances that promote low crime rates. To the extent that Sunday-closing Laws, in fact, contribute to a high quality of life that, in turn, promotes lower crime rates, the state is justified, in an economic sense, in implicitly taxing individuals (through the aforementioned higher implicit price of consumption) in order to provide an optimal (low) quantity of crime.

There are, of course, a number of factors that contribute to differential crime statistics across states, such as differences in the age distribution of the population, differences in state support for education, per capita income, and the like. A thorough examination of the causes of the types of crimes reported on is necessary to conclude that Sunday-closing Laws, by themselves, are responsible for lower crime rates.

Table 5–12 reports additional data that bear on the quality of life issue under investigation. The data reported includes death rates per 100,000 population due to accidents and suicides.

The figures with respect to the accident rate are virtually identical across the two types of states. However, the suicide rate in blue law states is lower, by a good 10 percent, than the rate in non-blue law states. Again, to the extent that a low suicide rate is considered a public good, and to the extent that blue laws may contribute to a quality of life that promotes low suicide rates, the state may be justified in regulating economic activity.

The statistics on marriages and divorces during the 1970s imply nothing definitive about the implicit quality of life in blue law states versus non-blue law states. These data are presented in tables 5–13 and 5–14 for marriages, and divorces and annulments, respectively.

Table 5–11
Crime Rates per 100,000 Population*

| State | Blue Law States | | | |
	1978	1979	1980	1981
Louisiana	4792	5359	5454	5268
Maryland	5814	6295	6630	6558
Mississippi	2555	2961	3417	3537
Missouri	4527	4940	5433	5351
New York	5792	6205	6912	6905
North Dakota	2405	2756	2964	2991
Oklahoma	4130	4703	5053	4837
Rhode Island	5262	5770	5933	5852
Texas	5557	5925	6143	6050
West Virginia	2270	2325	2552	2619
Average	4310.4	4723.9	5049.1	4996.8

| State | Non-Blue Law States | | | |
	1978	1979	1980	1981
Arkansas	3462	3621	3811	3796
California	7136	7469	7833	7590
Connecticut	4929	5780	5882	5837
Idaho	4015	4241	4782	4531
Illinois	5018	5169	5275	4950
Oregon	6075	6373	6687	7037
Pennsylvania	3185	3495	3736	3683
Tennessee	3690	4013	4498	4311
Vermont	3807	5299	4988	5061
Washington	6116	6530	6915	6742
Average	4743.3	5199.0	5440.7	5353.8

*Crimes reported include: murder, forcible rape, robbery, aggravated assault, burglary/ larceny/theft and motor-vehicle theft.

While the divorce/annulment rate has been uniformly lower in blue law states than in non-blue law states during the 1970s, the increase in the divorce/annulment rate over that decade was greater in blue law states. With respect to marriages, the number of marriages per 1,000 population was greater in blue law states than in non-blue law states in 1970 but by the end of the decade there was virtually no difference across the two categories of states. Over this time period (1970–79) we note that the marriage rate actually fell slightly in blue law states while rising slightly in non-blue law states. The directional movements in these statistics arguably reflect a worsening

Table 5–12
Death Rates per 100,000 Population — 1979

State	Blue Law States Accidents	Suicides
Louisiana	60.5	12.5
Maryland	37.5	10.8
Mississippi	68.8	9.7
Missouri	50.1	11.5
New York	32.2	9.4
North Dakota	47.3	11.6
Oklahoma	59.9	13.8
Rhode Island	35.5	12.3
Texas	56.1	12.2
West Virginia	57.7	12.9
Average	50.56	12.3

State	Non-Blue Law States Accidents	Suicides
Arkansas	48.7	15.6
California	54.1	11.4
Connecticut	35.5	8.6
Idaho	68.5	13.7
Illinois	41.5	9.3
Oregon	56.3	13.9
Pennsylvania	40.7	11.4
Tennessee	54.5	13.7
Vermont	54.2	17.8
Washington	51.5	14.2
Average	50.55	12.96

overall quality of life in blue law states relative to non-blue law states, although the magnitudes do not argue strongly for such an interpretation.

One final statistic sheds meaningful, if indirect, light on the issue of quality of life. The *Statistical Abstract of the United States — 1982–83* (p. 13) provides data with respect to total net migration into a state over the period 1970–1980. During that decade, total net migration into the ten blue law states was 938,000, which, as a percent of the 1970 population, constitutes a rate of net inmigration equal to 1.9 percent. Total net inmigration for non-blue law states over that same period was 2,991,000, which represents a rate of 5.1 percent. To the extent that this type of statistic can be taken as a mea-

Table 5–13
Marriage Rates per 1,000 Population in the United States, 1970–79

State	Blue Law States 1970	1979	% change
Louisiana	9.7	10.3	6.2
Maryland	13.3	11.1	– 16.5
Mississippi	11.9	11.2	– 5.9
Missouri	10.7	10.9	1.2
New York	8.9	8.1	– 9.0
North Dakota	8.6	9.2	7.0
Oklahoma	15.2	15.4	1.3
Rhode Island	7.9	7.9	0.0
Texas	12.5	12.9	3.2
West Virginia	9.1	9.4	3.3
Average	10.78	10.64	– 1.3

State	Non-Blue Law States 1970	1979	% change
Arkansas	12.1	11.9	– 1.7
California	8.6	8.8	2.3
Connecticut	8.2	8.2	0.0
Idaho	15.3	14.8	– 3.3
Illinois	10.4	9.7	– 6.7
Oregon	8.3	8.7	4.8
Pennsylvania	8.0	8.0	0.0
Tennessee	11.6	13.5	16.4
Vermont	10.2	10.5	2.9
Washington	12.1	12.0	– 0.8
Average	10.48	10.61	1.2

Source: *Statistical Abstract of the United States—1982–83*, p. 83.

sure of revealed preference of the population, this suggests that people prefer to live in states with no restrictions of commercial activity rather than in states that do regulate Sunday activity.

Hours of Work, Labor Force Participation, and Unemployment

One of the stated concerns of proponents of Sunday-closing laws is that workers would be forced by employers to provide involuntary labor services

Table 5–14
Divorces and Annulments per 1,000 Population in the United States, 1970–79

State	Blue Law States 1970	1979	% change
Louisiana	1.4	3.7	164.29
Maryland	2.4	4.1	95.24
Mississippi	3.7	5.6	51.35
Missouri	3.8	5.7	50.00
New York	1.4	3.7	164.29
North Dakota	1.6	3.2	100.00
Oklahoma	6.6	7.9	19.70
Rhode Island	1.8	3.9	116.67
Texas	4.6	6.9	50.00
West Virginia	3.2	5.3	65.63
Average	3.05	5.00	63.93

State	Non-Blue Law States 1970	1979	† change
Arkansas	4.8	9.3	93.75
California	5.7	6.1	7.02
Connecticut	1.9	4.5	136.84
Idaho	5.1	7.1	39.22
Illinois	3.3	4.6	39.39
Oregon	4.6	7.0	52.17
Pennsylvania	1.9	3.4	78.95
Tennessee	4.1	6.8	65.85
Vermont	2.3	4.6	100.00
Washington	5.2	6.9	32.69
Average	3.89	6.03	55.01

Source: *Statistical Abstract of the United States—1982–83*, p. 84.

on Sundays if such laws were repealed. This claim is based, to our knowledge, upon no solid evidence that workers are forced to work on Sundays (or any other days) in states that do not have blue laws. Indeed, we find such an argument to be highly implausible.

The exploitation of labor argument runs essentially as follows. Repeal of Sunday-closing legislation permits sellers to open and compete on Sundays, just as they do every other day of the week. If any proprietors decide to sell, competitive pressure will force other producers to open as well—if they do not open they risk losing some portion of their business to the sellers who do take advantage of this opportunity. The sellers who open voluntarily on Sundays in the search for greater profits obviously are better off from the changed legal environment. Proprietors who would rather not open on Sundays but feel they must do so to remain competitive are worse off. Those employers that do open must have labor to operate; employers will force their employees to work on Sundays whether or not they want to, or else they will get rid of uncooperative employees and hire laborers who are willing to work on Sundays.

The crux of this issue is whether employers who open on Saturdays and Sundays hire full-time or part-time employees to meet their labor requirements. There are a number of possibilities: (1) hire full-time employees only and stagger their work schedules to provide coverage during all days the establishment is open for business (each employee works only forty hours per week), (2) hire full-time employees to work the regular Monday through Friday work week and hire part-time personnel to work on the weekends, or (3) hire full-time employees to work the regular work week and induce them to work additional hours on Saturdays and Sundays. To the extent employers respond to their labor needs through scenarios (1) and (2), the end result is increased overall employment; current employees are not made worse off in any respect. The question is, how do employers "induce" employees to work overtime hours—via threat or reward? Surely the latter answer is the correct one. First of all, no individual can be forced to work when he or she does not want to—the individual always has the option of finding alternative employment under more favorable working conditions. This fact forms the basis for wage differentials for late-hour shift work, for weekend or holiday work, and for risky or otherwise undesirable occupations. Second, federal law prohibits wage employees from working more than forty hours per week unless they receive special compensation from their employer. The bottom line is that an employer must offer positive inducements to persuade workers to accept weekend assignments.

Whether an employer pays his existing workforce overtime wages to provide weekend labor or hires additional employees, Sunday hiring must lead to increased per capita income, *ceteris paribus*. That is, of course, exactly what we found in the income statistics presented in table 5–7—per capita income is higher in non-blue law states than in blue law states. Additional investigation with respect to hours worked per week, labor force participation, and unemployment rates indicates that, in fact, employers tend to respond to an increased need for labor by hiring additional workers, not by attempting to induce or force their current employees to work additional, undesirable weekend hours. We turn first (in table 5–15) to the data with respect to hours worked per week.

If employers are exploiting their laborers in unregulated states by forcing

Table 5–15
Hours Worked per Week

State	Blue Law States				
	1972	1975	1979	1980	1981
Louisiana	NA	42.8	41.3	41.2	42.2
Maryland	40.2	39.1	40.0	39.6	39.9
Mississippi	41.1	39.3	39.6	39.3	39.3
Missouri	39.8	39.0	39.5	39.2	40.3
New York	39.6	38.9	39.6	39.4	39.4
North Dakota	40.2	39.9	39.1	37.5	38.1
Oklahoma	40.5	40.0	40.5	40.1	40.1
Rhode Island	39.5	38.9	39.1	39.3	39.3
Texas	NA	NA	41.1	41.2	41.3
West Virginia	40.0	39.0	39.6	39.2	39.4
Average	40.11	39.66	39.94	39.60	39.93
State	Non-Blue Law States				
	1972	1975	1979	1980	1981
Arkansas	40.2	38.8	39.6	39.3	39.4
California	40.1	39.4	39.9	39.5	39.6
Connecticut	41.5	40.5	42.0	41.8	41.6
Idaho	39.4	38.8	38.3	37.1	37.8
Illinois	41.0	39.7	40.7	39.8	40.0
Oregon	39.4	38.4	38.5	38.1	37.7
Pennsylvania	49.8	38.8	39.9	38.8	39.2
Tennessee	40.6	39.8	39.7	39.7	39.9
Vermont	41.5	40.4	40.8	40.6	40.0
Washington	39.6	38.7	38.6	38.5	38.8
Average	40.31	39.33	39.80	39.32	39.40

Source: *Statistical Abstract of the United States—1982–83,* 103rd edition, table 668, "Production Workers, Manufacturing Industries—Hours and Gross Earnings," p. 402.

them to work on weekends, as opponents of repeal fear will happen, average hours worked per week in non-blue law states should exceed those worked in blue law states. The statistics show just the opposite—throughout the 1970s and into the early 1980s the average number of hours worked per week by an employee in blue law states actually exceeded slightly the average number of hours worked by an employee in non-blue law states.

Turning to the labor force participation rate (table 5–16), it is immediately evident that the unrestricted commercial environment prevailing in non-

Table 5–16
Labor Force Participation and Unemployment Rates

State	Blue Law States Participation Rate (1981)		Unemployment Rate (1980)
	Male	*Female*	
Louisiana	76.3	47.4	6.7
Maryland	80.2	56.6	6.5
Mississippi	72.4	47.6	17.5
Missouri	75.2	51.9	7.2
New York	73.3	48.2	7.5
North Dakota	79.0	53.1	5.0
Oklahoma	78.4	50.0	4.8
Rhode Island	78.7	54.1	7.2
Texas	81.0	53.9	5.2
West Virginia	69.7	39.9	9.4
Average	76.42	50.27	7.70

State	Non-Blue Law States Participation Rate (1981)		Unemployment Rate (1980)
	Male	*Female*	
Arkansas	72.9	51.0	7.6
California	77.5	54.3	6.8
Connecticut	79.2	55.1	5.9
Idaho	78.4	50.6	7.9
Illinois	79.6	53.2	8.3
Oregon	79.0	55.3	8.3
Pennsylvania	74.7	47.5	7.8
Tennessee	74.1	50.4	7.3
Vermont	80.1	56.1	6.4
Washington	76.7	52.0	7.9
Average	77.22	52.55	7.42

Source: *Statistical Abstract of the United States—1982–83*, 103rd edition, pp. 378 and 393.

blue law states results in a higher labor force participation rate than occurs in blue law states. The higher rates are observed for males and females. The greater difference between women, suggests that women comprise the majority of part-time employees. The opportunity to work on Sundays apparently induces members of both sexes, but especially women, to voluntarily join the labor force.

Table 5–16 also includes a column that lists the rate of unemployment in each state in 1980. The average rate of unemployment in blue law states was slightly higher than was the average unemployment rate across non-blue law states, although if Mississippi is excluded as an unusual outlier, rates across both groups of states are almost identical. Thus, the unrestricted commercial activity on Sundays in non-blue law states stimulates a higher labor force participation rate, at a constant unemployment rate, compared to states that restrict business activity on Sundays. The higher labor force participation rate results in greater earnings per capita among the population of non-blue law states, which is reflected not only in per capita state income statistics, but also in a lower percentage of the population classified as living below the officially defined poverty line.

Two additional points deserve mention at this juncture. First, the exploitation-of-labor argument favored by opponents of blue law repeal is based on the notion that shop owners will feel compelled to open on Sunday, if any of their competitors avail themselves of the opportunity to open their doors for business. There is no law that requires firms to engage in commercial activity on any day, least of all Sunday, so any such compulsion is not mandated by the state. The question of whether competitive pressures force a firm to open on Sunday, even when the owner might not want to, is disputable. Elimination of restrictions on commercial activity on Sundays does not necessarily imply a redistribution of business from those stores closed on Sunday to those that open. Previously bottled up consumer demand may stimulate completely new sales on Sunday if restrictions are removed, generating greater commercial activity per se, than currently exists in states with Sunday-closing laws. Restaurants serve as a classic example. Certain individuals would dine out on Sundays, regardless of how many other times that week they might have eaten out, if restaurants were permitted to open, or permitted to open during more convenient hours. Moreover, individuals who shop very often frequent restaurants in the course of their excursion—this segment of business is lost by restaurants that may be permitted to open on Sundays when other stores are not so permitted.

Second, the issue of whether repeal of blue laws must inevitably result in employers forcing their employees to work undesirable days is very simply overcome by mandating that such conditions of employment are illegal. In fact, such complementary legislation is normally introduced into state legislatures by individuals seeking repeal of blue laws simultaneously with the repeal legislation.

Available data permit us to shed revealing light on the question of what happens to economic activity when a state repeals its Sunday-closing legislation. Since there is no basis for predicting that the total amount of commercial activity would decline when the opportunity to engage in trade is expanded to include Sundays, two realistic possibilities suggest themselves.

First, the amount of commercial activity that occurs in a state is constant, irrespective of the number of days per week sales are permitted. If true, this suggests that repeal of blue laws would simply redistribute individuals' shopping behavior in favor of Sundays to the detriment of sales on other days of the week. Small shopowners would be correct in their premise that competitive pressures would, in some sense, force them to open, since not doing so would cost them some portion of their business.

The second possibility is that the total amount of economic activity one engages in per week is a positive function of the number of legitimite days for selling. If the total size of the retail sales "pie" increases when Sunday sales are permitted, it is highly likely that all businessmen, both large and small, can benefit from repeal of blue laws.

Table 5–17 reports several categories of information that are pertinent to this question, including average annual retail sales per establishment, average annual retail sales per capita, and per capita income.

Businessmen experience 10.1 percent greater sales per outlet in states with no commercial restrictions on Sundays than do those living in blue law states. Even when these sales are standardized to a per capita basis, non-blue law states experience 8.1 percent greater retail sales than blue law states. To a certain extent this differential-spending pattern merely reflects the fact that average per capita annual income of individuals living in non-blue law states exceeds the average per capita annual income of individuals living in blue law states, as the income figures testify. Subtracting out this income differential, however, there remains the inescapable fact that per-person spending, as a percent of annual income, is over a full percentage point higher in states that do not restrict commercial activity on Sundays (49.4 percent vs. 48.2 percent). It appears, then, that opening Sundays to commercial activity has the net effect of increasing the total amount of economic activity, not just simply redistributing six days worth of sales across seven.

This increased economic activity is clearly going to benefit certain businessmen, specifically, the ones who decide to open their shops on Sundays. The question is whether the ones who decide to remain closed will actually be hurt. Small businessmen, in particular, have a big interest in the answer to this question, because there seems to be a widespread belief that failure to open would spell economic ruin for small proprietors. In contrast to the larger shops and chain stores, the typical small businessman relies much more heavily upon his or her own labor to cater to customers. The owner of a large department store can easily hire someone to run the store on Sundays whereas a small shop owner may not be able, for financial reasons, to hire outside labor to work on Sundays and thus is faced with the prospect of toiling seven days per week.

To some extent these hardships are part and parcel of the initial decision to start, buy into, or otherwise maintain a relatively small business enter-

Table 5–17
Retail Sales per Capita and Income per Capita—1977

State	Blue Law States Average Annual Sales Per Outlet	Average Annual Sales Per Capita	Income Per Capita
Louisiana	$387,440	$3,092	$5,913
Maryland	$507,240	$3,427	$7,572
Mississippi	$288,060	$2,514	$5,030
Missouri	$368,360	$3,286	$6,654
New York	$356,520	$2,840	$7,537
North Dakota	$336,740	$3,466	$6,190
Oklahoma	$328,180	$3,220	$6,346
Rhode Island	$344,330	$2,934	$6,775
Texas	$379,920	$3,473	$6,803
West Virginia	$380,640	$2,979	$5,986
Average	$371,010	$3,123	$6,481

State	Non-Blue Law States Average Annual Sales Per Outlet	Average Annual Sales Per Capita	Income Per Capita
Arkansas	$293,090	$2,892	$5,540
California	$431,380	$3,627	$7,911
Connecticut	$394,190	$3,376	$8,061
Idaho	$340,990	$3,414	$5,980
Illinois	$461,420	$3,438	$7,768
Oregon	$410,220	$3,832	$7,007
Pennsylvania	$377,270	$3,135	$7,011
Tennessee	$355,820	$3,114	$5,785
Vermont	$290,730	$3,388	$5,823
Washington	$423,670	$3,580	$7,528
Average	$408,580	$3,380	$6,841

Source: Compiled from U.S. Dept. of Commerce, Bureau of the Census, *County and City Data Book 1983,* table A, p. 13, and *Statistical Abstract of the United States 1978,* 99th edition, table No. 725, p. 449.

prise. But before we pity the small proprietor, let us examine what happens to him if he chooses to remain closed on Sundays.

The decomposed effects of increased overall retail trade in states that do not restrict Sunday sales range as follows:

1. All proprietors who open for business could experience a proportionate increase in sales.
2. Small shops could experience a more-than-proportionate share of the increased sales than large firms.
3. Small shops could experience a less-than-proportionate share of the increased sales.
4. Or, as feared by certain small businessmen, large chain stores could attract so much additional business on Sundays that gross sales receipts of small proprietors could actually drop, even if they opened seven days per week.

It is apparently true that large department stores attract a considerable amount of sales when they are permitted to open on Sundays. Total annual sales are nearly 17 percent higher for stores selling on Sundays than stores owned by the same chain operated in states with Sunday-closing laws. Moreover, Sunday is second only to Saturday in terms of total sales generated per day of the week. So the opportunity to sell on Sundays is clearly beneficial to large stores. Do they take business away from smaller firms? The answer is apparently not.

Table 5.18 reports on the number and size distribution of small firms in blue law states versus non-blue law states. The specific numbers are categorized according to the two alternative Small Business Administration (SBA) definitions of a small business: (1) those establishments employing less than 100 workers, and (2) those establishments employing less than 500 workers. Relative to these definitions of what constitutes a small business, the data indicate that there is virtually no difference in the number of small shops supported by a given population in one type of state versus the other. This suggests that, at the worst, repeal of blue laws would not prove harmful to small businessmen but would definitely be beneficial to large outlets.

Two alternative classifications of small businesses, recognized by the SBA, may be so broad as to obscure relevant information about more sharply defined size classes of firms. As the ensuing discussion reveals, although there are no appreciable differences between the number of small businesses per capita under either SBA size class, noticeable differences become apparent when firm size is disaggregated more finely.

Size of Business Establishment

In the state of Maryland, as well as in several other states, Sunday-closing legislation takes the form of restriction with respect to the size of a firm, as mea-

Table 5–18
Small and Large Firms per 1,000 Population—1979

| | Blue Law States | | | |
State	Less than 100 Employees	More than 100 Employees	Less than 500 Employees	More than 500 Employees
Louisiana	16.96	.35	17.28	.04
Maryland	15.96	.34	16.26	.04
Mississippi	16.15	.31	16.43	.04
Missouri	19.39	.42	19.76	.06
New York	19.70	.39	20.03	.06
North Dakota	23.19	.22	23.40	.01
Oklahoma	20.13	.32	20.41	.04
Rhode Island	20.81	.44	21.18	.06
Texas	19.59	.39	19.93	.05
West Virginia	16.11	.33	16.40	.05
Average	18.94	.38	19.26	.05

| | Non-Blue Law States | | | |
State	Less than 100 Employees	More than 100 Employees	Less than 500 Employees	More than 500 Employees
Arkansas	18.20	.32	18.49	.03
California	19.41	.37	19.73	.04
Connecticut	19.66	.44	20.03	.07
Idaho	21.35	.24	21.55	.04
Illinois	17.77	.47	18.17	.07
Oregon	21.95	.44	22.34	.03
Pennsylvania	17.24	.45	17.62	.07
Tennessee	17.44	.42	17.80	.06
Vermont	24.00	.35	24.32	.04
Washington	20.40	.35	20.71	.04
Average	18.75	.40	19.10	.05

Source: Compiled from National Federation of Independent Business *Fact Book on Small Business 1979*.

sured by number of employees. For example, in Balitmore County, Maryland, which comprises several suburbs to the west of the city, it is illegal for establishments with more than six employees and two guards to operate on Sundays, except for the four Sundays prior to Christmas. Not infrequently, it is the owners of the small shops in competition with the larger establishments, who turn in the larger establishments that violate the blue laws. The history of conflict between small businessmen and owners of large establishments over blue law repeal is apparent to anyone who has observed the public policy debates that have raged annually in Baltimore County (which still has its blue laws) and in Houston, Texas, which voted to repeal its blue laws in 1985. The redistributive consequences of repeal of Sunday-closing laws are potentially severe. Current law effectively protects small firms from the competition of larger, more efficient firms, at least on Sundays, which are prime shopping days for potential customers. Survival of many small firms may hinge on such legislation. It is not surprising, then, that small businesses tend to support blue laws while large chain operations actively lobby to repeal such legislation.

Abstracting away from all of the other nominal arguments in support of blue laws, and the efficiency aspects one way or the other, there is a positive question of ultimate justification for blue laws that remains to be addressed. Do blue laws constitute a de facto subsidy to small, less efficient producers of goods and services, a subsidy paid by consumers through implicitly higher prices of those commodities? If so, this should not be a surprise, given the history of strong popular sentiment toward small businesses in America and the degree of redistributive activity currently under way in the U.S. economy.

There is strong evidence in support of this redistributive theory of Sunday-closing laws. Tables 5–19 and 5–20 report various measures of firm size and the number of establishments per 100,000 population in 1972 and 1977, respectively.

The data reported were obtained from the *Census of Manufactures* for 1972 and 1977. Across the categories of firm size, number of employees per establishment, and value-added per establishment, the data demonstrate that firms are larger, on average, in non-blue law states than they are in blue law states. In both years, the difference in mean number of employees per establishment was roughly 26 percent, while the difference in value-added per establishment was nearly 20 percent. This suggests that the competitive pressures that serve to guarantee efficient economic production in an unregulated commercial environment favor survival of larger firms. Smaller firms can react to this unfavorable economic climate in one of two ways; they can take whatever economic steps are required to insure competitive survival (e.g., increased efficiency in production through internal growth or growth by merger, development of consumer loyalty through service, other types of product differentiation or advertising, or development of untapped customer markets), or they can attempt to eliminate or minimize the degree of competition from larger enterprises by political means. The economic response adapts small business to a changing environment; the political response alters the environment within which small businesses operate.

It is clear that Sunday-closing laws, whether intentionally designed to do so or not, protect small businessmen from their more efficient, larger competitors. That protection enables a larger-than-normal number of small busi-

Table 5–19
Firm Size and Number per 100,000 Population—1972

State	Blue Law States Employees per Establishment	Value-Added per Establishment	Establishments per 100,000 Population
Louisiana	48.95	1,168,444	92.21
Maryland	71.53	1,315,172	87.70
Mississippi	73.34	1,035,937	118.21
Missouri	64.47	1,213,458	141.64
New York	43.79	792,989	208.92
North Dakota	20.75	417,012	76.39
Oklahoma	47.01	746,220	114.49
Rhode Island	42.82	640,058	282.37
Texas	51.03	1,057,890	122.66
West Virginia	69.78	1,526,528	96.49
Average	50.03	936,043	155.31

State	Non-Blue Law States Employees per Establishment	Value-Added per Establishment	Establishments per 100,000 Population
Arkansas	62.48	966,517	143.56
California	43.31	873,834	173.42
Connecticut	68.37	1,169,979	190.10
Idaho	36.13	689,916	155.96
Illinois	70.15	1,388,388	165.38
Oregon	38.33	747,323	212.76
Pennsylvania	77.07	1,278,346	154.54
Tennessee	82.70	1,356,827	138.14
Vermont	43.02	699,767	185.75
Washington	42.28	883,255	155.06
Average	64.39	1,166,782	165.48

Source: *Statistical Abstract of the United States—1982–83*, pp. 770–71.

nesses to survive, when they would not be able to in an unrestricted commercial environment. The overall inefficiency of this arrangement, from an economic perspective, is reflected not only in the statistics regarding firm size in blue law versus non-blue law states, but also in the figures on number of firms per 100,000 population. In the unregulated environment of non-blue law states, the number of firms per 100,000 population is roughly 10 percent

Table 5–20
Firm Size and Number per 100,000 Population — 1977

State	Blue Law States		
	Employees per Establishment	Value-Added per Establishment	Establishments per 100,000 Population
Louisiana	45.60	2,202,526	106.47
Maryland	61.98	1,807,468	93.85
Mississippi	66.59	1,708,422	133.70
Missouri	58.88	1,773,457	151.79
New York	41.28	1,210,837	204.90
North Dakota	24.52	828,371	87.98
Oklahoma	42.95	1,221,058	133.22
Rhode Island	40.23	880,914	325.34
Texas	48.80	1,825,742	137.26
West Virginia	63.00	2,089,392	97.43
Average	47.13	1,500,555	156.59

State	Non-Blue Law States		
	Employees per Establishment	Value-Added per Establishment	Establishments per 100,000 Population
Arkansas	54.80	1,357,997	162.89
California	38.68	1,211,376	202.63
Connecticut	63.53	1,686,045	209.94
Idaho	34.78	956,522	169.31
Illinois	65.89	2,063,791	171.11
Oregon	35.34	1,073,828	151.54
Pennsylvania	70.94	1,922,445	157.68
Tennessee	75.54	1,952,058	147.36
Vermont	40.78	1,019,418	209.35
Washington	39.42	1,331,995	178.23
Average	58.73	1,720,240	174.15

Source: *Statistical Abstract of the United States — 1982–83*, pp. 770–71.

higher than the number of firms per 100,000 population in the regulated environment of blue law states. The regulation deters competition by hindering the ability of larger firms to operate in a profit maximizing fashion. This lowers expected profitability of larger businesses and, predictably, a relatively larger percentage of large businesses choose to operate in non-blue law states than choose to operate in blue-law states.

The detailed statistics on firm size in 1976 that are presented in tables 5–21 to 5–26 confirm the differential size distribution of firms between states with legal restrictions on Sunday selling and those without such restrictions. These data, available in the National Federation of Independent Business' *Fact Book on Small Business* (February 1979), report the total number of business establishments per state, as well as the number of businesses by size of firm, from which it was possible to calculate the percentages falling into each category. The data reported in the tables focus on retail establishments, service outlets, and total establishments. Across all three classifications, the numbers tell the same story: the size distribution of firms is skewed in favor of small firms in the sample of blue law states relative to the non-blue law states. A larger percentage of all firms falls into the one-to-four employees category in the former states than in the latter, with a very large difference noted among retail establishments.

These findings with respect to the number of business establishments per 100,000 population and the size distribution of firms square nicely with the findings of Moorehouse [1984], who found that (1) controlling for population density, income and other variables, there are fewer firms located in SMSA's (Standard Metropolitan Statistical Areas) covered by blue laws than operate in unregulated SMSA's, and (2) the size distribution of firms is skewed in favor of small firms operating in SMSA's located in states affected by Sunday-closing regulations as compared to firms operating in SMSA's in which economic activity was unrestricted, controlling for a number of factors.

The interpretation is basically indisputable — Sunday-closing laws constitute a political weapon with which small businesses circumvent the competitive pressures that might otherwise reduce their numbers. Production by smaller firms is clearly inefficient — competitive pressures result in larger firms, on average, in an unrestricted commercial environment than exist in the restricted environment.[3] From a distributive point of view it is useful to make two observations. First, there may be sociopsychological and political reasons that favor such a redistributive policy with respect to small businessmen. Society may place a positive value on having many small firms relative to large ones, irrespective of the implied efficiency, or inefficiency, in production. It is questionable whether such a value would be reflected by the patronage of each class of enterprise, because, in the "decision calculus" of private individuals, there is an incentive to "free ride" on the socially valued good that is provided. There is some reason to believe, then, that public subsidization of small businesses via blue laws may actually represent a coherent public policy. Second, if there is no societal value placed on the size distribution of firms in the economy, then blue laws merely reflect the proclivity, and ability, of small businesses to find the least-cost means to remain competitive with more efficient producers than themselves. Who can blame them for

Table 5-21
Number of Establishments by Employment Size—1976

Blue Law States

State	Total Outlets	1–4	5–9	10–19	20–49	50–99	100–499	500+
Louisiana	68,431	38,578	13,046	8,142	5,577	1,695	1,236	157
Maryland	68,011	36,249	13,885	8,723	5,888	1,848	1,240	178
Mississippi	40,009	24,245	7,407	4,274	2,525	803	662	93
Missouri	95,570	55,761	17,380	10,923	7,059	2,426	1,751	270
New York	361,198	222,227	61,299	37,272	25,016	8,311	5,981	1,092
North Dakota	15,101	9,301	2,767	1,647	972	269	137	8
Oklahoma	57,715	34,878	10,291	6,368	4,045	1,243	791	99
Rhode Island	20,182	12,206	3,501	2,131	1,401	527	355	61
Texas	257,710	150,057	46,821	29,487	19,712	6,650	4,380	603
West Virginia	30,872	18,368	5,570	3,441	2,178	687	539	89
Total	1,014,799	601,870	181,967	112,408	74,373	24,459	17,072	2,650

Non-Blue Law States

State	Total Outlets	1–4	5–9	10–19	20–49	50–99	100–499	500+
Arkansas	40,170	24,437	7,254	4,358	2,609	815	623	74
California	433,806	252,551	79,144	48,957	33,563	11,583	7,052	956
Connecticut	62,016	37,368	10,989	6,449	4,290	1,569	1,141	210
Idaho	18,502	11,067	3,573	2,045	1,260	348	179	30
Illinois	207,233	115,738	37,897	24,960	17,074	6,222	4,529	813
Oregon	53,118	31,581	9,749	5,990	3,778	1,146	972	82
Pennsylvania	210,237	120,122	38,952	23,988	16,130	5,751	4,474	820
Tennessee	77,328	44,483	14,439	8,860	5,804	1,903	1,572	267
Vermont	11,813	7,654	1,973	1,136	667	212	152	19
Washington	76,571	46,181	14,125	8,155	5,375	1,656	1,136	140
Total	1,190,794	691,182	218,095	134,898	90,550	31,205	21,650	3,411

Table 5–22
Percent of Establishments by Employment Size—1976

State	Total Outlets	1–4	5–9	10–19	20–49	50–99	100–499	500 +
			Blue Law States					
Louisiana	68,431	56.4	19.1	11.9	8.1	2.5	1.8	0.2
Maryland	68,011	53.3	20.4	12.8	8.7	2.7	1.8	0.3
Mississippi	40,009	60.6	18.5	10.7	6.3	2.0	1.7	0.2
Missouri	95,570	58.3	18.2	11.4	7.4	2.5	1.8	0.3
New York	361,198	61.5	17.0	10.3	6.9	2.3	1.7	0.3
North Dakota	15,101	61.6	18.3	10.9	6.4	1.8	0.9	0.1
Oklahoma	57,715	60.4	17.8	11.0	7.0	2.2	1.4	0.2
Rhode Island	20,182	60.5	17.3	10.6	6.9	2.6	1.8	0.3
Texas	257,710	58.2	18.2	11.4	7.6	2.6	1.7	0.2
West Virginia	30,872	59.5	18.0	11.1	7.1	2.2	1.7	0.3
Total	1,014,799	59.3	17.9	11.1	7.3	2.4	1.7	0.3
			Non-Blue Law States					
Arkansas	49,170	60.8	18.1	10.8	6.5	2.0	1.6	0.2
California	433,806	58.2	18.2	11.3	7.7	2.7	1.6	0.2
Connecticut	37,368	60.3	17.7	6.9	2.5	1.8	0.3	
Idaho	18,502	59.8	19.3	11.1	6.8	1.9	1.0	0.2
Illinois	207,233	55.8	18.3	12.0	8.2	3.0	2.2	0.4
Oregon	53,118	59.5	18.4	11.3	7.1	2.2	1.5	0.2
Pennsylvania	210,237	57.1	18.5	11.4	7.7	2.7	2.1	0.4
Tennessee	77,328	57.5	18.7	11.5	7.5	2.5	2.0	0.3
Vermont	11,813	64.8	16.7	9.6	5.6	1.8	1.3	0.2
Washington	76,571	60.3	18.4	10.7	7.6	2.2	1.5	0.2
Total	1,190,794	58.0	18.3	11.3	7.6	2.6	1.8	0.3

Table 5-23
Number of Retail Establishments by Employment Size—1976

Blue Law States

State	Total Outlets	1-4	5-9	10-19	20-49	50-99	100-499	500+
Louisiana	20,422	11,283	4,323	2,560	1,683	389	174	10
Maryland	19,803	8,951	4,967	2,931	2,073	612	249	20
Mississippi	13,622	8,402	2,769	1,491	733	124	62	1
Missouri	28,872	16,201	6,064	3,638	2,148	575	224	22
New York	96,584	58,966	18,749	10,072	6,368	1,607	743	79
North Dakota	4,745	2,673	1,013	618	343	73	25	0
Oklahoma	17,939	10,327	3,602	2,256	1,357	274	119	4
Rhode Island	5,590	3,266	1,120	647	396	122	35	4
Texas	77,901	42,896	16,722	10,077	5,896	1,559	705	46
West Virginia	9,429	5,271	2,013	1,207	696	182	57	3
Total	294,907	168,236	61,342	35,497	21,733	5,517	2,393	189

Non-Blue Law States

State	Total Outlets	1-4	5-9	10-19	20-49	50-99	100-499	500+
Arkansas	13,506	8,229	2,771	1,512	812	136	44	2
California	119,486	62,736	27,241	14,805	10,432	3,131	1,054	87
Connecticut	17,837	10,073	3,660	2,052	1,480	420	145	7
Idaho	5,433	2,903	1,272	744	403	89	22	0
Illinois	57,810	29,479	12,636	8,133	5,234	1,619	653	56
Oregon	14,326	7,558	3,224	1,925	1,230	280	103	6
Pennsylvania	62,758	34,191	13,869	17,930	4,904	1,265	548	51
Tennessee	24,204	13,876	5,079	2,902	1,691	466	179	11
Vermont	3,603	2,169	742	409	235	37	11	0
Washington	20,708	11,268	4,461	2,596	1,840	403	129	11
Total	339,671	182,482	74,955	43,008	28,261	7,846	2,888	231

Table 5-24
Percent of Retail Establishments by Employment Size—1976

| | Blue Law States | | | | | | | |
State	Total Outlets	1–4	5–9	10–19	20–49	50–99	100–499	500+
Louisiana	20,422	55.2	21.2	12.5	8.2	1.9	0.9	0.0
Maryland	19,803	45.2	25.1	14.8	10.5	3.1	1.3	0.1
Mississippi	13,622	61.7	20.3	10.9	5.7	0.9	0.5	0.0
Missouri	28,872	56.1	21.0	12.6	7.4	2.0	0.8	0.1
New York	96,584	61.1	1.4	10.4	6.6	1.7	0.8	0.1
North Dakota	4,745	56.3	21.3	13.0	7.2	1.5	0.5	0.0
Oklahoma	17,939	57.6	20.1	12.6	7.6	1.5	0.7	0.0
Rhode Island	5,590	58.4	20.0	11.6	7.1	2.2	0.6	0.1
Texas	77,901	55.1	21.5	12.9	7.6	2.0	0.9	0.1
West Virginia	9,429	55.9	21.3	12.8	7.4	1.9	0.6	0.0
Total	294,907	57.0	20.1	12.0	7.4	1.9	0.8	0.1

| | Non-Blue Law States | | | | | | | |
State	Total Outlets	1–4	5–9	10–19	20–49	50–99	100–499	500+
Arkansas	13,506	60.9	20.5	11.2	6.0	1.0	0.3	0.0
California	119,486	52.5	22.8	12.4	8.7	2.6	0.9	0.1
Connecticut	17,837	56.5	20.5	11.5	8.3	2.4	0.8	0.0
Idaho	5,433	53.4	23.4	13.7	7.4	1.6	0.4	0.0
Illinois	57,810	51.0	21.9	14.1	9.1	2.8	1.1	0.1
Oregon	14,326	52.8	22.5	13.4	8.6	2.0	0.7	0.0
Pennsylvania	62,758	54.5	22.1	12.6	7.8	2.0	0.9	0.1
Tennessee	24,204	57.3	21.0	12.0	7.0	1.9	0.7	0.0
Vermont	3,603	60.2	20.6	11.4	6.5	1.0	0.3	0.0
Washington	20,708	54.4	21.5	12.5	8.9	1.9	0.6	0.1
Total	339,671	53.7	22.1	12.7	8.3	2.3	0.9	0.1

Table 5–25
Number of Service Establishments by Employment Size—1976

Blue Law States

State	Total Outlets	1–4	5–9	10–19	20–49	50–99	100–499	500+
Louisiana	18,076	11,653	3,145	1,653	991	389	209	36
Maryland	20,513	12,900	3,621	2,041	1,206	209	294	46
Mississippi	9,761	6,645	1,646	443	159	85	6	
Missouri	25,967	17,036	4,395	2,243	1,376	495	359	63
New York	103,672	70,692	15,807	5,357	5,134	1,778	1,676	328
North Dakota	3,405	2,270	516	301	181	47	5	
Oklahoma	15,247	10,494	2,414	1,172	733	283	133	18
Rhode Island	5,565	3,965	811	241	88	65	13	
Texas	69,511	46,383	11,471	5,844	3,562	1,324	830	97
West Virginia	8,433	5,886	1,408	6289	330	88	77	15
Total	280,150	187,824	45,234	20,399	14,197	5,094	3,775	627

Non-Blue Law States

State	Total Outlets	1–4	5–9	10–19	20–49	50–99	100–499	500+
Arkansas	9,901	6,819	1,563	808	436	181	82	12
California	134,216	88,513	22,290	11,970	6,505	2,473	1,605	230
Connecticut	18,402	12,563	2,997	1,492 787	321	204	38	11
Idaho	4,618	3,179	825	353	165	56	29	
Illinois	57,204	36,005	10,109	5,586	3,267	1,242	826	169
Oregon	14,657	9,748	2,622	1,274	633	217	148	15
Pennsylvania	60,294	40,135	10,112	5,124	2,839	1,036	857	191
Tennessee	20,753	13,580	3,682	1,831	1,042	371	208	39
Vermont	3,390	2,402	499	246	74	54	6	
Washington	21,668	14,329	3,904	1,806	998	380	20	31
Total	345,103	227,273	59,233	30,490	16,781	6,351	4,033	842

Table 5-26
Percent of Service Establishments by Employment Size—1976

State	Total Outlets	1–4	5–9	10–19	20–49	50–99	100–499	500+
Blue Law States								
Louisiana	18,076	64.5	17.4	9.1	5.5	2.2	1.2	0.2
Maryland	20,513	62.9	17.7	9.9	5.9	2.0	1.4	0.2
Mississippi	9,761	68.1	16.9	8.0	4.5	1.6	0.9	0.1
Missouri	25,967	65.6	16.9	8.6	5.3	1.9	1.4	0.2
New York	103,672	68.1	15.2	5.2	5.0	1.7	1.6	0.3
North Dakota	3,405	66.7	15.2	8.8	5.3	2.5	1.4	0.1
Oklahoma	15,247	68.8	15.8	7.7	4.8	1.9	0.9	0.1
Rhode Island	5,565	71.2	14.6	6.7	4.3	1.6	1.2	0.2
Texas	69,511	66.7	16.5	8.4	5.1	1.9	1.2	0.1
West Virginia	30,872	59.5	18.0	11.1	7.1	2.2	1.7	0.3
Total	280,150	67.0	16.1	7.3	5.1	1.8	1.3	0.2
Non-Blue Law States								
Arkansas	9,901	68.8	15.8	8.2	4.4	1.8	0.8	0.1
California	134,216	65.9	17.2	8.8	4.9	1.8	1.2	0.2
Connecticut	18,402	68.3	16.3	8.1	4.3	1.7	1.1	0.2
Idaho	4,618	68.8	17.9	7.6	3.6	1.2	0.6	0.2
Illinois	57,204	62.9	17.7	9.8	5.7	2.2	1.4	0.3
Oregon	14,657	66.5	17.9	8.7	4.3	1.5	1.0	0.1
Pennsylvania	60,294	66.6	16.8	8.5	4.7	1.7	1.4	0.3
Tennessee	20,753	65.4	17.7	8.8	5.0	1.8	1.0	0.2
Vermont	3,390	70.9	14.7	7.3	3.2	2.2	1.6	0.2
Washington	21,668	66.1	18.0	8.3	4.6	1.8	0.1	0.1
Total	345,103	65.9	17.2	8.8	4.9	1.8	1.2	0.2

looking for that least-cost means in the political arena as opposed to the free-market arena?

Concluding Comments

The economic consequences of the subsidy implied by Sunday-closing legislation should be clear by now. The general level of economic activity in non-blue law states is higher than it is in blue law states. As a result, there is greater labor force participation and greater employment in states that do not regulate economic activity on Sundays, which is reflected in higher per capita income in those states. That higher income is due strictly to employment of larger numbers of people, and is not due to any exploitation of labor — average number of hours worked per week is actually slightly lower in non-blue law states than in blue law states. Finally, the unrestricted competition prevalent in non-blue law states gives rise to greater consumer choice of establishment to patronize.

Notes

1. The religious denominations examined in each state include: American Lutheran Church, Baptist General Conference, Brethren in Christ Church, Christian Church (Disciples of Christ), Christian Union, Church of God (Anderson, Indiana), Church of the Brethren, Church of the Nazarene, Conservative Congregational Christian Conference, Cumberland Presbyterian Church, Evangelical Church of North America, Evangelical Congregational Church, Evangelical Covenant Church of America, Evangelical Lutheran Synod, Evangelical Mennonite Brethren Conference, Lutheran Church in America, Lutheran Church (Missouri Synod), Mennonite Church, Moravian Church in America (Unitas Fratrum) North, Moravian Church in America (Unitas Fratrum) South, North American Baptist Conference, Presbyterian Church in the USA, Reformed Church in America, Seventh Day Adventists, Southern Baptist Convention, United Church of Christ, United Methodist Church, United Presbyterian Church (USA), Wisconsin Evangelical Lutheran Synod.

2. Real costs of purchasing an item include the nominal purchase price *plus* one's cost of opportunity-time spent, aggravation due to fighting the crowds or lack of sales staff, and so on. In this regard, Sunday-closing laws in the state of Maryland have actually increased local costs to consumers, because they restrict the number of employees that a store is legally allowed to have on active duty on Sundays to five or fewer.

The local Hechinger store, a lumber and hardware outlet, operates with a severely curtailed staff, and the variety of services they are able to offer on Sundays is minimal relative to the range of services offered on other days of the week. The added waiting time at the check-out register and the aggravation of not having a member of the staff available to assist in locating an item or with other problems adds to the price a shopper implicitly pays when shopping there on Sunday.

3. The notion that efficiency in production is reflected in the size of firms that survive over time was introduced by Stigler [1958].

6
Other English-Speaking Countries

On April 15, 1986, the House of Commons of the British Parliament voted 296–282 against repeal of Britain's decades-old Shops Act. The Shops Act, passed in 1950, is the British version of Sunday-closing legislation and is, impossible though it may be to contemplate, every bit as anachronistic and full of special-interest groups exemptions and contradictions as are the laws in the United States. In Australia weekend shopping is even more restricted than in either the United States or England, since shops are required to close at noon or 1:00 p.m. on Saturdays, not to re-open until Monday morning. Again, however, there are a myriad of anomalies, contradictions, and special exemptions from the law.

The purpose of this chapter is to trace the development of selling restrictions in England, Australia, and Canada, to identify special-interest groups in support of, and opposed, to such laws, and to review the arguments voiced by members of those respective groups. It will become apparent that the regulation of retail sales activity is strikingly similar from one English-speaking country to another.

England

History of the Shops Act

The Fairs and Markets Act of 1448 was the first prohibition of Sunday trading in England. Specifically, the Act forbade the showing of goods on Sunday and on various feast days. The Sunday Observance Act of 1627 forbade butchers to kill or sell meat on Sundays. A variety of additional restrictions on Sunday trading were mandated by the Sunday Observance Act of 1677. Ireland and Wales did not have Sabbath laws prior to their union with England in 1707; Scotland did establish a Sabbath law prior to that union. All of the early Acts applicable throughout the Commonwealth were repealed in 1969.

The Shops Act of 1912 was a consolidation of three previously enacted laws regulating employment in shops. The Shop Hours Regulation Act of 1886 provided that persons under eighteen years old should not work more than seventy-four hours a week. The Shop Hours Act of 1904 empowered local authorities to fix shop closing times, subject to the approval of two-thirds of the shops thereby affected. The 1911 Shops Act provided a half-day holiday per week for all employees and that shops must have at least one early closing day.

Certain restrictions on hours of operation were introduced during World War I and were codified formally by the Shops Act of 1928. This Act, known also as the Hours of Closing Act, set 8:00 p.m. as the closing time for shops, with provision for one day per week to have a 9:00 p.m. closing time. Numerous exceptions to this, as well as the 1911 Act, are noted. The Hairdressers and Barbers Act and the Retail Meat Dealers were passed in 1930 and 1936, respectively, principally on the strength of support by the trade associations for both industries. Both statutes mandate prohibitions on work by individuals employed in these trades. In 1936 the Shops (Sunday Trading Restrictions) Act was passed, applying only to England and Wales, which incorporated special provisions for Jews, street vendors, and seaside resorts.

The current Shops Act was passed in 1950, as a consolidation and clarification of previously enacted statutes. The five parts of the law address: (1) hours of closing, (2) conditions of employment, (3) exceptions, (4) Sunday opening, and (5) enforcement. There are seven schedules, all but one of which specify exemptions that are, or may be, granted from the general prohibition against Sunday sales or the prohibition against shops being open after 8:00 p.m., or 9:00 p.m. on one day. Anomalies in the law are rampant. The sale of pornographic magazines, for example, is legal on Sundays while the sale of Bibles is not; other items that may legally be sold on Sundays include postcards (but not birthday cards), whiskey (but not milk or baby food), Chinese carry-out food (but not fish and chips). In addition, as is the case in the United States, much claimed inequity results from disparities in the pattern of enforcement. Enforcement of the 1950 Shops Act is left up to local authorities assisted by Shops Inspectors. Many shops, including many small shops, open illegally on Sunday; certain local authorities press charges in an effort to enforce the law, others do nothing to enforce it. Illegal in name does not therefore imply illegal in fact, at least not with any degree of consistency. The implied inequity is obvious.

There have been many efforts to amend or repeal the 1950 Act, either in part or in whole. To date, however, only two minor changes have been permitted: the Shops Act of 1962 exempted airports from the restrictions on weekday opening hours, and the Shops Act of 1965 entitles the shopkeeper, as opposed to the local authority, to determine the shop's early closing day. Serious efforts to repeal the Shops Act entirely were mounted in 1982–1983 and 1985–1986; the 1982 attempt was turned down by the House of Commons after passage by the House of Lords; the 1985 attempt was killed in the Commons before any vote by the Lords.

Interested Parties and Arguments

A portion of the most recent debate in the Commons was exerpted in the *London Times* (April 15, 1986) and is highlighted in the following paragraphs. Virtually all of the statements and claims parallel those raised whenever the repeal issue is debated in America. As a preface to the discussion to follow, certain facts regarding the 1950 Act and the repeal bill are advisedly known in advance;

1. The 1950 Act, with its arbitrary enforcement and many contradictions, does not command respect or compliance.
2. There is no formal Sunday closing law in Scotland.
3. The repeal bill would not have required shops to open on Sundays; it would have repealed existing restrictions.
4. The repeal bill would have advanced protection for workers who refused to work late hours or on Sundays.
5. As determined by opinion polls taken in 1981, 1982, and 1983, the large majority of popular opinion (63, 69, and 73 percent, respectively) favored permitting shops to open when they choose, including late evenings and Sundays.

Exerpts from the debate:

Mr. Gerald Kaufman (Labor—chief opposition spokesman on home affairs): "This bill would enable shops to open for twenty-four hours a day seven days a week. Yet under it shop workers would have no immediate legal protection against disciplinary action or even dismissal if they refused to work late at night."

A job application from in Mr. Kaufman's possession asked applicants to sign the declaration: "I agree to work on bank holidays, Sundays and overtime as required." He went on to note that, in the considered view of the Association of Chief Police Officers, Sunday trading would increase crime.

Mr. Donald Stewart (leader of the Scottish National Party): "The government can have no pretense after this Bill about belief in Christian morality. The Bill goes directly against God's plan for living. The Fourth Commandment is an integral part of the law of God: the Sabbath Day should be kept holy."

Authors' note: we reiterate the fact that Scotland has no formal Sunday closing law. In a "do as I say, not as I do" sense, this casts serious doubt on the
power of the argument. Moreover, we question whether issues of economic
interest might really underlie his position. A certain percentage of Scotland's
Sunday sales are to Britishers who shop in Scotland because the 1950 Shops
Act prevents them from doing so in England. Repeal of the British law would
have an obvious, adverse effect on business activity in Scotland.

Sir Paul Bryan (Conservative): "The Archbishops' case is too much concerned with a fantasy of Sunday, Sunday as it used to be once upon a time
and long ago—and what they would like it to be. Long ago a lot of people
used to go to church. There was nothing else to do then. But revolution had
come from the motor car and the fact that a lot of people now own their own
homes. Now, people garden, watch television, engage in do-it-yourself, and
go shopping on Sundays for, among other things, do-it-yourself items. Yet
despite such activity Sunday remains a much quieter day than others. Will
the opening of a few shops on Sundays change that?"

Mr. Thomas Torney (Labor): "Shop workers have always been down-
trodden, poorly paid, and required to work long and unsocial hours. This
Bill should be renamed the Exploitation of Workers in Shops, Open All
Hours, Including Sundays, Bill. With nearly four million people unemployed
and with things like promotion prospects to be considered, shop owners can
quickly suppress any conscientious or religious objections by shop workers
to the notion of working on Sundays. Away will go premium payments,
overtime, and so on for those called upon to work Sundays."

Sir Peter Blaker (Conservative): He did not think that the Bill would destroy
the special character of Sunday. "It is not right to try to prevent the people of
England and Wales [from] following the life they want to by means of the
criminal law, especially when the law is in such disrepute."

Mr. David Young (Labor): "People will see this Bill as bowing to the pressure
of a few large, influential retailers to attack small distributors."

Sir Bernard Braine (Conservative): He said the Bill would lead to full-scale
business activity of Sundays. "It is a surrender to large retail concerns who
would weep no tears if all of our small traders were put out of business."

Viscount Cranborne (Conservative): He said he had a share in a number of
shops which already opened on Sundays. "All of us know in this debate that
the law is an ass. Since it is recognized as such, it brings the rest of the law
into disrepute."

Mr. Roy Hughes (Labor): He opposed the measure on religious, social, and
union grounds. "With a serious crime wave, delinquency, drug-taking, glue-
sniffing and so on, if Sunday opening becomes the norm—meaning mother

working part-time in a shop—Sunday would no longer be the day when families could be expected to come together and that would be highly detrimental to society."

The Law

Closing of shops on Sunday: Every shop shall, save as otherwise provided by this Part of this Act, be closed for the serving of customers on Sunday:

Provided that a shop may be open for the serving of customers on Sunday for the purposes of any transaction mentioned in the Fifth Schedule to this Act. Shops Act 1950, section 47, *Halsbury's Statutes of England,* third edition, vol. 13, 1969, as amended by the Criminal Law Act 1977, Vol. 47, section 31 (6).

Sections 48–56 specify exemptions to the provisions of section 47, including exemptions for London, for persons observing the Jewish Sabbath, for holiday resorts, and for restaurants:

Offenses connected with Sunday trading:
1. In the case of any contravention of any of the foregoing provisions of this Part of this Act, the occupier of the shop shall be liable to a fine not exceeding—

(a) in the case of a first offense, fifty pounds;
(b) in the case of a second or subsequent offense, two hundred pounds.

2. A person who carries on the business of a shop, or carries on retail trade or business at any place not being a shop, on Sunday in accordance with the foregoing provisions of this Part of this Act, shall not be deemed to commit an offense against any of the following enactments, namely—

(a) the Sunday Fairs Act; 1448; or
(b) the Act of the third year of His late Majesty King Charles First, chapter 3, for the further reformation of sundry abuses committed on the Lord's Day commonly called Sunday; or
(c) the Sunday Observance Act, 1677.

Fifth Schedule—Section 47

Transactions for the purpose of which a shop may be open in England and Wales for the serving of customers on Sunday:

1. The sale of—
    (a) intoxicating liquors;
    (b) meals or refreshments whether or not for consumption at the shop at which they are sold, but not including the sale of fried fish and chips at a fried fish and chip shop;

(c) newly cooked provisions and cooked or partly cooked tripe;

(d) table waters, sweets, chocolates, sugar confectionery and ice-cream (including wafers and edible containers);

(e) flowers, fruit and vegetables (including mushrooms) other than tinned or bottled fruit or vegetables;

(f) milk and cream, not including tinned or dried milk or cream, but including clotted cream whether sold in tins or otherwise;

(g) medicines and medical and surgical appliances—

   (i) at any premises registered under section twelve of the Pharmacy and Poisons Act, 1933; or

   (II) by any person who has entered into a contract with an Executive Council for the supply of drugs and appliances;

(h) aircraft, motor, or cycle supplies or accessories;

(i) tobacco and smokers' requisites;

(j) newspapers, periodicals, and magazines;

(k) books and stationary from the bookstalls of such terminal and main line railway or omnibus stations, or at such aerodromes as may be approved by the Secretary of State;

(l) guide books, postcards, photographs, reproductions, photographic films and plates, and souvenirs—

   (i) at any gallery, museum, garden, park or ancient monument under the control of a public authority or university; or

   (ii) at any other gallery or museum, or any place of natural beauty or historic interest, or any zoological, botanical or horticultural gardens, or aquarium, if and to the extent that the local authority certify that such sale is desirable in the interest of the public; or

   (iii) in any passenger vessel within the meaning of Part II of the Finance (1909–1910) Act, 1910, while engaged in carrying passengers'

(m) photographs for passports;

(n) requisites for any game or sport at any premises or place where that game or sport is played or carried on;

(o) fodder for horses, mules, ponies, and donkeys at any farm, stables, hotel or inn.

2. The transaction of—

(a) post office business;

(b) the business carried on by a funeral undertaker.

Australia

It is a distinct anomaly that restrictions on retail-selling activity exist at all in free, democratic societies which, according to polls of public sentiment, favor repeal by better than a two-to-one margin. It is even more difficult to understand why such laws prohibit retail trade during precisely those days and times that working persons find most attractive for shopping, namely in the evenings and on weekends. In this respect, Australia is perhaps the most peculiar of the countries with restrictive domestic-selling laws, because shops are restricted in their hours of evening operation and forbidden to open on Saturday afternoon or on Sunday. The congestion this begets during Saturday morning must be experienced in order to understand the impact of the law.

As always, exceptions to the law and differences between the states with respect to the law and its enforcement combine to produce a maze of conflicting behavioral restraints.

History of Shopping Restrictions

Restriction of retail trading in Australia dates back to 1885, when the colony of Victoria approved legislation requiring shopkeepers to close by 7:00 p.m. on weekends and 10:00 p.m. on Saturdays, with Sunday sales outlawed entirely. By the end of the nineteenth century, most of the other colonies had passed legal restrictions on retail trade. Moves to close shops for half a day each week, in addition to the Sunday closing, were argued in New South Wales and Victoria starting in the 1890s and continuing into the 1920s. The timing of the half-holiday was the major concern; for some time Wednesday was a popular alternative to Saturday. Also considered was a plan that would have permitted shopkeepers within local government areas to designate the half-holiday by majority vote. By the 1920s most of the states had adopted legislation requiring shops in metropolitan areas to close at 6:00 p.m. Monday through Thursday, at 9:00 p.m. on Friday, and at either noon or 1:00 p.m. on Saturday. Observance of the half-holiday on weekdays continued to persist for some time in rural areas, with the usual exemptions granted to pharmacies, coffee houses, fish shops, and greengrocers.

These regulations continued basically intact up to World War II, when, in 1941, all shops were required to close by 6:00 p.m. each day of the week throughout the country. This was no great hardship for hotels, which had been required to close no later than 6:00 p.m. since World War I. After World War II, the prohibitions on evening hours continued in effect, thanks mainly to legislation passed in each of the states. Finally, Victoria and New South Wales re-introduced evening shopping for one day of the week in the late 1960s, and were quickly followed by the other states.

Interested Parties and Arguments

Some evidence suggests that at least part of the motivation for the early restrictions on shopping hours came from a desire to limit the hours of work demanded of shop employees by their employers. According to Hogbin

[1983], transcripts of evidence presented to Royal Commissions inquiring in-to shop trading hours in the late 1800s and early 1900s contain numerous references to the adverse effects of long hours of work on the health of shop assistants and on the well-being of their families. The health consequences of being shackled to one's job from sunup to sundown, argues Hogbin, suggest strongly that legislative action to improve working conditions could scarcely fail to be in the public interest and that any inconvenience suffered by con-sumers would be comparatively trivial.

It has been suggested, however, that concern for the public welfare may not have been the sole motivation underlying the initial restrictive legislation. If exploitation of labor was indeed the only concern, that concern could sure-ly have been met more directly by setting limits on the number of hours a shop employee could be asked to work per day or per week, as was done in the United States.

Indirect evidence casts doubt on the exploitation of labor theory of shop restrictions. References in the same transcripts mentioned above indicate that certain employers had difficulty finding people willing to work on Saturday afternoons. Many retailers, in fact, were voluntarily closing their shops for half a day each week, in addition to Sundays, before they were required to do so by law. This suggests that labor-market conditions were not so favorable to employers that they could impose limitless demands upon their employees. Why, then, the restriction on shop hours?

Hogbin argues that the profit motive of shopkeepers was the real mover-and-shaker in the arly debates over shop closing-hours and the half-holiday. He notes that most of the recorded evidence in the early inquiries and Parlia-mentary debates were provided by the shopkeepers themselves rather than employees or other citizens. When the first measure restricting retail selling was introduced, businessmen were split over its passage. Similarly, shopkeepers came down on both sides of the issue when the idea of compul-sory half-holiday was debated. Any proposal to introduce or change a regula-tion governing shopping hours was accompanied by claims that the proposed measure would be inflationary, that small proprietors would be disadvan-taged relative to large businesses (or vice versa), that shops in suburban areas would suffer relative to those in the inner city, or that family business enter-prises would benefit, or suffer, relative to others. Hogbin concludes that while concern for the welfare of shop assistants may have triggered moves to regulate shopping hours, that does not preclude the possibility that the inter-ests of the shopkeepers themselves played a major role in determining the ini-tial form of the legislation as well as subsequent modifications.

The Law

There is no national law governing Sunday, Saturday, or evening trade in Australia. It appears, however, that each of the states that comprise Australia have enacted restrictions that encompass a broad spectrum of activity. Sales of liquor have long been regulated by all of the states. Similarly, all states maintain versions of a Factories and Shops Act, which originated from the British law. The Sabbath laws of Australia are derived—law by law, amendment by amendment—from successive British monarchs so that the root of each law and amendment may begin with a different monarch. Any change from the original law, which may have been enacted decades ago, is passed by the state in question as a supplement to the original law, with the whole package given the same name as the original. Thus, the fifteenth supplement to the Factories and Shops Act of 1920, to pick a fictional example, might be the Factories and Shops Act of 1985. So that the full import of each law will not be lost, we abstain from listing the specific laws for each of the states comprising Australia. We refer especially interested readers to the Australian consulate in Washington, D.C. and to the Library of Congress, also in Washington, D.C

Canada

In contrast to Australia, Canada has a national law that regulates Sunday trading—the Lord's Day Act of 1970. Not surprisingly, exemptions and exceptions permit numerous activities to take place on Sunday and numerous shops and enterprises of various sorts to open on Sunday. The guise under which one may gain exemption from the law is as a "work of necessity or charity," which is the standard guise of exemption in all of the English-speaking countries, including America. Canada's Sunday-closing law originates from the British law applicable during the reign of King George III.

The Law

1. This Act may be cited as the *Lord's Day Act*. R.S., c. 171, s.1.

2. In this Act "employer" includes every person to whose orders or directions any other person is by his employment bound to conform; "Lord's Day" means the period of time that begins at midnight on Saturday night and ends at midnight on the following night; "performance" includes any game, match, sport contest, exhibition, or entertainment; "person" has the meaning that it has in the Criminal Code; "provincial Act" means the charter of any municipality, or any public Act of any province, whether passed before or since Confederation; "railway" includes steam railway, electric railway, street railway, and tramway; "vessel" includes any kind of vessel or boat used for conveying passengers or freight by water. R.S., c. 171, s.2.

3. (1) Nothing herein prevents the operation on the Lord's Day for passenger traffic by any railway company incorporated by or subject to the leg-

islative authority of the Parliament of Canada of its railway where such operation is not otherwise prohibited.

(2) Nothing herein prevents the operation on the Lord's Day for passenger traffic of any railway subject to the legislative authority of any province, unless such railway is prohibited by provincial authority from so operating. R.S., c. 171, s.3.

Prohibitions

4. It is not lawful for any person on the Lord's Day, except as provided herein, or in any provincial Act or law in force on or after the first day of March 1907, to sell or offer for sale or purchase any goods, chattels, or other personal property, or any real estate, or to carry on or transact any business of his ordinary calling, or in connection with such calling, or for gain to do, or employ any other person to do, on that day, any work, business, or labour. R.S., c. 171, s.4.

5. Except in cases of emergency, it is not lawful for any person to require any employee engaged in any work of receiving, transmitting or delivering telegraph or telephone messages, or in the work of any industrial process, or in connection with transportation, to do on the Lord's Day the usual work of his ordinary calling, unless such employee is allowed during the next six days of such week, twenty-four consecutive hours without labour. R.S., c. 171, s.5.

6. (1) It is not lawful for any person, on the Lord's Day, except as provided in any provincial Act or law in force on or after the 1st day of March 1907, to engage in any public game or contest for gain, or for any prize or reward, or to be present thereat, or to provide, engage in, or be present at any performance or public meeting, elsewhere than in a church, at which any fee is charged, directly or indirectly, either for admission to such performance or meeting, or to any place within which the same is provided, or for any service or privilege thereat.

(2) When any performance at which an admission fee or any other fee is so charged is provided in any building or place to which persons are conveyed for fire by the proprietors or managers of such performance or by any one acting as their agent or under their control, the charge for such conveyance shall be deemed an indirect payment of such fee within the meaning of this section. R.S., c. 171, s.6.

7. It is not lawful for any person on the Lord's Day, except as provided by any provincial Act or law in force on or after the 1st day of March 1907, to run, conduct, or convey by any mode of conveyance any excursion on which passengers are conveyed for hire, and having for its principal or only object the carriage on that day of such passengers for amusement or pleasure, and passengers so conveyed shall not be deemed to be travellers within the meaning of this Act. R.S., c. 171, s.7.

7. 1(1). Where an activity referred to in section 4, 6, or 7 is permitted within a province on the Lord's Day by a provincial Act or law, it shall be lawful for any person to engage in that activity on the Lord's Day on any Indian reserve in that province.

(2) In subsection (1), "Indian reserve" includes Category IA land and Category IA-N land, as defined in the Cree-Naskapi (of Quebec) Act. R.S., c. 171, s.7.1(1-2).

8. (1) It is not lawful for any person to advertise in any manner whatever any performance or other thing prohibited by this Act.

(2) It is not lawful for any person to advertise in Canada in any manner whatever any performance or other thing that if given or done in Canada would be a violation of this Act. R.S., c. 171, s.8.

9. It is not lawful for any person on the Lord's Day to shoot with or use any gun, rifle, or other similar firearm, either for gain, or in such a manner or in such places as to disturb other persons in attendance at public worship or in observance of that day. R.S., c. 171, s.9.

10. It is not lawful for any person to bring into Canada for sale or distribution, or to sell or distribute within Canada, on the Lord's Day, any foreign newspaper or publication classified as a newspaper. R.S., c. 171, s.10.

Works of Necessity and Mercy Excepted

11. Nothwithstanding anything herein contained, any person may on the Lord's Day do any work of necessity or mercy, and for greater certainty, but not so as to restrict the ordinary meaning of the expression "work of necessity or mercy," it is hereby declared that it shall be deemed to include the following classes of work:

(a) any necessary or customary work in connection with divine worship;

(b) work for the relief of sickness and suffering, including the sale of drugs, medicines, and surgical appliances by retail;

(c) receiving, transmitting, or delivering telegraph or telephone messages;

(d) starting or maintaining fires, making repairs to furnaces and repairs in cases of emergency, and doing any other work, when such fires, repairs, or work are essential to any industry or industrial process of such a continuous nature that it cannot be stopped without serious injury to such industry, or its product, or to the plant or property used in such process;

(e) starting or maintaining fires, and ventilating, pumping out, and inspecting mines, when any such work is essential to the protection of property, life or health;

(f) any work without the doing of which on the Lord's Day, electric current, light, heat, cold air, water, or gas cannot be continuously supplied for lawful purposes;

(g) the conveying of travellers and work incidental thereto;

(h) the continuance to their destination of trains and vessels in transit when the Lord's Day begins, and work incidental thereto;

(i) loading and unloading merchandise at intermediate points, on or from passenger boats of passenger trains;

(j) keeping railway tracks clear of snow or ice, making repairs in cases of emergency, or doing any other work of a like incidental character necessary to keep the lines and tracks open on the Lord's Day;

(k) work before 6:00 in the morning and after 8:00 in the evening of yard crews in handling cars in railway yards;

(l) loading, unloading and operating any ocean-going vessel that otherwise would be unduly delayed after the scheduled time of sailing, or any vessel that otherwise would be in imminent danger of being stopped by the closing of navigation; or loading or unloading before 7:00 in the morning or after 8:00 in the evening of any grain, coal or ore-carrying vessel after the fifteenth day of September;

(m) the caring for milk, cheese, and live animals, and the unloading of, and caring for, perishable products and live animals arriving at any point during the Lord's Day;

(n) the operation of any toll or drawbridge, or any ferry or boat authorized by competent authority to carry passengers on the Lord's Day;

(o) the hiring of horses and carriages or small boats for the personal use of the hirer or his family for any purpose not prohibited by this Act;

(p) any unavoidable work after 6:00 in the afternoon of the Lord's Day, in the preparation of the regular Monday morning edition of a daily newspaper;

(q) the conveying of Her Majesty's mails and and work incidental thereto;

(r) the delivery of milk for domestic use, and the work of domestic servants and watchmen;

(s) the operation by any Canadian electric street railway company, whose line is interprovincial or international, of its cars, for passenger traffic, on the Lord's Day, on any line or branch that is, on the first day of March 1907, regularly so operated;

(t) work done by any person in the public service of Her Majesty while acting therein under any regulation or direction of any department of the Government;

(u) any unavoidable work by fishermen after 6:00 in the afternoon of the Lord's Day in the taking of fish;

(v) all operations connected with the making of maple sugar and maple syrup in a maple grove;

(w) any unavoidable work on the Lord's Day to save property in cases of emergency, or where such property is in imminent danger of destruction or serious injury; and

(x) any work that the Canadian Transport Commission, having regard to the object of this Act, and with the object of preventing undue delay, deems necessary to permit in connection with the freight traffic of any transportation undertaking. R.S., c. 171, s.11; 1966–67, c. 69, s.94.

Offences and Penalties

12. Any person who violates any of the provisions of this Act is for each offence liable, on summary conviction, to a fine of not less than $1 and not exceeding $40, together with the cost of prosecution. R.S., c.171, s.12.

13. Every employer who authorizes or directs anything to be done in violation of this Act, is for each offence liable, on summary conviction, to a fine not exceeding $100 and not less than $20, in addition to any other penalty described by law for the same offence. R.S., c.171, s.13.

14. Every corporation that authorizes, directs, or permits its employees to carry on any part of the business of such corporation in violation of this Act, is liable, on summary conviction before two justices of the peace, for the first offence, to a penalty not exceeding $250 and not less than $50, and, for each subsequent offence, to a penalty not exceeding $500 and not less than $100, in addition to any other penalty prescribed by law for the same offence. R.S., c.171, s.14.

Procedure

15. Nothing herein shall be construed to repeal or in any way affect any Act or law relating in any way to the observance of the Lord's Day in force in any province of Canada on the first day of March 1907; and where any person violates this Act, and such offence is also a violation of any other Act or law, the offender may be proceeded against either under this Act or under any other Act or law applicable to the offence charged. R.S., c.171, s.15.

16. No action or prosecution for a violation of this Act shall be commenced without the leave of the Attorney Genreal, or his lawful deputy, for the province in which the offence is alleged to have been committed, nor after the expiration of sixty days from the time of the commission of the alleged offence. R.S., c.171, s.16.

7
Final Thoughts

There is mounting evidence that suggests that restrictions of commercial activity on Sunday, in America at least, will soon be no more. In the mid-1980s several states that had rebuffed all previous attempts at repeal of their statutes including Louisiana, Massachusetts, and Texas, repealed their blue laws with respect to commercial activity. There is every indication that the state of Maryland, with one of the most powerful pro-blue laws traditions, will soon relax its restrictions on Sunday-selling. The political forces which had for years successfully opposed repeal efforts have now disintegrated, and it appears that the Baltimore-metropolitan-area shoppers will soon be free to shop on Sundays without having to trek to the southern counties bordering on Washington, D.C.

It seems to us that, in light of the dying importance of blue laws, a number of important concluding thoughts are in order. First and foremost, we harken back to chapter 5, with an ever-more-secure knowledge that the arguments put forth by those parties opposed to repeal of blue laws are simply, for the most part, specious. The passage of time has demonstrated that church attendance, for example, does not suffer unduly merely because individuals have alternative shopping possibilities presented to them. Whether or not the church ought, in good conscience, to rely upon restriction of competition to fill their collection plates, is a separate, but intriguing, issue. Similarly, it is abundantly clear that employees of firms that choose to open on Sunday are not forced to work on Sunday without some type of compensatory remuneration. In the many months of detailed research that went into this volume, we did not ever encounter evidence that employees were exploited in this fashion by shopkeepers.

Has the possibility of shopping on Sunday torn the social fabric asunder? Has peaceful family life been victimized by Sunday-selling? There is no evidence that we are aware of to support the long-held view that society is worse off when Sunday shopping is legalized. To the extent that the generalized happiness a well-being of society is a legitimate concern of state legislators, those lawmakers can, if it is within their power of comprehension, take a good lesson from the history of blue laws repeal in America. Social unhappiness does not follow repeal; rather, repeal follows social unhappiness. The facts are inescapable; there is a strong and increasing demand for Sunday shopping by the consumer population in America, fueled in great degree by the steady addition of women to the workforce. This movement of women into the labor force implies that time in general, and time for shopping in particular, has become more valuable both to men and women. As the demand for Sunday shopping increased over time, merchants found Sunday selling to highly profitable. Merchants who chose not to open found themselves in the same predicament that all sellers who ignore the public pulse do—the peril of nonpatronage. Moreover, stores located in states with enforced blue laws that bordered on states with no such selling restrictions on Sundays found that they were losing business to their brethren across the state lines. One can choose to be unresponsibe to consumer demand and die the slow death that surely awaits; that same slow death awaits those who are forced by irresponsible laws to be less than immediately responsive to consumer demand. To the rising clamor for repeal of blue laws was added the voice and political clout of organized businessmen, who, by the nature of their enterprise, are not normally known for stupidity. It should be clear from the foregoing chapters that the repeal movements in each political jurisdiction that restricted Sunday trading faced entrenched opposition from interest groups that benefited, in fact or fancy, from the laws. Equally clearly, the repeal movement was, and is, demand-driven.

Much has been written in recent years about the power of special-interest groups to influence political outcomes, that, in turn, may affect economic outcomes. It is of singular interest to realize that the free market has an inherent power to protect consumers against protracted efforts of special-interest, or producer, groups to restrict competition. Market forces dominate the political process in the long run; politicians must be responsive to constituents. Although small, well-organized groups of constituents may receive special favors from a legislative body to the detriment of the overall population in the short run, competition from alternative producer groups will inevitably doom the original special-interest legislation. This is the story of blue laws in a nutshell. Regardless of their original intent, such laws have, for years, been supported by a politically well-organized minority, to the detriment of the larger population of would-be consumers and restricted sellers.

As is well-known, by economists at least and eventually by politicians who need revenues to finance state operations, consumers and voters exercise their will through dollar voting and "voting with their feet." Favorable treatment in one political jurisdiction attracts those made miserable by the policies of another. It does not take much movement—of business or population— between political jurisdictions before incumbent officeholders foreswear previous allegiances in order to re-secure their offices or else new political entrepreneurs offer their wares to the voters and outcompete the incumbent brands. In either event, the power of the market in securing outcomes generally favored by the consuming public is evident. To be sure, that natural power operates in the long run rather than the short run. Still, the prospect of no recourse in the short or long run is repugnant. Under the circumstances, the market alternative looks pretty good.

References

The Baltimore Sun, letter to the editor, January 14, 1986.

The Baltimore Sun, letter to the editor, December 27, 1985.

Barron, Jerome A. "Sunday in North America," *Harvard Law Review,* Vol. 79, November 1965, pp. 42–54.

Bembry, Jerry. "Carroll Video Renters Irked by Blue Laws' 'Never on Sunday'," *The Baltimore Sun,* February 3, 1986, p. 12D.

Blakely, William A. *American State Papers Bearing on Sunday Legislation,* New York, NY.: DeCaro Press, 1970.

Dilloff, Neil J. "Never on Sunday: The Blue Laws Controversy," *M aryland Law Review,* Vol. 39, no. 4, 1980, 679–714.

Earle, Alice M. *The Sabbath in Puritan New England,* Williamstown, MA.: Corner House Publishers, 1891.

Elverum, Ken. *Blue Laws,* Research Monograph, Legislative Research Office, State of Oregon, February 1, 1980.

Gorman, Kit. "The Assault on Louisiana's Blue Laws Continues," *Citibusiness,* May 2, 1983, 10–14.

The Greenville (S.C.) *News,* September 16, 1986, p. 3c.

Halsbury's *Statutes of England,* 3rd Edition, vol. 13, 1969.

Harris, George E. *A Treatise on Sunday Laws,* Littleton, CO.: F.B. Rothman, 1892.

Harris, Ralph, and Arthur Seldon, "Shoppers' Choice: An Essay in the Political Economy of Obstruction by Sectional Interests to the Repeal of the Shops Acts," Occasional Paper No. 68, Institute of Economic Affairs, London, 1984.

Hegstad, Roland R., "Why I Oppose Sunday Laws," *Liberty,* January/February 1975, pp. 20–23.

Henman, R.R. *The Blue Laws of New Haven Colony,* Hartford, CT.: Case, Tiffany & Co., 1838.

Hogbin, Geoffrey. *Free to Shop,* Australia: Centre for Independent Studies, 1983.

Johns, Warren L. *Dateline Sunday, U.S.A.,* Mountain View, CA.: Pacific Press Publishing Association, 1967.

Lewis, Abraham H., *A Critical History of Sunday Legislation from 321 to 1888 A.D.,* New York, NY.: D. Appelton and Company, 1888.

The London *Times,* April 15, 1986, p. 4.

The London *Times,* November 16, 1985, Financial section, p. 3.

Marylanders for Blue Laws Repeal, Position Paper, Fall 1985.

Maxwell, A. Graham. "The Day of Freedom," *Liberty,* January/February 1975, pp. 23–25.

McGowan et al. v. Maryland, 220 Md. 117, 151A.2d 156, Maryland State Supreme Court, May 29, 1961.

Moorehouse, John C. "Is Tullock Correct About Sunday Closing Laws?" *Public Choice,* 1984, 197–204.

National Federation of Independent Business. *Fact Book on Small Business,* Washington, D.C.: 1979.

Novotney, John. "The Energy Crisis and Sunday Closing Laws," *Liberty,* January/February 1975, pp. 4–7.

Odom, Robert L. *Sabbath and Sunday in Early Christianity,* Washington, DC: Review and Herald Publishers Association, 1977.

Paine, Donald F. "Sunday, the Sabbath, and the Blue Laws," *Tennessee Law Review,* 30, 1963, pp. 249–71.

Posner, Richard. "Theories of Economic Regulation," *Bell Journal of Economics and Management Science,* Vol. 5, Autumn 1974, pp. 335–358.

Price, Jamie and Bruce Yandle, "Labor Markets and Sunday Closing Laws," *Journal of Labor Research,* forthcoming, 1987.

Prince, Walter F. *Annual Report of the American Historical Association for the Year 1898,* Washington, D.C.: U.S. Government Printing Office, 1899.

Quinn, Bernard, Herman Anderson, Martin Bradley, Paul Goetting and Peggy Shriver. *Churches and Church Membership in the United States-1980,* Atlanta, GA.: Glenmary Research Center, 1982.

Rordorf, Willy. *Sunday: the history of the day of rest and worship in the earliest centuries of the Christian church,* Translated by A.A.K. Graham from the German. Philadelphia, PA.: Westminister Press, 1968.

Shelsby, Ted. "Retail Merchants Join Move to End Blue Laws," *The Baltimore Sun,* November 29, 1985, p. 1C.

Simon, Roger. "State Law Gives Shoppers a Case of Sunday Blues," *The Baltimore Sun,* December 9, 1985, p. 1D.

Solis, Diana. "If You Want to Make a Retailer Red-Hot, Talk About Blue Laws," *The Wall Street Journal,* February 4, 1985, p. 25.

Statutes of the fifty states.

Statutes and revisions of Australia.

Statutes and revisions of Canada.

Statutes and revisions of England.

Stigler, George. "The Economies of Scale," *Journal of Law and Economics,* October 1958, pp. 54–71.

Trumbull, J. Hammond (ed.), *True-Blue Laws of Connecticut and New Haven and the False Blue Laws Invented by the Rev. Samuel Peters,* Hartford, CT.: American Publishing Company, 1876.

Tullock, Gordon. "The Transitional Gains Trap," *Bell Journal of Economics,* Vol. 6, no. 2 (1975), pp. 671–78.

United States Department of Commerce, Bureau of the Census. *County and City Data Book-1983,* Washington: U.S. Government Printing Office, 1984.

United States Department of Commerce, Bureau of the Census. *Statistical Abstract of the United States, 1982-83,* 103rd Edition, Washington: U.S. Government Printing Office, 1984.

United States Department of Commerce, Bureau of the Census. *Statistical Abstract of the United States, 1978,* 99th Edition, Washington: U.S. Government Printing Office, 1979.

Index

About the Authors

David N. Laband is currently associate professor of economics at Clemson University. He received his Master's and Ph.D. degrees in economics from Virginia Tech. He is an active researcher in the areas of political economy, public policies toward business, and labor economics, with contributions in several of the leading economics journals.

Deborah Hendry Heinbuch received her Associate in Arts degree from Anne Arundel Community College and her Bachelor of Arts degree as a double major in economics and history from the University of Maryland, Baltimore County.